God Now

God Now

— Christianity and Heresy —

C. Fred Alford

RESOURCE *Publications* • Eugene, Oregon

GOD NOW
Christianity and Heresy

Copyright © 2019 C. Fred Alford. All rights reserved. Except for brief quotations in critical publications or reviews, no part of this book may be reproduced in any manner without prior written permission from the publisher. Write: Permissions, Wipf and Stock Publishers, 199 W. 8th Ave., Suite 3, Eugene, OR 97401.

Resource Publications
An Imprint of Wipf and Stock Publishers
199 W. 8th Ave., Suite 3
Eugene, OR 97401

www.wipfandstock.com

PAPERBACK ISBN: 978-1-5326-9716-6
HARDCOVER ISBN: 978-1-5326-9717-3
EBOOK ISBN: 978-1-5326-9718-0

Biblical quotations are from the New International Version, © 2019 HarperCollins Christian Publishing. In one or two cases, I have used the King James Version.

Manufactured in the U.S.A.   10/15/19

To Elly, whose constant questions about Christianity have helped me figure out my own beliefs.

The relativization of all moral norms, the crisis of authority, the reduction of life to the pursuit of immediate material gain without regard for its general consequences . . . originate not in democracy but in that which modern man has lost: his transcendental anchor, and along with it the only genuine source of his responsibility and self-respect. . . . Given its fatal incorrigibility, humanity probably will have to go through many more Rwandas and Chernobyls before it understands how unbelievably shortsighted a human being can be who has forgotten that he is not God.

—Václav Havel

Contents

Introduction | xi

Part I: Why I Pray

1: Why I Pray | 1
2: He Only Promises We Do Not Suffer Alone | 4
3: Simone Weil and Donald Trump | 6
4: Would You Forgive a Nazi Mass Murderer? | 10
5: Forgiving a Mass Murderer: The Amish | 14

Part II: Theologians

6: Luther | 18
7.1: Bonhoeffer: Religionless Christianity | 22
7.2: Bonhoeffer: Can I Just Be a Second-Rate Christian? | 27
7.3: Basics of Bonhoeffer | 31
8: Bultmann: What Does It Matter if the Bible Is a Myth? | 35
9.1: Kierkegaard: The Leap to Faith | 38
9.2: Kierkegaard: The Tragedy of Grace | 42
9.3: Kierkegaard Is Wrong: An Absurd God Is Not Good | 45
10.1: Did Camus Believe in God? | 49
10.2: Did Camus Want to Be Baptized? | 53
10.3: Camus's Absurdism Lacks Imagination | 58
11.1: Moltmann: Heaven on Earth and My Heresy | 62
11.2: Moltmann's Ecological God | 66

12.1: Niebuhr and the Scandal of the Twentieth Century | 70

12.2: Niebuhr and Original Sin | 74

12.3: Niebuhr and the Things That Are Not | 77

13: Tillich and Existential Christianity | 81

14: Niebuhr, Barth, Bultmann, Bonhoeffer, and Tillich: What They Share | 85

15: Hauerwas and the End of Socially Responsible Christianity | 91

16.1: Merton Is Wrong: Christian Mysticism Is a Bad Idea | 95

16.2: The Unknown Thomas Merton | 98

17.1: C. S. Lewis Is Wrong: We Are Not Little Christs | 101

17.2: Thoughts While Reading *A Grief Observed*, by C. S. Lewis | 106

17.3: Why We Need Pain: A Bad Answer by C. S. Lewis | 110

18.1: Pagels and the Gnostic Gospels | 114

18.2: Pagels: *Why Religion?* A Fine But Flawed Book | 118

19: Smith: Does Religion Matter Anymore? | 122

20: Levinas Says We Cannot Talk to God, Only Each Other | 125

21: Buber: *I and Thou*; Dialogue or Touch? | 129

22.1: Weil Is Not a Christian Mystic | 133

22.2: Weil and the Need for Roots | 137

22.3: Paying Attention with Weil | 140

22.4: Weil: "The great mystery of life is not suffering, but affliction" | 143

23: Berger: A Sociologist Who Turned to God But Never Understood Faith | 146

Part III: On Some Books of the Bible

24: The Book of Job: The Most Puzzling | 150

25: Ecclesiastes Is a Dark Book | 155

26: Book of Mark: Apocalypse Now | 158

27: Gospel of John: Christ's Return Is Now | 163

28.1: Paul: The First Jew for Jesus | 167

28.2: Paul and Martin Luther King: Two Revolutionaries | 172

29: The Book of James: Simply Right and Simply Wrong | 177

30: The Book of Revelation Subverts the Spirit of Christianity | 181

Part IV: Psychology and God

31: "Do You Believe in God?" Is the Wrong Question | 185
32: Psychology, God and Death | 190
33: Psychology and the New Atheists | 194

Part V: Natural Law

34: Does Natural Law Exist? | 200
35: Three Stories About Natural Law | 204
36: Do Human Rights Depend on God? Natural Law? | 210

Part VI: Topics and Heresies

37: Process Theology | 214
38: God Is the One Who Remembers | 219
39: What Is So Great About Faith? | 222
40: Do you Have Soul? | 226
41: "The Grand Inquisitor," Then and Now | 229
42: What Is So Great About Eternity? | 232
43: Christianity and Technology | 235

Part VII

44: Conclusion | 239

Bibliography | 243

Introduction

THE FIRST CHAPTER, WHY I PRAY, contains a lot of what the reader may want to know about me, but here's a little background about me and this book. I was baptized a Christian and am a member of my local Episcopal church; but I attend services rarely. I occasionally attend services at a Franciscan shrine and priory near me. I am sympathetic to Catholicism, but have no intention of converting.

I spend a lot of time thinking about how to come to terms with Christian doctrine, particularly as expressed in the Nicene Creed. I like doctrine (it states the issues clearly), but often I just can't go along.

When people ask me what I believe, or what religion I am, I generally answer that I'm a practicing Christian. What I don't usually add is that I'm not always a believing one. Oh, I believe in God and Jesus Christ, but about much church doctrine I am dubious. I am not dubious about the Christian idea of a God who came to earth in order to suffer as humans do; that is a breathtaking achievement.

Though I have published a book on natural law, another on Emmanuel Levinas (a Talmudic scholar and philosopher), as well as a chapter on the Book of Job, I am not a theologian. For forty years, I taught ancient and classical political theory at a large state university. If you want to learn more about me, see my University of Maryland, College Park webpage, where I am Professor Emeritus: https://gvpt.umd.edu/facultyprofile/alford/c-fred

My Greek is not nearly as good as I would like, but I can often manage to make up my own mind about the meaning of a doubtful term or sentence, especially with the help of Strong's Concordance, a list of how every Greek root word used in the New Testament is employed. Strong's Concordance also lists every Hebrew word, but since I don't know Hebrew, I cannot use the Hebrew Strong's as it is meant to be used, as a guide for someone who already knows the basics of the language.

This book is unusual in that it contains many relatively short essays, each averaging about 1,400 words, some more. About some authors I've written two, three, or four essays, which I indicate like so: chapter 7.1, 7.2, 7.3. I wrote the essays over a period of several years, which means that there is some repetition. Though I have positions I believe in, I don't have an overall position to defend. I inquire in order to learn, and I write not just in order to share what I've learned, but to figure out what I have learned in the first place.

While I don't have a position to defend, many Christians would surely regard me as a heretic, at least about some matters. For me, Christ's life and death are far more important than his resurrection. I am aware that for most Christians, Christ's resurrection is at the center of the *kerygma*, which means preaching, but generally refers to the teaching of the Gospels. Without the resurrection, according to most Christians, Christianity would be meaningless, the promise of eternal life empty.

I disagree. Christianity is a great religion because God became fully human in order to participate in what it means for humans to love and suffer, God's "strength made perfect in weakness." The Trinity, which explains (or rather asserts) how God could become a man yet remain fully God, is a great idea.

The question that has occupied my mind as I wrote, and still does, is, what does it mean to believe in God? The answer I have come up with is that it is good to believe in God (unless one is a fanatic), even though his existence can never be proven. Søren Kierkegaard, D. W. Winnicott (a psychoanalyst), Reinhold Niebuhr, and Dietrich Bonhoeffer, about whom I have written at least one essay, and often several, have been helpful to me. Almost every theologian I have written about has been helpful. Most atheists seem overwrought.

Though I've written about what faith might be, the question still puzzles me. "What type of knowledge is faith?" is the way I formulate the issue, for I'm sure that faith isn't the mere assertion of what I don't know, unless, perhaps, all knowledge has this quality to some degree.

Along the way, the reader may notice that I am fond of psychoanalytic explanations, even if very few of the chapters concern psychoanalysis. Along with my forty years' teaching undergraduates, I spent a number of those years teaching psychoanalytic social theory to graduate students. In one way or another, it is the topic of many of my books. I've tried not to make it central to this manuscript, but it creeps in from time to time. One thing I should make clear is that psychoanalysis has nothing to say, and can have nothing to say, about God's existence. The psychoanalytic study of religion is primarily about how we participate in the God experience, even if it is to reject it.

Though I explicitly address the question in only a few essays, it is clear to me that the Christian experience is the Judeo-Christian experience. Much of the New Testament is an attempt to make the Christian experience conform to the Hebrew Testament's predictions about the Messiah, for Christ seems such an unlikely one. This is one reason I argue that it is a good thing that Gnosticism did not make it into the Bible. Gnostics abandon the connection of the New Testament to the Old.

This brings up a final point. So much of the Bible has been redacted over the years, often in regard to the changing historical circumstances of its readers, that it is hard to decide when and whether to stick with the original version; if, that is, we even know what the original version is. My approach has been to go with what's on the page, generally in the New International Version, unless a number of experts believe that a text was materially altered. Occasionally I have called upon my own knowledge of Greek to help make up my mind.

Consider, for example, the Book of Job, in which the last verses (42:10–17), often called Job's restoration, are almost certainly a later addition in order to restore a human concept of justice to God. Other parts of the Book of Job are also certainly additions, but as they don't fundamentally alter the meaning of the text, I leave them be.

The book is organized into seven parts, the first six into chapters.

Part I: Why I Pray begins with the essay of that title, and includes posts on Donald Trump and Simone Weil, as well as an essay on whether you would forgive a Nazi mass murderer. Think of Part I as an appetizer for those with strong stomachs.

Part II: Essays on a number of theologians, including men and women not usually considered theologians, such as Albert Camus.

Part III: On some books of the Bible. From Job to Revelation, I include some of the books I have found most curious and interesting.

Part IV: Psychology and God. Psychology has nothing to say about whether God exists. It does have something to say about the nature of belief.

Part V: Natural Law. I'm fond of the natural law, and regret that it has gone out of style. Only Catholics, and then only some, seem to still find it relevant. I find it essential in thinking about morality.

Part VI: Topics and Heresies. From an essay on God having limited powers (process theology), to an essay on Christianity and God, I consider some topics that fascinate me.

Part I

1

Why I Pray

BECAUSE I DO NOT believe in a God who intervenes in everyday life, I am not sure why I say my prayers every night. Yet I continue to pray, and there is still so much I do not understand.

Why do we ask God's blessings, on those near and dear to us, as well as refugees and displaced persons far away whom I will never meet?

About asking God's blessings. If there were an interventionist God, why would He be more likely to intervene if I asked Him to? He does not take recommendations from me.

One answer is that what I am really asking is for God to feel present in another person's life, as well as my own. Not that he change their journey, or mine, but that he accompany us along the way. But the problem remains. Why would God be more likely to accompany someone on their perilous journey just because I ask Him to? Or if a thousand people ask Him to?

What I Believe

I believe that the universe is a miracle, and that my life, as well as everybody else's life, is a gift. The universe did not have to be. I did not have to be. That I am—even for a moment in time, before I become ashes and dust again—is an incredible miracle, and an incredible gift. And so I believe in the One who gives life, a distant God.

How distant? That puzzles me. On the one hand, when I look around the world and see so much suffering and misery, I can only believe in the

God of Job. The God who created the universe out of matter (not *ex nihilo*; that is Genesis, not Job), not for our satisfaction, but for His. Or as the liberation theologian Gustavo Gutiérrez puts it about the God of Job,

> the speeches of God have brought home the fact that human beings are not the center of the universe and that not everything has been made for their service.[1]

Along with many theologians, I hold that Job 42:10–17 was an addition by later redactors to encourage the faithful. The Book ends with Job despising himself for his arrogance in questioning God, not with God rewarding his faithfulness.

Another way of saying much the same thing is that I believe in a God who has stepped back from his creation. It is up to us what we make of it. The best thing we can do is help and comfort each other in a world that was not made for the human being.

Jesus

I also believe in the story of Jesus, not merely that He was a good man, but that He represents that part of God who let Himself feel the suffering of humanity, and so can accompany us on our journey, for He understands it.

The idea of a God who comes not in glory, but in all humbleness and vulnerability, "his strength made perfect in weakness," is a great God story. Nevertheless, I do not find myself praying to Jesus very often, but to that much more abstract and distant being, God.

I belong to the Episcopal Church, but attend services rarely. My favorite is on Ash Wednesday, for it reminds me of my mortality, against which my modest achievements in this world, other than loving and caring for family and friends, mean little. Caring for the stranger would make me a better person, and I should do that more.

So Why Do I Pray?

Strangely enough, for someone whose faith is so fragile, I never feel that I am talking to myself when I pray. I feel (I think) that I am helping create a relationship that would not exist if I didn't pray. Aggressive atheism makes no sense to me. How could we know?

The question is not whether God exists. The question is whether it is worthwhile to act as if He does, and so create a richer world, a numinous

---

1. Gutiérrez, *On Job*, 74.

world, a world of wonder. I rarely succeed, and my most religious experiences are often in nature. When I could still kayak, and the wind rippled the surface of the lake, I could see His face upon the waters.

What Do I Pray?

I pray for my wife, a couple of friends who are ill, a mentally ill relative, and then depending on what has happened during the day, I pray for the hungry, the homeless, and refugees and displaced persons all over the world. I pray for people in pain. These seem to me about the worst things, and there are so many who suffer.

I do not pray that I give more to charity—though I should—because I would feel hypocritical. That is something in my hands, one of the few things I can control.

I thank God for my existence, and generally try not to pray for myself. Somehow it seems selfish or impolite. If I do it right, then I must always pray, "if it be Thy will, then . . . " But if it is God's will, then what will my pleading change?

I try to remember the reason Jesus introduced what we call "The Lord's Prayer." To keep it simple. Do not babble on, for God knows what you need better than you do (Matthew 6:7–8).

So Why Pray?

I pray to create, establish, and maintain a relationship with a God who seems to have stepped back from this world. And the relationship I seek is one of felt presence. So that when I ask God to bless this or that person, or thank God for my existence, as well as that of those I love, I am asking God to accompany us on our journeys, to let his presence be felt.

I do not ask God for grace, which I understand as the unmerited favor of God, though that would be nice (Romans 3:22–24). I ask that if I am ever able to open myself to God's presence (usually I am too preoccupied and anxious) that He be there waiting for me.

And then I stop.

2

He Only Promises We Do Not Suffer Alone

"Twenty centuries of Christianity," I said. "You'd think we'd learn . . . In this world, He only promises we don't suffer alone."[1]

A Marine chaplain says this in a short story by Phil Klay about the Iraq War. The story is fiction but the point is real. Most people pray for God to protect them, their families, and their friends. Many pray only in moments of death and desperation. But it is the wrong thing to pray for. Pray to feel the presence of God. Period.

Of course, it is not this simple. Lots of people, including me, pray for more. Some pray for salvation. It is perfectly human, but it's the wrong way to think about God.

Religion is about meaning, and religion is about suffering. Buddhism has one answer: don't cling. Do not cling to life, don't cling to attachments, and do not cling to yourself. Christianity has another answer: God will suffer with you. Your suffering will not be lessened, but you will not be alone. You will be less subject to your suffering.

Nietzsche argued that God is dead because there is no longer a convincing answer to the question, "Why do I suffer?"[2]

But if man is given a meaning for his suffering, then it has a purpose, and suddenly it is worthwhile to suffer. The meaning of suffering is everything. Nietzsche said this too, and he was right. The question is whether the answer "God accompanies you in your suffering" is really an answer. I think it is.

One could elaborate, along the lines of "God has a plan, one that you will never know, but from a God's eye view, there is a meaning to your

---

1. Klay, *Redeployment*, 167.
2. Nietzsche, *Genealogy of Morals*, III.28.

suffering." That is the answer of the Book of Job. But I do not think it is very convincing.

There is something about being human that makes "God accompanies you in your suffering" a perfectly complete and adequate answer to the question, "Why do I suffer?" If this does not seem like an answer, think about it.

A suffering child is comforted by the presence of his parents. What makes an adult is not the absence of the need for comfort and presence, but the ability to use the idea or feeling of another's presence as comfort. That is not childish. That is the imagination of an adult at work. The grace of God is the ability to use this imagination to feel His presence.

Christianity, the Religion of the God Who Suffers

I think the answer "God accompanies you in your suffering" is the basis for a complete religion, and one of the great attractions of Christianity is its emphasis on Christ's suffering. The cross was a torture instrument, as the chaplain says. Christ is a great instance and exemplar of God suffering with us. To me, that is a lot more important that Christ dying for my sins.

Christ died so that we do not suffer alone. That is enough.

3

Simone Weil and Donald Trump: The World as Force and Affliction

SIMONE WEIL WROTE DURING the years leading up to the Second World War. She died in 1943. There is much that is curious and troublesome about her life—and death. She died of starvation by her own hand. Born a Jew, Weil is generally regarded as a Christian mystic. Throughout her life, she refused baptism. I see her as a woman with deep insight into the experiences of force and affliction. We all know who Donald Trump is.

"The *Iliad*, Or the Poem of Force," her most well-known work, addresses the founding document of Western Civilization. Generally seen as an epic of war and heroes, Weil reads it as an account of what force does to people: those who use force, and those who suffer it. It subjects both to the empire of might.

> Whoever does not know just how far necessity and a fickle fortune hold the human soul under their domination cannot treat as his equals, nor love as himself, those whom chance has separated from him by an abyss. The diversity of the limitations to which men are subject creates the illusion that there are different species among them which cannot communicate with one another. *Only he who knows the empire of might and knows how not to respect it is capable of love and justice.*[1]

We live in an age of force, and contempt for those who suffer it. "Loser" has become a common term of abuse. About the concept of a loser, Weil reminds us that Christ was the greatest "loser" of them all. He lost so that we might be saved.

Weil's is a heretical reading of the New Testament. Christ is the incarnation of God, come to earth to suffer as men and women suffer, and to

---

1. Weil, "The *Iliad* or the Poem of Force," 181, author's emphasis.

die as testimony to this fact. The resurrection, so central to Christianity, is unimportant to her.

> If the Gospel omitted all mention of Christ's Resurrection, faith would be easier for me. The Cross by itself suffices for me.[2]

Resurrection is unimportant because Christ represents not God's power, but his willing weakness, a rejection of all who equate God with might. Instead of being a God of might, God is the one who becomes one with the victims of history.

Affliction

> The great mystery of human life is not suffering but affliction.

> It is not surprising that the innocent are killed, tortured, and displaced, put in concentration camps or prison cells. For there are always enough servants of might to do this work. Surprising is that affliction has the power to seize the souls of the innocent. "He who is branded by affliction will only keep half his soul."

> Our senses attach to affliction all the contempt, all the revulsion, all the hatred which our reason attaches to crime.... Everybody despises the afflicted to some extent, although practically no one is conscious of it.... Thought is constrained by an instinct of self-preservation to fly from the sight of affliction, and this instinct is infinitely more essential to our being than the instinct to avoid physical death.[3]

It is, I believe, the proper task of politics to counteract this contempt, consoling and comforting the afflicted with justice, as well as the necessities of life. Both are the political version of love. Nothing is more important than that in everyday life.

Instead, contemporary politics seems to be a contest in who can inflict the most affliction, and so liberate himself from the forces of fate masquerading as political power. "Masquerading," because even in the realm of politics, no one is immune to fate, ultimately the fatefulness of nature and death. The wealthy in the United States live about 15 years longer than the poorest among us.[4] Nevertheless, we are all dead for eternity. Death is the

---

2. Weil, *Letter to a Priest*, 55.
3. Weil, *God and Affliction*, 443, 457.
4. https://www.nytimes.com/interactive/2016/04/11/upshot/for-the-poor-geography-is-life-and-death.html?_r=0

great equalizer, and much of life is an attempt to deny this fact, as though we could get others to do our dying for us.

Affliction as Gift?

For Weil, affliction is a gift. In this regard, politics and religion are opposites. Politics should comfort the afflicted, and afflict the comfortable, as the saying goes. But we should thank God, says Weil, for giving us necessity.

Because Weil understands the soul in its Greek meaning, *psyche*, the death of the soul is good. For the death of the self is good. This sounds a little bit like Buddhism, and perhaps it is. Weil was fascinated by Buddhism; that it might contain part of a truth about God is one reason she did not convert to Christianity.

It is impossible to accept the death of the soul unless one has placed one's love and attention elsewhere, "in the hands of our Father." The goal is that there be nothing left over that could be called oneself, one's will, one's "I." The goal is to "become nothing other than a certain intersection of nature and God."[5]

An Unselfie Stick

Unselfing is actually not quite as weird as it sounds. The novelist and Oxford don, Iris Murdoch, influenced by Weil, recommended unselfing, which is in many ways simply the opposite of our selfie culture, in which everything I do is a reflection of me, a presentation of myself. Beauty, for both Murdoch and Weil, is an unselfie stick.[6] For Murdoch, wild beauty is an especially effective medium of unselfing.

> I am looking out of my window in an anxious and resentful state of mind, oblivious of my surroundings, brooding perhaps on some damage done to my prestige. Then suddenly I observe a hovering kestrel. In a moment everything is altered. The brooding self with its hurt vanity has disappeared. There is nothing now but kestrel. And when I return to thinking of the other matter it seems less important.[7]

For Weil, attention to others is the unselfie stick. The Holy Grail, says Weil, belongs to the one who first asks its guardian, a king almost completely

---

5. Weil, *God and Affliction*, 458.

6. A selfie stick is attached to a smartphone camera in order to better take pictures of oneself.

7. Murdoch, *Sovereignty of Good*, 82.

paralyzed by a painful wound, "What are you going through?"[8] Who would think to ask that today, especially when one is in hot pursuit of knowledge, power, or money? Most of our interactions with others are about trying to fit them into our familiar categories.

The Difference Between Politics and Religion

Religion is about unselfing, living as though one were forever exposed to God in His awesome, terrible mystery. In everyday life, unselfing is about paying attention to the reality of others. Beauty reminds us of this, but so do the needs of others.

Politics is about meeting the needs of others, which of necessity categorizes them into familiar classes, such as citizens, the poor, the abused, the widow, orphan, and stranger.

It is easy to see how unselfing can prepare us to experience the needs of others, but we need enough self left to do the work of helping them. Starving oneself to death, as Weil did, eating no more (and often less) than her compatriots in occupied France, did no one any good.

Politics Today

Politics in the era of Trump (and to be fair, politics always tends in this direction) is about the exaltation of force, and the imposition of affliction on others. Not only Trump's followers, but so many, respect only the empire of might, as though this might save the meaning of their lives, or life itself. Trump is unique in his worship of force, and his contempt of the powerless, offering his followers a chance to share in his immunity to affliction. But not for long. For as Weil reminds us, there is a geometry of virtue that, much like Karma, punishes automatically the abuse of strength.[9] Too bad so many innocents get hurt along the way.

---

8. Weil, *Reflections on School Studies*, 51. The Holy Grail is traditionally the cup from which Jesus drank at the last supper.

9. Weil, "The *Iliad*" 164.

4

Would You Forgive a Nazi Mass Murderer?

It is difficult to state clearly the New Testament's view of forgiveness. New Testament views would be more like it. Nevertheless, the central claim seems to be that forgiveness should be offered as many times as it is needed. Peter asks Jesus how many times he should forgive someone who sins against him, suggesting the answer might be seven. (Matthew 18:21–22) Jesus replies, "I tell you, not seven times, but seventy-seven times." (Or seventy times seven in some versions.) Seven represents the number of completeness and perfection in the Bible, and the point of course is that, for forgiveness to be perfect, it must be impossibly generous. Jesus expresses much the same point when he states that when people pray, they must forgive anyone anything and everything, so that "your Father in heaven may forgive your sins." (Mark 11:25)

The Sunflower, or Would You Forgive a Nazi Mass Murderer?

Little in Christ's teachings suggests that I am required to forgive someone for an act against a third party. Yet this issue comes up often in discussions of forgiveness. It is the main issue that seems to divide Christians and Jews in their responses to *The Sunflower*, a story told by Simon Wiesenthal.[1]

The gist of the story is straightforward. A young Nazi is dying in a hospital located near a concentration camp where Wiesenthal is imprisoned. While being marched past the hospital in a work detail, a nurse selects Wiesenthal from the group of inmates and takes him to the room of the dying Nazi, who wants "a Jew" to hear his confession and grant him forgiveness. Evidently brought up in a good Catholic home, the young Nazi had willingly committed

---

1. Wiesenthal, *Sunflower*, 8.

terrible atrocities against innocent Jewish civilians, burning many to death. Will Wiesenthal grant him forgiveness before he dies?

Wiesenthal silently leaves the dying man's bedside, and the book turns on the question of whether he should have forgiven the Nazi, who seems genuinely repentant. Wiesenthal's bunkmates rightly point out that he was in no position to forgive, primarily because he was selected simply because he was "a Jew," and not because he was personally a victim of this particular Nazi's crimes. Furthermore, a man under a death sentence is not free to forgive. The remainder of the book is taken up by the answers of dozens of famous theologians, teachers, philosophers, and writers to the question of "What would I have done?" had I been in Wiesenthal's place.

It is widely held that whether to forgive the dying Nazi is divided down the middle between Christians and Jews, with few exceptions. Solomon Schimmel puts it this way:

> Most of the Jews felt that only the victim of a crime has the right to forgive the perpetrator and that in the absence of repentance as defined in Jewish tradition, which includes remorse, confession, apology, and reparation, there is no *obligation* to forgive. Most of the Christians felt that a third party could forgive a sinner, especially if he has confessed and expressed remorse for his deeds, even if he hasn't made reparation or apologized to his victim, and that Christian love mandates forgiveness by a victim, even where the perpetrator hasn't repented.[2]

Although it is difficult to generalize, it is safe to say that, for most Jews, Wiesenthal was under an obligation *not* to forgive.

This is hardly the case for many Christians. In his response, the priest and former president of Notre Dame, Theodore Hesburgh, says "if asked to forgive, by anyone for anything, I would forgive because God would forgive."[3] Gregory Jones writes about *The Sunflower*, suggesting this response to the Nazi, assuming that he was as truly repentant as he appears to be.

> I cannot speak for your victims. However, I am called on to speak to you as a child of God, and as such I am empowered as a disciple of Jesus Christ to pronounce forgiveness in God's name. ... In the name of God I embrace you and tell you "Your sins are forgiven. ... May the peace of Christ be with you forevermore."[4]

---

2. Schimmel, *Wounds Not Healed*.
3. Hesburgh, *Sunflower*, 164.
4. Jones, *Sunflower*, 288.

This is not an easy issue for Christians. Jesus clearly gives to his disciples the power to forgive sins, and many Christians, such as Jones, believe this power extends to all believers. (John 20:23) Catholics would confine this power to the priesthood, recognizing with Jones that no human forgives in his own name, but only in the name of God, who remains the final judge.

Certainly, I am in no position to pronounce on this issue, and yet something about the forgiveness offered here is deeply troubling. If Jesus Christ was hesitant, as evidently he was, to grant forgiveness in his own name, but only in the name of the father, then who are we to forgive in the name of the father?[5] One does not have to be a student of theology to recommend that Christians hesitate before offering forgiveness, particularly to those whose crimes are odious, as well as to those whom we do not know well, and so are unable to form a judicious judgment about whether they are truly repentant.

Jews Have a Great Idea

The steps of forgiveness, outlined below, are loosely based on *teshuvah*, as they are laid out by Maimonides's *Laws of Forgiveness*, or *Hilkhot Teshuvah*. The term *teshuvah* means return: to God, Torah (the Old Testament), and the good. It is similar in meaning to *metanoia* in the New Testament, which refers to the changed state of mind brought about by repentance. (Mark 1:15) I chose the *Hilkhot Teshuvah* primarily because Jewish teachings approach forgiveness as a relationship between human beings, rather than focusing on forgiveness as a relationship between humans and God. Jewish teachings are also more specific about the obligation to forgive if the proper steps are taken.

The steps of forgiveness according to my loose, contemporary interpretation of Maimonides:

1. The offender acknowledges his or her offense in such a way as to demonstrate an understanding of why the offense was so hurtful.

2. The offender expresses remorse and regret to the victim, as well as those close to the victim. Expressions of remorse and regret to the victim's family are especially important when the victim is no longer

---

5. It is sometimes difficult to tell in whose name Jesus is acting, as he frequently speaks in the present passive, as in "your sins have been forgiven," without specifying by whom. See Mark 2:5–9. Bash, in Forgiveness and Christian Ethics (90–1), argues that Jesus in not claiming divine status as the one who forgives, but that can't be right. Jesus claims the authority to forgive sins at least three times. But in either case, we are not talking about human forgiveness. (Matthew 9:6; Mark 2:10; Luke 5:24)

in a position to acknowledge remorse (for example, when the victim is dead, whether or not he or she has been killed by the offender).

3. Making compensation when possible and relevant. The compensation must be directed to the victim and victim's family. Compensation to substitutes, such as acts of contrition aimed at the poor and destitute, are appropriate, but only if the victim and his or her family agree with the substitute, or if the victim and family are unavailable or unreceptive.

4. Living differently in the future, demonstrating that one is a changed person. A drunk driver who killed someone might give up drinking and join Alcoholics Anonymous, for example. For some interpreters of the Hebrew Bible, this is the step that validates all the others. Sometimes this is referred to as *teshuvah gemurah*, or complete repentance. Repentance is complete when opportunities to reoffend present themselves, and the offender refrains from doing so.

Forgiveness is a demanding human relationship. Forgiveness may be given freely, but that does not mean that it need not be earned. Though the point often seems lost in today's popular psychology of forgiveness, it is worth remembering that forgiveness requires someone to ask for forgiveness, and someone else to grant it. Forgiveness requires someone who will act the part of the penitent, and a victim who is willing to offer forgiveness if certain conditions are met. Each depends on the other. Without someone to ask forgiveness, it is hard to see what sense it makes to grant it.

What Forgiveness Is Not

Popular psychology, which spills over into popular theology, argues for forgiveness along the following lines: "Forgive, so that you will not carry this terrible burden of hate with you but can finally feel free." It is an awful answer from any perspective, forgiveness turned into a strategy of psychological self-help. I do not believe it is necessary to remove God from forgiveness, but the Jewish perspective has the great advantage of not being easily transformed into "cheap grace," as Dietrich Bonhoeffer called it (or cheap forgiveness).[6]

---

6. Bonhoeffer, *Cost of Discipleship*, 47, 53.

5

Forgiving a Mass Murderer: The Amish

I WANT TO TELL you a story about forgiveness. It begins with the murder of five Amish school girls, and the critical wounding of five others, at a one-room Amish schoolhouse in Nickel Mines, Pennsylvania, on October 2, 2006.

The girls, the oldest of whom was thirteen, were murdered by a demented local man named Charles Carl Roberts IV, who brought with him to the schoolhouse a semiautomatic pistol, six hundred rounds of ammunition, a shotgun, a stun gun, plastic ties to use as handcuffs, sexual lubricant, and a board with nails to barricade the school door shut. The teacher managed to slip out the side door almost immediately and ran for help; three policemen arrived within minutes. Ten more police arrived several minutes later. Negotiations were brief. Hearing shots from inside, they stormed the school. Roberts had shot himself in the head, but not before shooting the ten girls.

That evening, three Amish men went to visit Amy Roberts, Roberts's widow, who was staying with her parents. "We just talked with them for about ten minutes to express our sorrow and told them that we didn't hold anything against them," said one of the Amish visitors.[1] Several miles away, an Amish man went to see Carl Roberts's father, spending about an hour with him. A spokesman for the Roberts family later said, "He stood there for an hour, and he held that man [Mr. Roberts] in his arms and said, 'We forgive you.'" Presumably Mr. Roberts's father did not need forgiveness in any of the ways we ordinarily understand the term today, but perhaps that was not as important as the visit and the holding.

Acts of forgiveness and grace by the Amish continued. The parents of several of the slain children invited members of the Roberts family to attend their daughters' funerals. When Charles Roberts was buried, more than half of the seventy-five mourners were Amish. Most impressive, perhaps because

---

1. Kraybill, *Amish Grace*, 44.

it required that forgiveness be organized by thought, the Nickel Mines Accountability Committee, which received thousands of dollars in donations from all over the country and the world, decided to delete the name "Amish" from the committee, and direct a significant portion of the donations to the Roberts family for the support of Roberts's widow, and the education of the Roberts children. Many Amish also contributed to the Roberts Family Fund established at a local savings bank.

When asked why they forgave so rapidly, all the Amish cited the example of Jesus. While many aspects of the life and death of Jesus were mentioned, most prominent was the parable of the unforgiving servant. A servant who owed much (a staggering amount), was forgiven by his king, but the servant in turn did not forgive a lesser servant, who owed the forgiven servant far less. "In anger," said Jesus, the king "handed [the forgiven servant] over to the jailers to be tortured, until he should pay back all he owed. This is how my heavenly Father will treat each of you unless you forgive your brother or sister from your heart." (Matthew 18: 23–35) The lesson that you must forgive in order to be forgiven is explicit in Matthew 6:14–15, Mark 11:25, Luke 6:37. It is implicit in the Lord's Prayer. (Matthew 6:9–13; Luke 11:2–4)

With so much media attention directed to their acts of extraordinary forgiveness, the local Amish leaders wrote to their local newspaper to explain.

> There has been some confusion about our community's forgiving attitude, [but] if we do not forgive, how can we expect to be forgiven? By not forgiving, it will be more harmful to ourselves than to the one that did the evil deed.[2]

Reading about the extraordinary forgiveness offered by the Amish in this case, as well as a number of other cases, one has no sense that forgiveness is being offered out of fear, religious blackmail (forgive or go to Hell), or anything other than a deep commitment to a particular religious identity, an identity organized around the principles of nonresistance, forgiveness, discipleship, caring, and martyrdom. Or as one Amish woman put it, "You mean some people actually thought we got together to plan forgiveness?" The Amish did not plan forgiveness, because it was woven into their everyday lives.

The Amish are not perfect. Certain aspects of the mass murder actually made forgiveness easier. The murderer was not Amish, and was clearly deeply disturbed, if not insane. He was dead, and his family was not complicit. On the contrary, they were ashamed and deeply wounded by Charles Roberts IV's

---

2. Kraybill, *Amish Grace*, 44.

act. The Amish seem to struggle more with forgiveness when the offense occurs within Amish families, especially when it involves child abuse.[3]

Far from perfect, the Amish are unusual in that they truly believe their salvation is bound up with their willingness to forgive others, and that deeds, not words, are the measure of one's faith. The result is not an anxious toting up of sins on one side, acts of forgiveness on the other. The result is a community and way of life in some ways the opposite of that, one in which forgiveness comes with awesome speed, and frequently with genuine good will. This is the result, I believe, of the way in which community and tradition humanize an otherwise not terribly generous and gracious theological doctrine: forgive or be tortured in Hell.

A Different Interpretation of Forgiveness: Prolepsis

There are other Christian interpretations of forgiveness. My favorite is the *proleptic* interpretation of forgiveness. Prolepsis means assuming or acting as if something anticipated has already happened. Widely held, it is especially prevalent among Methodists and Lutherans, or at least among those who think about such things.

In the proleptic interpretation, forgiveness serves not primarily to absolve guilt, but to remind us what communion with God and each other can be. Why is communion so central? *Because we are already forgiven.* The forgiveness has happened. What we have to do is live up to our forgiveness, not just by forgiving others, but by living a life worthy of discipleship and Christ's sacrifice. We are already forgiven; we do not need to earn it, but we need to learn how to behave in its light. This is the real meaning of communion. Living up to our forgiveness is the opposite of what Dietrich Bonhoeffer called cheap grace.

> Cheap grace is not the kind of forgiveness of sin which frees us from the toils of sin. Cheap grace is the grace we bestow on ourselves. Cheap grace is the preaching of forgiveness without requiring repentance.... When he spoke of grace, Luther always implied as a corollary that it cost him his own life, the life which was now for the first time subjected to the absolute obedience of Christ.... Luther had said that grace alone can save; his followers took up his doctrine and repeated it word for word. But they left out its invariable corollary, the obligation of discipleship.[4]

3. Kraybill, *Amish Grace*, 113.
4. Bonhoeffer, *Cost of Discipleship*, 47, 53.

From a Christian proleptic perspective, repentance does not precede forgiveness. We are already forgiven, but the gift is not cheap, for we have to know, act, and live as though we earned it in order to be worthy of what we have been given through Christ's sacrifice. The doctrine is different from that of the Amish, which stresses salvation through forgiveness, but as the practice of the Amish suggests, doctrine may be less important than the community it is practiced in.

Conclusion: Most Christians and the Amish

What makes the Amish so extraordinary? The close community they live in, and the tradition they come from. The Amish stem from the Anabaptists, who were persecuted by the Lutherans and other protestant denominations during the Reformation. As a result, they have a long history of martyrdom, to which the dead girls were quickly assimilated, particularly the oldest, Marian, who according to the surviving children stepped forward and said, "Shoot me first."

Most Christians probably believe in a combination of the two doctrines. Christ suffered and died so that we might be forgiven. But we still have to forgive others, as the Lord has forgiven us. I also imagine that most Christians do not think about the details of forgiveness very much. That is not bad. Doctrinal inconsistencies don't matter very much as long as they do not lead to "cheap grace." Too often they do.

Part II: Theologians

Among theologians, I have included a couple of people generally not considered theologians, such as Albert Camus. If you think and write seriously about God, then you are a theologian.

6

Martin Luther

CAN HISTORY DEPEND ON just one man? Was Martin Luther that man? October 2017 was the 500th anniversary of Martin Luther's posting of his 95 theses on the door of the Wittenberg church. Or so the story goes. It might even be true, but there is no need to be overly dramatic. The church door served as a kind of community bulletin board.

An Angry Man

Luther was an angry, troubled man, who brought not just the church, but the medieval world, to the threshold of the modern. In 2000, *Life* magazine ranked Martin Luther third among the one hundred most important figures of the millennium.[1] I do not think most people pay that much attention to Luther anymore, but he was a big deal.

What I cannot figure out is the relationship between Luther's life and the transformation he wrought. Perhaps it was time for these changes to happen

---

1. Kolb, *Confessor of the Faith*, 1.

anyway, and Luther just happened to be there. In any case, the transformation of the world that began in Luther's era made our world possible.

Erik Erikson, who wrote a marvelous psychological biography of Luther, puts the question simply but incorrectly:

> Did Luther have a right to claim that his own fear, and his feeling of being oppressed by the image of an avenging God, were shared by others? Was his attitude representative of a pervasive religious atmosphere, at least in his corner of Christendom?[2]

It is not a question of right. It is a question of fit. Let's assume for a moment that Luther's hatred of the Pope was an attempt to free himself from his dominating father, Hans. Why did his personal psychological solution resonate so broadly? The church (and there was only one church, what today we call the Roman Catholic church) was corrupt to the core. His 95 theses were concerned with the church's selling of indulgences. Pay to pray, or at least put your prayer on the fast lane.

Against the Pope, Luther set scripture and faith. You did not have to listen to the Pope or priests, he said. A careful reading of the scriptures coupled with faith in Christ would see you through this world and into the next. (In his free time, Luther translated the Bible from both Hebrew and Greek into German, so the laity could actually read it.) Gutenberg's recent invention of the movable type printing press was more transformative than the internet, allowing for wide distribution of the scriptures.

Grace, Not Works

Grace, not works, was Luther's lesson, and God's grace is given freely because he loves us. (Romans 5:5) We do not have to earn grace, we cannot earn grace, rituals do not help, not even prayer helps. But we can have it in our hearts to receive grace, and with it salvation.[3]

One can see how this might free Luther from his father if, as seems likely, Luther psychologically identified his father with the Pope.

> There remains one motive which God and Martin shared at this time: the need for God to match Hans, within Martin, so that Martin would be able to disobey Hans and shift the whole matter of obedience and disavowal to a higher, and historically significant, plane.[4]

2. Erikson, *Young Man Luther*, 74.
3. Luther, *Bondage of the Will*.
4. Erikson, *Young Man Luther*, 94.

Equally striking is how Luther transformed his hatred of the Pope into a doctrine of love: not just of other people, but of this world. For Luther, reality was not measured by heaven. Reality is about how we live and love now. Family life is important. So is caring for others. If people can read the scriptures, then we do not need the church's authority. We do not need anybody's authority. This was the heart of the Protestant Reformation. This, I think, was exactly what the tradesmen, craftsmen, and merchants, the rising middle class of Germany, wanted to hear.

Plant a Tree

If the world were to end at any moment, what would you do? According to a story that grew after Luther's death—but is entirely in accord with his thought—Luther had said, "Plant a tree and feed others from it." Luther would have planted the tree both to enjoy its beauty as a reflection of God's goodness, and to produce fruit for his neighbors. This world remains a reflection of God, but it is up to us to care for others.

If God gives his grace freely, then we have more time and energy to serve our neighbor, and need not spend so much on seeking salvation through prayer and ritual. Doing so, thought Luther, was selfish.[5]

Luther's Sin

All his life Luther was an angry man, but toward the end of his life he became a vicious anti-Semite. I think the best response is that of Roland Bainton, who wrote that "one could wish that Luther had died before [his treatise against the Jews] was written."[6]

It gets worse. Hitler and his minions often referred to Luther in their anti-Semitic tracts. Luther's anti-Semitism was doctrinal, not racial, based primarily on the Jews' refusal to recognize the Trinity, but the difference hardly mattered to those who misused him centuries later.

Luther and Hitler

It is possible to compare Luther and Hitler by asking the following question: without them, would German history have taken an entirely different path?

One wants to believe (or at least I want to believe) that big historical movements take big historical causes. Certainly, something like the

---

5. Kolb, *Confessor of the Faith* 172–4.
6. Bainton, *Here I Stand*, 297.

Protestant Reformation would have happened without Luther, for it is what the modern world and a rising middle class wanted. "*Laissez faire et laissez passer, le monde va de lui même.*" Let us do and let us pass; for the world goes on by itself. While not originally directed at the Pope, this attitude of "let us alone, we can figure it out by ourselves," was widespread. How different the reformation would have been without Luther is impossible to say, but it would have happened.

How different German history would have been without Hitler is also hard to say. Jews would have been persecuted, and the object of pogroms. That was hardly new. But without Hitler, there would have been no Holocaust.[7] At the right place at the right time (or in Hitler's case, the wrong place at the wrong time), the fate of millions can depend on one man. Hardly a comforting thought, then or now.

---

7. Alford, *After the Holocaust*.

7.1

Bonhoeffer: Religionless Christianity

Religionless Christianity may seem like a contradiction. It is not. Christ did not seek to establish a religion, but to speak for the oppressed and downtrodden, as well as to save our souls. He and his first followers sought to establish communities in the midst of empire.

The term "religionless Christianity" belongs to Dietrich Bonhoeffer, and because Bonhoeffer was murdered before he developed his ideas, it has sometimes been mistaken for something like the death of God. Not so.

Bonhoeffer was 39 years old when he was executed by the Nazis in Flossenbürg concentration camp in 1945. He co-founded the Confessing Church in 1934 when the German Lutheran Church adopted the Aryan paragraph, in which converted Christians were barred from the church. But he was murdered because he was involved in the plot to kill Hitler.

Bonhoeffer believed that the church will always submit to the state. The situation in Germany was extreme, Hitler eventually appointing the *Reichsbischof* of the Evangelical Church, the state Church.

But Bonhoeffer's view of history was longer than that. Ever since the thirteenth century, the Western world has found less need for the "God hypothesis," as he called it. Everyone from Machiavelli to Hobbes to Galileo, and every discipline from science and technology to medicine and law, created worlds with no place for God. The world, Bonhoeffer declared, has "come of age." In some ways this is good, as people take responsibility for their own fates instead of blaming God.

The co-optation of the Christian church began with the Roman Emperor Constantine (circa 300 CE), says Bonhoeffer, but its role as servant of empire has never changed. One might ask whether things are different now. The answer is yes, but not better. In the Islamic world, it is not always clear if religion serves the state or vice versa. In any case, they are all mixed up. In the United States, we still ask God to bless our soldiers as they go off to kill people. War may sometimes be necessary, but it should not be confused with the work of the Lord. People can't seem to help seeking God's justification for killing other people.

Karl Barth

Barth is generally regarded (at least by Wikipedia) as the greatest Protestant theologian of the twentieth century. While their views diverge, Barth's view of the relationship between Christ and church inspired Bonhoeffer.

> Jesus simply has nothing to do with religion. The meaning of his life is the actuality of that which is actual in no religion, the actuality of the unapproachable, unfathomable, incomprehensible.[1]

But whereas Barth sought an experience of the divine, Bonhoeffer turned to life in this world.

No Redemption, or, Not My Sunday School Class

For Bonhoeffer, religion is no longer about redemption. Religionless Christianity is interested in two things: prayer and righteous action.

Bonhoeffer came to admire the Old Testament (as Christians call it) more and more because it is not a teaching of redemption. "Myths of redemption search outside history for an eternity after death."[2] Emmanuel Levinas, whose thought converges with Bonhoeffer's in surprising ways, calls Judaism "a religion for adults," because there is no personal salvation at the end.[3] Our job is to care for others in this world. Bonhoeffer agrees.

No one ever taught me this in Sunday school.

Prayer and Righteous Action

What would remain of Christianity after its outer trappings have been stripped away?

---

1. Barth, *Word of God*, 94.
2. Bonhoeffer, *Letters from Prison*, 336.
3. Levinas, *A Religion for Adults*.

Prayer

Bonhoeffer believed that intercessory prayer (prayer on behalf of others) created a sense of empathy and solidarity with the people one prays for. "In prayer," said Bonhoeffer, "I move into the other man's place. I enter his life . . . his guilt and distress. I am afflicted by his sins and his infirmity."[4] Only if we identify with the suffering of others will we act to make their lives better.

I wish it were so. My experience with prayer is that it just as often lets people off the hook. "Oh, those poor people in Yemen. I must remember them in my prayers." Well, that is nice, but it is not going to help them. Bonhoeffer does not share my cynicism; he thinks prayer leads to action.

Action

Bonhoeffer did not believe that prayer generally or usually leads to action. It leads to action only when we understand God properly. God is not strong, but weak.

God's participation in Christ, his identity with Christ, meant for Bonhoeffer that God chose to become weak and powerless so as to identify with and represent the suffering of this world. Bonhoeffer believed, and I think he was right, that this vision of a weak God who depended on humans to do his work in this world was a uniquely valuable aspect of Christianity. God not only speaks for the outcast; he became one.

Conversely,

> Bonhoeffer knew that a category such as God's omnipotence was not to be seen as an authentic aspect of God's nature, but was our understanding of power extended out into the world.[5]

Prayer leads to righteous action when we understand that if people are going to be saved from lives of living hell (right now I am thinking of Yemen, but there are many living hells, some private), then other people are going to have to save them. Our prayers should ask for the strength and courage to care for others, and support others who do, for no one else is going to do it for us.

---

4. Bonhoeffer, *Sanctorum Communio*, 133.
5. Pugh, *Religionless Christianity*, 99.

What Happened to the Church?

Sometimes it seems that, for Bonhoeffer, we could get by on prayer and social service agencies. Not so. His alternative to the church seems to be small ecclesiastical communities such as Finkenwalde, the illegal seminary he established for the Confessing Church from 1935–1937, when it was closed by the Gestapo. There students and faculty lived together as well as studied and worshipped together. His experience there was the basis of his book, *Life Together*.

Perhaps the best contemporary, or at least recent, model is the Christian base communities in El Salvador and elsewhere, including Eastern Europe, associated with liberation theology. The theological stance of these communities is that of Bonhoeffer, in which God becomes man in order to speak

> from the perspective of the outcast, the suspects, the maltreated, the powerless and oppressed, the reviled—in short, from the perspective of those who suffer.[6]

Another possibility, especially in the city, would be intentional communities in which people would be united in aim, not location, coming together in prayer and to donate their time, energy, and skills to others.

The Secret

Bonhoeffer writes of the "secret discipline" that constitutes prayer and worship in the absence of religion. "In prison, he seems to be moving back to the community in Finkenwalde," implying that God's self-revelation is realized most fully in "the community that was able to keep the discipline of the secret."[7]

Pugh thinks the secret is the Eucharist. I think the secret is best expressed in God's weakness, for anytime God becomes part of the world, he becomes an icon of power. Still, Pugh is not far from this view.

> The community formed by the discipline of the secret is able to ask the world why it remains oblivious to the screams of its victims.[8]

---

6. Bonhoeffer, *Letters*, 18.
7. Pugh, *Religionless Christianity*, 144–5.
8. Pugh, *Religionless Christianity*, 150.

What Happened to God?

Does Bonhoeffer still believe in God? Yes, the question is how he believes. It depends on whether you focus on *The Cost of Discipleship* (original 1937), or the late *Letters and Papers from Prison*, collected after his death less than ten years later. In *Discipleship*, Bonhoeffer's belief is conventional, if severe. In *Letters*, Bonhoeffer believes in an unconventional God, similar in some respects to the God of Levinas (chapter 20 of this work); that is, knowable only through the suffering of the other person. As Bonhoeffer puts it,

> the transcendental is not infinite and unattainable tasks, but the neighbour who is within reach in any given situation.[9]

The transcendent is here and now, in the desperate needs of others. Not a bad way of thinking about something otherwise so abstract.

---

9. Bonhoeffer, *Letters*, 381.

7.2

Bonhoeffer: Can I Just Be a Second-Rate Christian?

DIETRICH BONHOEFFER WAS 39 years old when he was executed by the Nazis in Flossenbürg concentration camp in 1945. He co-founded the Confessing Church in 1934, when the German Lutheran Church adopted the Aryan paragraph, in which converted Christians were barred from the church. But he was murdered because he was involved in the plot to kill Hitler.

His most well-known book, *The Cost of Discipleship*, argues against cheap grace.

> Cheap grace is the preaching of forgiveness without requiring repentance, baptism without church discipline, Communion without confession, absolution without personal confession. Cheap grace is grace without discipleship.[1]

Cheap grace completely, and perhaps intentionally, misunderstands Martin Luther.

> When he spoke of grace, Luther always implied as a corollary that it cost him his own life, the life which was now for the first time subjected to the absolute obedience of Christ. Only so could he speak of grace. Luther had said that grace alone can save. His followers took up his doctrine and repeated it word for word. But they left out its invariable corollary, the obligation of discipleship.[2]

The obligation of discipleship is complete. God asks everything of us, including our lives. Bonhoeffer practiced what he preached.

---

1. Bonhoeffer, *Cost of Discipleship*, 47.
2. Bonhoeffer, *Cost of Discipleship*, 53.

Can I Just Give Some of My Money Away?

In Bonhoeffer's account, giving everything means just that. In a well-known Biblical story, a rich man goes up to Jesus and says that he has fulfilled the Ten Commandments, what more can he do? Jesus answered, "If you want to be perfect, go, sell your possessions and give to the poor, and you will have treasure in heaven. Then come, follow me." (Matthew 19:21–22) When the young man heard this, he went away sad, because he had great wealth.

The man went away sad, I imagine, because he knew he was not going to give his wealth away and follow Jesus. The Ten Commandments are easy compared to that.

Bonhoeffer takes the Bible seriously. If Christ says to give all your money away to the poor, then that is what you do. This is how religion remains relevant.

Letters from Prison

In his letters from prison, written shortly before his execution, Bonhoeffer goes even further. The church itself should give away all its property. The difference in tone between *Discipleship* and *Letters* is remarkable, and I commented on "religionless Christianity" in my previous chapter. But the basic idea remains the same. Do not just pray. Work at being a Christian; do something.

But I Do Not Want to Be Perfect

When I read Christ's response to the rich man, I struggle for an out, an escape. After all, Christ did say if you want to be *perfect*, give all your money away. What if I do not want to be a perfect Christian? Can I then just give some of my money away; can I just tithe ten percent?

I do not think my response is in the spirit of Christ's advice. Sometimes I pray for forgiveness for not giving more of my money to the poor. But then I realize that I cannot ask for forgiveness for something I am not willing to change. Perhaps if I had more money, but of course that's a cop-out too.

The United States is not a good country in which to be old and poor, and it is getting worse. I do not want to spend my money on a Mercedes, or a thirty-foot boat, both of which I see frequently here on Cape Cod. I just want to have financial security in my old age.

Can I just will the money to charity after my wife and I are gone? That is possible, I suppose, though it does not seem to be what Christ meant either. And in any case, the obligation of the young man was not only to give away his wealth, but to abandon his previous life.

Bonhoeffer took the Bible seriously, but he took Christ more seriously. There is no distinction between faith and works. Or if there is, works comes first, from which emerges faith. One does works in order to have faith. That tired distinction is not going to help me out either, as in "Well, I do not give much money to the poor, but I have great faith." Yet another cop-out.

Bonhoeffer and Peter Singer

> The issue can no longer be evaded. It is becoming clearer every day that the most urgent problem besetting our Church is this: How can we live the Christian life in the modern world?[3]

At first, I say to myself that I have no idea how to live a Christian life in today's world. But if I am being honest with myself, then I realize I have a pretty good idea, and Peter Singer is a good example. Singer is a professor of ethics at Princeton University and the University of Melbourne. He has nowhere said he is a Christian. His parents were Austrian Jews who immigrated to Australia in 1938.

Singer himself seems to give away about twenty percent of his income, maybe more. In arguing that you should give more (not more than Singer, just more than you do), Singer uses an analogy, a less cryptic version of Christ's parables.

Suppose you see a child drowning in a muddy pool. You can rescue the child with no danger to yourself, but at the cost of ruining your expensive new suit.[4] Clearly you are morally obliged to rescue the child. Your new suit hardly figures in the moral equation. If you do not donate ten to twenty percent of your money to charities that feed, clothe, and shelter the poor, such as Oxfam or Care, then you are ignoring the drowning child. In one way or another, hundreds of millions are drowning around the world, and it is your obligation to save as many as you can. What a difference in my life, and yours, that would make.

By the way, it does not count if you give to public radio, or the art museum, charities of, by, and for the middle classes. I would say this raises a real problem for those who give their money to their church or synagogue, but I will not pursue it here.

---

3. Bonhoeffer, *Cost of Discipleship*, 60.
4. Singer, *Practical Ethics*, 199.

Conclusion

Singer's is not a religious argument. It is an argument about collective well-being. Jesus is, in any case, more stringent. Give all you have and follow Christ. Bonhoeffer gave his life. What have I given? What should I give? More than I do, I'm sure. And you?

7.3

Basics of Bonhoeffer

DIETRICH BONHOEFFER WAS NOT a systematic thinker, and I have had difficulty finding the themes that connect his thoughts. One problem is that his early writings, such as *The Cost of Discipleship*, differ from his latter writings, especially his *Letters and Papers from Prison*, written in the two years between his arrest and later murder by the Gestapo when his link to the plot to assassinate Hitler was uncovered.

I have focused on his *Letters*, which ask how a Christian is to live in a world that barely pretends to believe in God, a question that has become more pressing in recent years, at least in the Western world. I believe these themes summarize the thought of the mature Bonhoeffer, who died at the age of 39. To speak of the "mature Bonhoeffer" who died so young might sound silly, but by then he had been a mature thinker for years.

An earlier chapter addresses *The Cost of Discipleship*; another addresses his "religionless Christianity."

Live as if There Is No God?

For Bonhoeffer, we must live as if there is no God. By this he means several things. First, that in the modern world, there is no place for God. Some people still go to church and observe the rituals, but religion is confined to a small corner of life. The real issues of making a living, raising a family, and dealing with the problems of everyday life no longer have much to do with religion. But, Bonhoeffer argues, this is not entirely bad. In a world "come of age," we must do God's work for him. "Religionless Christianity," as he calls it, means action, not worship. In a letter to a nephew about the world he would inherit, Bonhoeffer wrote:

Our earlier words . . . [will] lose their force and cease, and our being Christians today will be limited to two things: prayer and righteous action among men.[1]

God Chose Weakness

In writing about the role of religion, Bonhoeffer is not just making an observation about our churches. More important is his theological point that God chose weakness. That is the significance of Christ. God did not send a powerful leader to save us, but one who died like the least of us, alone, tormented, abandoned, like a refugee dying of thirst in the Sonoran Desert. This man or woman is close to Christ. Our task is to grasp this image of Christ, which means understanding that God is weak, but we can be strong if we dedicate ourselves to serving him.

The God who emptied himself into Jesus (*kenosis*), becoming weak and powerless, so as to know and feel our suffering, is perhaps the most difficult concept for Christians to bear, and the most important.

The "Secret Discipline"

By this way of thinking, the church is redundant. Give the property of the church to the needy, and gather in each other's homes as the original Christians did.[2] Dedicating your life to others and prayer are the only essentials to Christianity. Prayer is so important not because God answers every prayer, but because it is the way we keep the needs of others in mind, putting ourselves in their shoes. Previously, I questioned whether this is true about prayer, but it is Bonhoeffer's view, and the best way to understand what he means by religionless Christianity.

Bonhoeffer writes of the "secret discipline" that constitutes prayer and worship in the absence of religion. Some have interpreted this as a reference to the Eucharist. I think it refers to the discipline required of Christians once the familiar institutions of religion are gone. Without these institutions, it is doubly difficult, and doubly important, to follow the path of Christ, while reinterpreting what that means in today's world. One thing it means is to stop worshipping success.

> In a world where success is the measure and justification of all things the figure of Him who was sentenced and crucified

---

1. Bonhoeffer, *Letters*, 300.
2. Bonhoeffer, *Letters*, 382–3.

remains a stranger and is at best the object of pity. . . . The figure of the Crucified invalidates all thought that takes success for its standard.[3]

The Transcendental Is Our Neighbor

Bonhoeffer asks us to reinterpret basic religious concepts in a worldly way, concepts such as repentance, faith, justification, rebirth, and sanctification. This would truly be, says Bonhoeffer, "the word became flesh." (John 1:14) Bonhoeffer was murdered before he could elaborate this theme. Seventy-five years later, the task remains undone, hardly begun. Still, we can imagine what it might look like. Faith is no longer expressed by observing the rituals of the church, but by helping to feed the hungry and house the homeless. By this measure, men and women of great faith may belong to no church at all. This is a familiar idea, but the idea that this is the true meaning of "the word became flesh" helps us think about it differently.

> The transcendental is not infinite and unattainable tasks, but the neighbor who is within reach in any given situation.[4]

We desire to have an immediate experience of Christ. What we get is a chance to serve others. It takes a grownup to accept this and act accordingly.

Not the Afterlife, But this Life

Is there any concern at all in the Old Testament about saving one's soul, asks Bonhoeffer? No, and that too is good. Not with the beyond should we be concerned, but this world as it is now, this world as it could be reconciled and restored. That is what salvation looks like, and what a worldly reinterpretation of sanctification might resemble.

Say Yes to God's Earth

If there is any theme that ties all this together, it is in his letter to his fiancée on their upcoming marriage, which was not to be. Marriage, he says, is a "'yes' to God's earth."[5] We celebrate God when we celebrate human life together. Marriage is an act of faith, not just in each other, but in God's world. Marriage is a prayer.

3. Bonhoeffer, *Ethics*, 77.
4. Bonhoeffer, *Letters*, 381.
5. Bonhoeffer, *Letters*, 456.

The Man

Focusing on Bonhoeffer's theology risks missing the extraordinary man who made it. A comrade who shared his last days, confined in a special prison in Buchenwald concentration camp, knowing they would almost certainly be killed, wrote of him this way:

> He always seemed to me to diffuse an atmosphere of . . . deep gratitude for the mere fact that he was alive. . . . He was one of the very few men that I have ever met to whom his God was real and ever close to him.[6]

---

6. Metaxas, *Bonhoeffer*, 514.

8

Bultmann: What Does It Matter if the Bible Is a Myth?

> We cannot use electric lights and radios and, in the event of illness, avail ourselves of modern medical and clinical means and at the same time believe in the spirit and wonder world of the New Testament.

WHO WROTE THIS ABOUT the wonder world of the New Testament? One of the many aggressive atheists who contend with religion these days? No, one of the most distinguished theologians of the twentieth century, Rudolf Bultmann.[1] The mythological world of the New Testament was the everyday world of men and women over two thousand years ago. Demons were everywhere, and heaven and hell were real places. Many Christians no longer believe in this magical world. The result is to question the relevance of the gospel. Needed, says Bultmann, is a demythologizing interpretation that retains the truth of the *kerygma*.

> What sense does it make to confess today "he descended into hell" or "he ascended into heaven," if the confessor no longer shares the underlying mythical world picture of a three-story world?[2]

What Is *Kerygma*?

Kerygma means preaching, and it refers to the message of the gospels. Whatever that is, it's not the Apostles' Creed or Nicene Creed, both of which refer to the three-story world. For Bultmann, the *kerygma* refers to God's decisive act in Christ, above all his death and resurrection. The question of

1. Bultmann, *New Testament*, 4.
2. Bultmann, *New Testament*, 4.

course is, why is this not just as mythical as a three-story world filled with angels and demons?

Bultmann argues that the message of the gospels will change in form depending on the world in which it lives. In a mythical world, the gospel will use mythical themes. In a scientific and technological world, we must depend more on faith. Not about everything. Christ was a real historical man who was crucified. But about his resurrection, faith is required. Demythologizing, says Bultmann,

> seeks to bring out the real intention of myth, namely, its intention to talk about human existence as grounded in and limited by a transcendent unworldly power, which is not visible to objectifying thinking.[3]

Now It Gets Complicated

It gets complicated because myth, while better understanding human limits, also objectifies. Its stories are situated in time and place, and transcendent powers are often represented by gods who look, act, and think like more powerful people.

Faith is concerned with a world that cannot be objectified or signified.

> Demythologizing in the sense of existentialist interpretation seeks, in critically interpreting the mythical world picture of scripture, to bring out the point of its statements by freeing them from the conceptuality of objectifying thinking—the objectifying thinking of myth.[4]

Bultmann still uses the word "salvation," but his is really an existential view of religion, and he prefers the term "authentic." Belief is all about my experience now. Religion is not about a faith community's experience, or shared doctrine and belief. And salvation is not about our final destination. It is about how we live our lives every day, recognizing that the salvific event is neither past nor future, but now. This is how a world of faith can do the work once done by a world of myth.

The advantage of this view is that faith, while somewhat more at home in a mythological world, is really about no world. Faith requires the surrender of security; the abandonment of a world one can grab hold of. Faith says that the *kerygma* is nevertheless true, even if everything around us says no. Faith is the willingness to fall endlessly, in the belief that God will catch us.

3. Bultmann, *New Testament*, 99.
4. Bultmann, *New Testament*, 102.

The Eschaton Is Now

Bultmann argues that the eschaton (the end of history, when Christ returns) has already happened. Instead of waiting for the end of history, we should recognize that the end, by which I mean goal or purpose of history, has already happened with Christ's death and resurrection. "Paradoxically, the community of faith looks ahead to an event that has already happened."[5]

At Christmas season, many of us celebrate and remember Christ's birth. But if one takes Bultmann seriously, then Christ's birth was already the end (purpose) of history, the beginning and the end at the same time. For me, this makes Christmas a more solemn occasion; Christ's birth was the gift of his death for humanity.

The Gospel Is Freedom from this World

> And what is the gospel? In a word: freedom from this world. The gospel has the power to grant freedom from the world.[6]

Bultmann's focus on the de-objectified gospel encourages us to step back from the world, and all that it offers. There is no security but God. (Matthew 9:16–20) Certainly, this is true from the perspective of eternity. But in everyday life, material security matters. Religious people who work on behalf of the poor are doing God's work. I do not think Bultmann has enough to say about this. He is more worried about authenticity than community.

Bultmann's perspective is one from which we can distance ourselves from the world. That is the greatest freedom: to have a place to be, a place to rest that does not depend on our place in the world. Christ's inbreaking, the experience of *kerygma*, allows that freedom. Perhaps it is the only perspective that does. More broadly, a religious perspective is the only perspective that puts the world in its place. And while it is not the only freedom (one's daily bread comes first), it is the most important one.

---

5. Congdon, *Bultmann*, 147.
6. Bultmann, *This World and Beyond*, 156.

9.1

Kierkegaard: The Leap to Faith

ONE OF THE BEST ways to understand religion is in terms of what Søren Kierkegaard called the "leap."[1] He never used the term "leap of faith." I am still struggling with Kierkegaard, and am particularly interested in the religious implications of his earlier works, those not explicitly Christian. When people refer to Kierkegaard as the first existentialist, it is to these earlier works that they refer. One influence on my decision to study Kierkegaard was reading some of Reinhold Niebuhr's sermons, prayers, and religious essays. Far from being a "Christian realist," as he is sometimes called, Niebuhr was first of all a man of faith. But what does this mean?

Truth as Subjectivity

It means that through an act of "imaginative reorientation," one chooses to see the world as gift, and Christ as our savior, because doing so makes life more meaningful. Reasons can be given, but the world as gift and Christ as savior becomes a reality by acting as if it were so. This is what Kierkegaard means by "truth as subjectivity."

Truth is not just a proposition. Truth becomes a way of life. This is exemplified in Christ's claim that "I am the way, the truth, and the life." (John 14:6) Christ not only claims to teach the truth; His life *is* the truth. Our lives can never be the truth, but we can seek to make the ideals represented by Christ's life and teachings our own, insofar as this is humanly possible. In this way, faith becomes a reality.

---

1. Kierkegaard, *Postscript*, 340.

Abraham and Isaac: Attempted Murder or Sacrifice?

If Abraham is taken as a model of faith, then the story of the binding (*Akedah*) of Isaac is an unethical act.

> The ethical expression for what Abraham did is that he intended to murder Isaac; the religious expression is that he intended to sacrifice Isaac. But in this contradiction lies precisely the anxiety that indeed can make a person sleepless, and yet Abraham is not who he is without this anxiety.[2]

If Abraham is justified in sacrificing Isaac, then there must be something higher than the ethical. Kierkegaard calls this the "teleological suspension of the ethical." (Sometimes I find Kierkegaard's terminology almost unbearable.)

Kierkegaard seeks to find a place to stand outside society, which for him is identical with the ethical. The ethical is whatever society says it is, what Hegel called *Sittlichkeit*, the ethical order that makes society possible. But truth is the word of God. Abraham is a "knight of faith," one who obeys only himself and God. The morality of society has nothing to do with it. For Kierkegaard, that is good.

Less frequently commented on is another version of this story told by Kierkegaard in which Abraham knew he was willing to do God's bidding, but he also knew that God should never have asked it of him. For the rest of his life, Abraham was depressed by this knowledge.

> Isaac throve as before; but Abraham's eye was darkened, he saw joy no more.[3]

Do we not have a right to expect that a just and merciful God would not put us to such a terrible test in the first place? Or should we say with the Lord that His thoughts are not our thoughts, and His ways are not our ways. (Isaiah 55:8–9) For nothing is changed in this story when an angel steps in at the end, halts Abraham's hand at the moment he would slit his son's throat, and substitutes a ram caught in a thicket. Abraham would have killed his adored son, and he knows it. That is what pains him forever, or so Kierkegaard imagines. He has a good imagination.

---

2. Kierkegaard, *Fear and Trembling*, 20.
3. Kierkegaard, *Fear and Trembling*, 46.

To Be Fit for Eternity

We can worry about whether something called "eternal life" exists. At the committal of the body to the grave, one of the rites of the Anglican Church (shared by other churches) refers to "the sure and certain hope of the resurrection to eternal life," a wording that has always struck me as odd. A sure and certain hope is still just a hope, one that sounds a little desperate.

Kierkegaard would say that we are worrying about the wrong thing. The right thing to worry about is not whether eternal life exists, but whether I am worthy of it. As he faces his death, Socrates is uncertain about eternity, but it does not worry him. Life after death may be nothingness, an endless sleep, or it may be his version of heaven, questioning the great heroes of the past (*Apology*, 40b-41e). What Socrates worries about is whether he has ordered his life so that he might be fit for eternity. In worrying about his fitness for eternity, Socrates is creating eternity. We can do the same.

The Incarnation *Is* Christianity; It Is Not a Paradox

For Kierkegaard, the central doctrine of Christianity is that at a certain point in history, God took on human form and loved us from a position of utter vulnerability, feeling human pain in every bone of his body. This vulnerability destroyed him, or would have, if Christ were fully human, but he was not, and so he saved us by giving us a plan for how to live and die, and the faith to believe in him.[4]

The contradiction of the incarnation is that something cannot be eternal and temporal at the same time. But there is no contradiction, for contradiction can only be logical, and the incarnation is simply unbelievable. But that does not speak against it either, for much that is unbelievable is true, such as the scientific claim that 93% of our bodies were originally stardust.

This means that I can experience the incarnation through faith, or I can think reasonably about it. If I can think about it, then it is not a contradiction like a square circle, which is a logical contradiction based on the definition of terms. That God became man is actually closer to a historical claim about an event in time, albeit one that can never be proven. But we do not even need to prove it; we just have to live as though it were true. Doing so is faith.

---

4. Kierkegaard, *Philosophical Fragments*, 108–9.

What Would Kierkegaard Say to Western Intellectuals Today?

What would Kierkegaard say to Western intellectuals who believe that we live in a post-Christian world? The first thing he would say is that questions of faith have nothing to do with the time in which one lives. Conversely, one cannot conclude that Christianity was true merely because it has endured for millennia. Kierkegaard detested Christendom, the establishment religion. It means nothing to believe in Christianity because others do, or disbelieve because others do not.

Is not the loss of faith really the decline of the mythic imagination, by which I mean the ability to tell good stories about the meaning of life? Myths are neither true nor false; they are either rich or impoverished in narrative, symbol, and meaning. Science tells us about a marvelous and fantastic world. Science also gets things done. But it has nothing to say about faith, and the fact that we live in a so-called scientific world only means that we have to work harder to make our faith real. That is the real meaning of subjective truth.

9.2

Kierkegaard: The Tragedy of Grace

MOST CHRISTIANS AGREE THAT we cannot save ourselves. God offers his grace freely, not because we merit it, but because God loves us. As Paul puts it,

> For it is by grace that you have been saved, through faith—and this is not from yourselves. It is the gift of God—not by works. (Ephesians 2:8–9)

The difference among Christians is how we earn grace. Faith or works is the usual distinction, but of course that is too crude. I am going to follow Kierkegaard (as far as I can). Because Kierkegaard is generally considered the first existentialist, choice must be important.

Love or Adversity?

Kierkegaard begins "Strengthening in the Inner Being," his most sustained treatment of grace, with a quotation from Paul, one that comes just a few verses after that quoted above:

> And I pray that you, being rooted and established in love, may have power, together with all the Lord's holy people, to grasp how wide and long and high and deep is the love of Christ. (Ephesians 3:17–18)

From here, Kierkegaard goes on to write about how adversity can lead you to God's grace, whereas Paul, who was experiencing real adversity (house arrest, and worse to come) when he wrote the Ephesians, wrote about love.[1]

---

1. Paul's authorship of the Letter to the Ephesians is contested. Many regard it as Deutero-Pauline; that is, a letter written by another who deeply understands Paul's ideas. Many believe Paul himself wrote the letter. I don't think it makes much difference; the tone and spirit are Paul's.

Though Kierkegaard wrote a fine book on love (*agape*) late in life,[2] there is not much love when Kierkegaard writes of grace. For Kierkegaard, grace comes from adversity.

What Is the Problem with Kierkegaard?

Kierkegaard is such an individualist that he does not allow for tragedy. Some people live in circumstances that lead them to be unreceptive to God's grace. Kierkegaard insists on radical individual responsibility. (In his journals, Kierkegaard wrote, "I wish that on my grave might be put 'the individual'"; it was not.) Other people, thought Kierkegaard, cannot do much to lead you to God, or keep you away from him.

At the close of "Strengthening in the Inner Being," Kierkegaard writes, "blessed is the person who could truthfully say: God in heaven was my first love."[3] Well, no one can say this. Ever. We are all embodied beings attached to those who care for us as children, even when this care is bad. It is only this early love that makes the adult acceptance of grace possible. Absent this early love, we do not love God first. We do not love, at least not well.

I would say this is the key error in Kierkegaard's thinking about grace. He understands that we have to choose to accept grace, and that doing so involves a leap to faith. But he nowhere admits that external forces can make us too blind and scared to leap.

Calvin argued that some people are barred from grace because they are not members of God's elect. In my account, God does not choose, but society may. Consider the following:

- a lack of love
- extreme poverty
- abuse, and even torture
- severe trauma

All these may close a person within him- or herself, impoverishing the spiritual imagination. Some people will overcome this adversity; many will not. The external practice of religion, such as going to church or synagogue, has relatively little to do with whether one has experienced grace. Grace is an inner experience that requires external support; it is not demonstrated by ritual, though ritual may help support it.

---

2. Kierkegaard, *Works of Love*.
3. Kierkegaard, *Inner Being*, 101.

One More Barrier for the Intellectual Elite

There is one more barrier to grace. An impoverished culture among intellectual elites, some of whom take pride in the destruction of "grand narratives," as they are called. Poverty comes in at least two forms: deprivation of love (including the love of neighbors, who fail to notice and care for those in need), and the deprivation imposed by an intellectual culture that destroys the spiritual imagination.

Tragedy and Grace, Heaven and Hell

In earlier times, people wondered if the pagan, someone who had never heard of the Judeo-Christian God, is doomed to Hell. It hardly seems fair. Well, what if we imagine there is no heaven or hell? Then those who are unable to receive God's grace live in a tragic world, in which the richness of belief is unavailable. This is not Calvin's tragedy of being excluded from the elect. It is a social and spiritual tragedy, and we ought to recognize what a disaster it is, emptying the world of mystery and faith. This emptying began with the Enlightenment (which was originally progress), and has accelerated in recent years: from faith in reason to faith in nothing.

The Obligation of Grace

The obligation of grace to which Bonhoeffer refers obligates us to foster ways of life and love that open all of us to the experience of grace. Not evangelism, but social, intellectual, and economic change on a large scale is needed. We live in a tragic world, but blindness to grace is primarily a social problem. Not just a social problem. Some will be forever closed to the experience, for that is who they are. But it is the social barriers that we can do something about.

Doing something about these barriers is how we express our gratitude for grace. In other words, it is how we become worthy of the gift.

9.3

Kierkegaard Is Wrong: An Absurd God Is Not Good

Kierkegaard says that there are three stages to life: the aesthetic, the ethical, and the religious. The aesthetic life is concerned with pleasure. The ethical life is concerned with living by principle. If married, I should follow the principles of marriage, which are loyalty, care, and love. The ethical man acts in a way he would want others to act. It is actually pretty close to the golden rule, which in turn is pretty close to what Immanuel Kant called the "categorical imperative."

The religious stage is where it gets complicated, because Kierkegaard subdivided the religious stage into A and B. We reach the religious stage when we see that the principles that guide our lives are not merely a product of human reason, but a divine imperative. Failing to live up to these principles is not only unethical; it is an insult to God.

Kierkegaard makes a big deal out of the difference between what he calls "religiousness A and religiousness B."[1] The main difference is that in religiousness A, God is thought of as comprehensible by humans, and understandable by reason, at least to a certain degree. There is continuity between the ethical and religiousness A.

Stage B, which Kierkegaard sometimes calls simply Christianity, is where God is beyond human reason, infinitely different and utterly inexplicable. Kierkegaard frequently uses the term "absurd" to characterize this God and his commandments. The experience of God as absurd is good, for it means we have abandoned trying to understand him. To act on the absurd is to act completely on faith.

---

1. Kierkegaard, *Postscript*, 556–82.

Religion Is a Bad Idea

We should not expect God to be a larger and more powerful version of a human. To fail to recognize and appreciate God's otherness is a mistake. Nevertheless, God's commandments, his presence in our lives, must be recognizably good, decent, and moral, or he is no longer a God whom humans can worship.

Consider the Ten Commandments, particularly the last five, which concern human relationships. The tenth commandment not to covet or envy another's relations or possessions is probably impossible for humans to fill, and perhaps not even always desirable. Thoughts and deeds are two different things. Nevertheless, the commandments overall make moral sense. They accord with our natural feelings about lying, cheating, stealing, and murder, even if there are contextual differences. Murder is not always murder, as any soldier knows. Sometimes these natural feelings are called the "natural law," things that every normal human knows just by growing up in a decent society with decent parents (see part V).

Is It Good to Worship the Gods?

At about the same time as the middle books of the Old Testament were being written, Socrates asked a simple but important question: Is it good to worship the gods, or do we worship the gods because they are good? (Plato, *Euthyphro* 10a-10e) The second choice is the only answer that makes sense, and it means that there must be some continuity between human categories of goodness and those of God. Otherwise, we could not answer the question, for humans would have no independent concept of goodness by which to evaluate the gods.

Perhaps "evaluating God" sounds arrogant, but what it really means is that the faith is not a matter of submission, but trust. We have faith in God because God is good. The Old Testament, especially, has lots of examples where God is not so good (1 Samuel 15:2–3), but that is probably best interpreted as part of the historical process by which the Hebrews came to make sense of their (that is, our) God, one in which God gradually became less anthropomorphic.

Jesus Christ raises the same problem. Consider his explanation of why he speaks in parables: because outsiders might understand him, and so be forgiven. (Mark 4:10–12) But his basic lesson, to love God and to love your neighbor as yourself, corresponds with cultivated human intuition, even if it would have made no sense in some cultures, such as the competitive (agonal) culture of ancient Greece as represented in the *Iliad*.

It is neither necessary nor desirable that everything God says be already known by humans, or fit our moral categories. But there must be overlap, otherwise it would make no sense to worship God. Recall, we worship God because he is good. Were God not good in terms humans could understand, humans would still be in awe of him. But unless God is good as well as powerful, it makes no sense to worship him, except perhaps as a way of escaping his wrath, and that is not really worship, is it?

Abraham and Isaac

Kierkegaard retells the story of Abraham and Isaac. God tells Abraham to go up to Mount Moriah and sacrifice his beloved son, Isaac. Abraham loves no one in the world as much as his son. But Abraham is willing to go through with the act, binding Isaac on the sacrificial altar (Isaac evidently does not protest). As Abraham raises his knife to slaughter his son, an angel of the Lord seized his hand and said, "now I know you fear God." Abraham looks up, sees a ram caught in a thicket, and sacrifices the ram in place of Isaac. (Genesis 22:1–19)

Attempts have been made to rationalize this story. For some it is an anthropological myth, designed to demonstrate humanity's progress from human to animal sacrifice. For others, Abraham's faith was so strong that he knew the Lord would stop him. But nothing in the Biblical account supports this interpretation. Abraham valued the Lord's commandment over the life of his son. For Kierkegaard, this makes Abraham a "knight of faith." Abraham surrendered himself to the

> paradox which is capable of transforming a murder into a holy act well-pleasing to God. . . . Abraham believed and did not doubt he believed the preposterous. He believed by virtue of the absurd; for all human reckoning had long since ceased to function.

He was called upon to renounce the moral for the religious, the finite for the infinite. "This is . . . clear to the knight of faith, so the only thing that can save him is the absurd, and this he grasps by faith."[2]

I do not believe there is any such paradox. I do not believe it is a virtue to believe in the absurd, "for all human reckoning had long since ceased to function." I do not believe it is necessary or desirable to renounce the moral for the religious. The knight of faith may feel justified by submitting the absurd, but all he has done is abandon human responsibility.

---

2. Kierkegaard, *Fear and Trembling*, 43, 65, 97; Blanshard, *Reason and Faith*.

Conclusion

The knight of faith abandons his humanity. Loving, caring, and the simple but profound knowledge that one should never kill one's child (or any child)—the abandonment of these virtues is not a courageous act of absurdity. Nor is it simply absurd. It is immoral and irresponsible. We must never give up our basic values unless deep reflection and changed circumstances require.

I believe these humble but profound virtues are fully realized in the teachings of Jesus Christ. But whatever their source, perhaps in that mysterious human nature itself, it is never a virtue to abandon them, particularly for the absurd. The absurd is no good thing. We may be caught up in absurd situations, the absurd exists, but it is our job to escape it or remake it, not to idealize it.

10.1

Did Camus Believe in God?

OF ALL THE EXISTENTIALISTS, Albert Camus came closest to believing in God, becoming closer in his later works. Camus would object to two parts of this statement. He objected to being labeled an existentialist, preferring the term "absurdist." And he would say he was not close to God. He admired (and once said "loved") Jesus Christ.[1]

Since Camus did not believe in an afterlife, what I mean by "close to God" and what most Christians believe is quite different. Yet even with all these qualifications the statement stands. Certainly, he has been many Christians' favorite atheist, primarily because he was comfortable with religious language and imagery. For Camus, "it is possible to be Christian and absurd."[2] All one has to do is disbelieve in an afterlife.

Most Christians, perhaps all, would reject this possibility, but in a time of militant atheism like our own, there is a vast difference between Camus and someone like Richard Dawkins. Camus had sympathy and respect for Christianity, above all for Christ. I think that is the best way of putting it.

Does Death Make Life Absurd?

Death makes life absurd. Camus says so, but what he really means is that life makes life absurd because there is no larger meaning to our existence. We want a world that is in some way made with the human being in mind. The human wants the world to respond, and the cosmos is silent. The result is not only absurdity, but a loss of freedom.

---

1. Jean-Baptiste Clamence, a character who seems to represent Camus in this respect (he is the novel's only character), says this in *The Fall*, 114.
2. Camus, *Myth of Sisyphus*, 112.

> "What freedom can exist in the fullest sense without assurance of eternity?"[3]

For Camus, we are slaves to death. As Ecclesiastes said (chapters 12), we are born and cut down after a few short years. "Vanity, vanity, all is vanity." Only, this is a bad translation. The Hebrew original is *hevel*, which literally means fog and lack of clarity.[4] "Absurdity, absurdity, all is absurdity" would be a more accurate translation.

But does death make life absurd? Would the only meaningful life be an eternal one, with its implication that I am one with the universe? Or as Camus puts it,

> I should *be* this world to which I am now opposed by my whole consciousness and my whole insistence upon familiarity.[5]

This does not make sense. The meaning of my life does not depend upon being one with the universe. Life is meaningful when I share in values that transcend my life, and act in accord with these values. In this way, I participate in a world beyond myself, a world that will be there long after I, my children and grandchildren are gone. Whether these values are eternal is open to question, for not even the universe is eternal, but perhaps that is not the point.

> It is essential to die unreconciled and not of one's own free will.[6]

This does not make sense either, unless it is read simply as an argument against suicide; but Camus means more. Life must forever fight death. But think about the difference between a man or woman cut down in his or her prime (as Camus was)[7], and one who dies after living a long, fruitful life. We are not meant for eternity. On the contrary, it is an enormous privilege, a miracle really, to exist for a nanosecond of eternity (of which, of course, there is no such thing). Why is that not enough?

Life Against the Universe: *The Plague*

Camus's view changes between *The Stranger* (begun before the war) and *The Myth of Sisyphus* (both published in 1942), and *The Plague* (published

---

3. Camus, *Myth of Sisyphus*, 57.
4. Strong, *Concordance*, 1892.
5. Camus, *Myth of Sisyphus*, 51, his emphasis.
6. Camus, *Myth of Sisyphus*, 55.
7. Camus died in a car crash at the age of 46. The car was being driven by his publisher. Camus was in the back seat.

five years later). About *The Plague*, Camus has the protagonist and narrator, Dr. Rieux, say, "Rieux believed himself to be on the right road—in fighting against creation as he found it."[8] This Camus calls "revolt," humanizing man and nature (as much as possible, for nature exists in its own right). His biographer, Olivier Todd, quotes Camus as saying that, out of a novelist's characters, one comes closest to representing the author. "Rieux is the one who represents me," says Camus.[9]

Rieux says, "the good man, the man who infects hardly anyone, is the man who has the fewest lapses of attention."[10] Paying attention is helped when we use clear language, and so say clearly what we are doing to whom and why. This is a mundane version of Simone Weil's concept of attention, discussed in chapter 22.3 of this work. It is the most human of all the spiritual things we can do: believe in and experience the reality of others. Camus was a great admirer of Weil, calling her "the only great spirit of our times."

In addition to paying attention, Camus has the narrator (Dr. Rieux) say,

> [a]s every decent person should, he deliberately took the side of the victim and wanted to meet others, his fellow-citizens, on the basis of the only certainties they all have in common, which are love, suffering and exile. Thus, there is not one of the anxieties of his fellows that he did not share and no situation that was not also his own.[11]

Of all the existentialists, Camus is also the most humane, understanding that needless suffering is the worst thing.

What if We Say We Were Wrong?

At a meeting of intellectuals at André Malraux's house in 1946, one that included Jean-Paul Sartre and Arthur Koestler, Camus said what French intellectuals (and intellectuals in general) hardly ever say: we were wrong.

> Don't you believe that we are all responsible for the absence of values?... [i]f we publicly say we were wrong and that moral values exist, and henceforth we shall do what we must to establish

---

8. Camus, *The Plague*, 120.
9. Todd, *Camus*, 230.
10. Camus, *The Plague*, 236.
11. Camus, *The Plague*, 232.

> and illustrate them, don't you think that would be the start of hope?[12]

There is something charmingly unphilosophical about Camus, or rather he was more a man than a philosopher. That is a compliment.

How can a humanist of the absurd have anything to do with Christianity? Are there degrees of being a Christian? Certainly, there are degrees of living a religious life, but are there degrees of adherence to Christian doctrine, or is it all or nothing? I am not sure, but I do know that Camus would fail the doctrine test.

> Tear out the final page of the Gospel and you have a human religion, a cult of solitude and of greatness is offered to us.[13]

By tearing out the last page, Camus means everything up to but not including Christ's resurrection. For it is at this point that the afterlife begins, not just for Christ, but for the rest of us. Simone Weil held a similar view: the incarnation and the crucifixion are enough (see chapter 22.1 of this work).

To stop there is, of course, not to be a Christian, but it is a way of thinking about Christianity that I have found inspirational and challenging. The afterlife is a reward. But one can live a Christian life in this world by caring for the widow, the orphan, and the stranger, and by following the example of Christ insofar as humans are able. Why is that not reward enough?

---

12. Todd, *Camus*, quoting Camus, 232.
13. Camus, *Notebooks*, 206; Onimus, *Camus and Christianity*, 49.

10.2

Did Camus Want to Be Baptized?

FIRST A DISCUSSION OF the religious beliefs of Jean-Baptiste Clamence in Albert Camus's novel, *The Fall*. Then a discussion of Camus's request to be baptized according to Howard Mumma in *Albert Camus and the Minister*. There is a connection. It has to do with faith.

The Fall, Camus's last novel, is set in Hell. Well, not exactly. It is set in Amsterdam, where the canals are laid out in concentric circles. That and the foggy atmosphere are both intended to remind us of Dante's version of Hell. Mexico City, a bar in the innermost circle of hell is where Clamence holds forth. He is the novel's only speaking character, but he is an unreliable narrator. He would have us think he is in a type of Hell, but he may be playing games with the reader, and himself.

I will not summarize the book. The only thing you need to know is that Clamence was a wealthy and successful Parisian lawyer and all-around good guy (lawyer and good guy are not automatically antonyms). After a series of minor mishaps, culminating in the not-so-minor mishap of ignoring a drowning woman's cry, he exiles himself to one of the seedier bars in Amsterdam, where he tells his tale to any who will listen. His goal, it seems, is to justify his drinking and whoring by constantly pointing out how bad he is. An odd strategy, designed it seems to preempt judgment.

About Christ's Guilt

Clamence tells us that not only is he guilty, but even Jesus Christ was guilty, merely by being born in a certain time and place. Consider the massacre of the innocents, in which Herod orders all male children in Bethlehem under two to be killed in order to avoid a prophecy about the "King of the Jews," who he believed threatened his throne. (Matthew 2:16–18) Was that not the source of the sadness one sometimes sees in Jesus?

> ... wasn't it the incurable melancholy of a man who heard night after night the voice of Rachel weeping for her children and refusing all comfort? The lamentation would rend the night, Rachel would call her children who had been killed for him, and he was still alive![1]

Clamence's point is that, just by being born into the midst of history, everyone is guilty. In this sense, affluent Westerners are guilty of the starvation of children in Yemen. Sure, we should each contribute money to relieve the starvation, but the famine's cause is not lack of food but politics. How do we live with that when living in this world is all it takes to be guilty? Or as Tarrou puts it in *The Plague*, Camus's previous novel, we are all accidental murderers; the best we can do in life is not to murder others intentionally, or through carelessness.

The Last Seven Words of Christ

Clamence continues, arguing that Christ was more human than we know.

> Yes, it was the third evangelist, I believe, who first suppressed his complaint. "Why hast thou forsaken me?"—it was a seditious cry, wasn't it?[2]

It was seditious because it showed Christ to be not only fully human (consistent with Christian doctrine), but human too in the sense that he was abandoned by God.

Clamence's view of Christ is complex. I can do no better than quote him one final time.

> And he was not superhuman, you can take my word for it. He cried aloud his agony and that's why I love him, my friend who died without knowing.[3]

Died without knowing what? That God would save him? Or that he would not, because he was not there? Camus is unclear. My belief is that Camus was unclear in his own mind. Consider Camus's late request to be baptized.

---

1. Camus, *The Fall*, 112–3.
2. Camus, *The Fall*, 113.
3. Camus, *The Fall*, 114.

Did Camus Want to Be Baptized?

Sometime in his early to mid-forties, just a few years before his death, Camus had a crisis of faith, or perhaps we should call it a crisis of lack of faith. Perhaps the world was not so meaningless as he had believed, and he wanted to understand what religion really claimed about God. A Catholic, Camus knew little of his own faith, and was fortunate to find a liberal Protestant minister, Howard Mumma, from Ohio, a guest minister at the American Church in Paris. Camus began attending the church, ostensibly to hear the widely admired organist, Marcel Dupré.

Camus approached Mumma, asking for a private conversation. Mumma agreed, and over a period of a couple of years, they talked about God and faith. Eventually, Camus asked to be baptized, but only in private.

Mumma tells a good story, and I am inclined to believe him, but there is a problem. The best way I can explain it is by means of an analogy. Both Xenophon and Plato wrote down the dialogues of Socrates, as Socrates never wrote a word of his own. Reading Xenophon, Socrates comes across as an extraordinary man, but not extraordinarily clever or deep. Reading Plato, Socrates comes across as an intellectual giant, challenging a whole way of thinking and being. It seems as if who Socrates was depends upon who writes his story.

It's the same with Mumma. Camus comes across as a serious searcher, open to new ideas. But there is nothing extraordinary about his intellect or his understanding. Occasionally, Camus comes across as one of Socrates's not-too-bright interlocutors. Reading Mumma's Camus and reading Camus himself is like reading about two different men. As one sees in *The Fall*, Camus is open to Christian experience. But there is an ambiguity and subtlety to his position missing in Mumma's account. Possibly it is the difference between Camus the author and Camus the man.

Mumma quotes Camus as saying,

> Something is dreadfully wrong. I am a disillusioned and exhausted man. I have lost faith, lost hope, ever since the rise of Hitler. Is it any wonder that, at my age, I am looking for something to believe in? . . . [t]o lose one's life is only a little thing. But, to lose the meaning of life, to see our reasoning disappear, is unbearable. It is impossible to live life without meaning.[4]

---

4. Mumma, *Camus and the Minister*, 14. Mumma published his book almost fifty years after his conversations with Camus, when Mumma was 90 years old. He writes that he took extensive notes after each conversation, but admits that his quotations of Camus are often paraphrases.

To Camus, Mumma presented the story of the Garden of Eden as a fable about men and women trying to put themselves in the place of God. Humanism can easily slide into the worship of the human. This made sense to Camus. How could God allow the suffering of innocents, especially children, a key theme of *The Plague*? Mumma answers in terms similar to what is called "process theology" (chapter 37 of this work), though he never uses that term. We live in a world that is incomplete. God is still in the process of perfecting it, and that requires our help. We are the hands and arms of God. We are co-creators with God.

God is not omnipotent in the sense that he could create a square circle, or grant humans freedom and eliminate evil at the same time. (About natural evils, like the plague, Mumma says nothing.) "God cannot create an independent thing and still have complete control over it or limit it."[5]

About all this, Camus seems convinced (it took a couple of years), but not in any conventional way. Camus's view seems closest to that of his character Dr. Rieux in *The Plague*, whom he quotes to Mumma.

> Since the order of the world is shaped by death, mightn't it be better for God if we refuse to believe in Him and struggle with all our might against death without raising our eyes toward the heaven where He sits in silence?[6]

Finally, Camus asks to be baptized, and Mumma wisely says no. Camus was baptized as an infant, and one baptism is enough. More than that, Mumma seems wary. Camus wants the baptism to be private, and refuses to join the church and participate in the rite of confirmation.

Why? In Mumma's version, there are two reasons. First, Camus had a literary reputation to protect. Second, and more important, he was an independent thinker who could never be an active member of any church.

Let's wait, says Mumma to Camus. Not long after, Camus had his fatal accident. It is unfortunate that Mumma perpetuates the myth that Camus committed suicide by driving into a tree. He did not. Camus's publisher, Michel Gallimard, was driving a crowded car. Camus was in the back seat, the only one to be killed.[7] I suspect that Mumma valued a good story over getting the facts straight. How much this influences the rest of his account is hard to say. More than a little, one suspects.

---

5. Mumma, *Camus and the Minister*, 74.
6. Camus, *The Plague*, 81.
7. Mumma, *Camus and the Minister*, 98; Todd, *Camus*, 412–3.

Conclusion

So what is one to conclude about Camus, faith, and God? No more, certainly, than that Camus struggled with the question of belief in God, whereas the man to whom he was so often linked, Jean-Paul Sartre, never entertained the possibility. Camus's seems the wiser choice.

10.3

Camus's Absurdism Lacks Imagination

CAMUS INSISTS THAT HE is an absurdist, not an existentialist. OK, but it is important to figure out what he means. Camus thinks a Christian can be an absurdist. I do not. I do think that absurdism is the leading alternative not only to Christianity, but religion. Religion is said to be based on faith, as it is. Camus's absurdism is based on a particular heroic ideal, a man who faces the truth head-on, as if it were that simple.

The World Is Not Absurd

> I said that the world is absurd, but I was too hasty. This world in itself is not reasonable, that is all that can be said. But what is absurd is the confrontation of this irrational and the wild longing for clarity whose call echoes in the human heart. The absurd depends as much on man as on the world.[1]

Though Camus writes about clarity (*clarté*), that could be misleading. What he means is that humans long for this world to be where we belong, that we are placed here for a reason, even if we lack clarity about it. This belief underlies the Judeo-Christian tradition. The absurd says there is no purpose; we just happen to be here.

The Plague, discussed previously, is about what it means to live without this underlying assumption. It means that humanity's job is to fight creation as we have found it (compare Genesis 1:28). We fight creation best when we work together. Absurdism is not a doctrine of individualism. If you remember *The Plague*, you will recall that even the absurd M. Grand, who spent years rewriting the first sentence of his novel (he never gets any further), is an everyday hero, volunteering to serve in the Sanitary Squad at some

---

1. Camus, *Myth of Sisyphus*, 21.

risk to himself.[2] Camus's point seems to be that even if the Sanitary Squad accomplished little in fighting the plague, it is noble for humans to work together to make this world a more fit place for human beings.

From this perspective, religion is a communal creation, a story people tell each other about why we are meant to be here. One reason religion is effective is because it is reinforced with shared rituals; another is because most of us learn it as children. By the way, this account of religion, which is mine, says nothing about whether God exists. We have religion, or we do not. God is in his heaven, or he is not. The first sentence is logically unrelated to the second.

There Is Only this Life

An absurd sensitivity requires that there be only this life. If a Christian accepts this, he or she can also be an absurdist. So says Camus.[3] First of all, a Christian could not accept this. Second, Christianity is not just, or even primarily, about an afterlife. Christianity denies the fundamental tenet of absurdism, asserting that we are meant to be here, and God provides the answer as to why, even if his answer is not always transparent. God also tells us how we should live. None of this is compatible with absurdism. I have been unable to figure out why Camus says a Christian could be an absurdist, except that he never wanted to completely disavow faith. In other words, he had nostalgia for Christianity.

A World without Appeal

Recognizing the claims of absurdity, many religious thinkers—and Søren Kierkegaard is my favorite—argue that there is a world beyond clarity, reason, and objective truth. Kierkegaard calls it subjective truth.[4] We know it through our feelings, our intuition, our desires. We know that we are in love when we feel it, not when someone measures our endorphin levels, or whatever. Faith works much the same way. Love's knowledge is faith's knowledge.

Camus's response is that religious belief requires that we deny observation, logic, and experience. Religious belief requires "philosophical suicide," as he calls it. Mass hunger, starvation, disease, and endless war somewhere

---

2. The absurd has practical as well as philosophical implications. Here it refers to the disproportion between M. Grand's skills and the task of writing a novel. See *Myth of Sisyphus*, 29, for a similar example.

3. Camus, *Myth of Sisyphus*, 112.

4. Kierkegaard, *Postscript*.

on this planet every hour of every day, is an experience of a world without appeal, as Camus puts it, a world in which we have to work out our own meaning, as the characters do in *The Plague*. Absurdism does not mean not one's life is subjectively absurd, only that its meaning is not given, and so we must find it for ourselves in a world that means only what we put into it.

> Hence, what he demands of himself is to live *solely* with what he knows, to accommodate himself to what is, and to bring in nothing that is not certain. He is told that nothing is. But this at least is a certainty. And it is with this that he is concerned: he wants to find out if it is possible to live *without appeal*.[5]

Revolt

Camus has an old-fashioned sense of virtue, what the ancient Greeks called *arete*. We live best and most nobly when we face the fact of a world without meaning and struggle against it in the way we live, as well as the way we think and feel. Camus calls this way "revolt," and sometimes "manliness," an echo of an earlier era.

> . . . [r]evolt gives life its value. Spread out over the whole length of a life, it restores its majesty to that life. To a man devoid of blinders, there is no finer sight than that of the intelligence at grips with a reality that transcends it.[6]

The Flaw in Camus's Project

Camus's courage in facing a world without appeal is admirable. And yet there is something equally admirable in facing an uncertain world, or rather living with uncertainty.

> I want everything to be explained to me or nothing. . . . If one could only say just once: "This is clear," all would be saved.[7]

Camus understands that clarity is impossible, that it is the cry of a man stranded on the island named absurdity.

But how much difference is there between the clarity of the absurd and the demand that humans accept only what is certain, even if that is nothing

---

5. Camus, *Myth of Sisyphus*, 53.
6. Camus, *Myth of Sisyphus*, 55.
7. Camus, *Myth of Sisyphus*, 27.

but uncertainty itself? Camus gets certainty by simplifying the world. For hardly anything in this world is certain, including Camus's assertion that there is only this world (or at least we should live as though this were the case). There are more things in heaven and Earth, Camus, than are dreamt of in your philosophy, as someone famous almost put it.

Camus risks becoming the scientist he criticizes. But Kierkegaard was right to begin with: much of what we call "knowledge" is subjective truth. It is a subjective truth that the noble man is one who lives his life in revolt. Why not acceptance, even acquiescence? No reason, it is a preference, just as it is a preference of some to find meaning in God. If Camus wants to know if he can live a life without appeal, then good for him. But if that is nobler than some pursuits, such as hypocrisy, it is no more noble than others, including religious pursuits.

Conclusion

Camus is not writing about what we know, or even what we should believe. He is writing about his view of "virile behavior," as he calls it. In many respects, I find his view admirable, and agree with it. It is a contemporary version of what the ancient Greeks called *arete*, or excellence at being a human. But it is certainly not the only version of a good or authentic life.

11.1

Jürgen Moltmann: Heaven on Earth and My Heresy

JÜRGEN MOLTMANN IS 93 years old as I write this. He is of the same generation as the well-known theologians I write about, such as Karl Barth and Reinhold Niebuhr. Like them, he was born in Germany and came of age in Nazified Germany. Unlike them, he stayed, served in the Wehrmacht (Nazi army, not the SS), and seems to have experienced profound guilt and remorse when he learned about the concentration camps after the war. That is his story, and I have no reason to doubt it.

In some ways, he is the most interesting of the five German theologians I have written about (Barth, Niebuhr, Bultmann, Bonhoeffer, and Tillich). I wish I understood why the most influential Christian theologians in the United States grew up in Nazified Germany, but I do not.[1] Moltmann is interesting not because he is right, but because he is different. Moltmann is different not only because he believes in heaven, but in heaven on earth.

Heaven on Earth and the Theology of Hope

Eschatology is the study of last things, the eschaton, the end of this world and the beginning of the next. Central to Moltmann's eschatological vision is that life in heaven is embodied. It is marked by the physical resurrection of the dead, who will be joined by those still living in what can only be called heaven on earth.

Heaven on earth is important, because the salvation of our disembodied selves would deprive us of bodily experience, a central part of being human, and a source of great pleasure as well as pain.

---

1. Stanley Hauerwas is the exception. He grew up in Texas.

> The reduction of salvation to souls is a gnostic vision that disregards the social, political, and physical needs of human beings.[2]

The Gnostics were a sect that regarded all things having to do with the body as evil (see chapter 18.1 of this work).

At first this makes sense. Physical experience is central to being human, so heaven, being good, should preserve that experience. In fact, it is a bad idea, for it leads to a world in which mortal humans are no longer mortal. If, as Moltmann argues, death and transience are no more, then we no longer live under the horizon of mortality. But it is mortality, transience, that makes human life human. We value experiences such as love precisely because they will not go on forever. Even the most loving relationship will be parted by death.

Moltmann Believes Original Creation Was Incomplete

Death and transience will be no more, not because of sin, but because the original creation was incomplete. The new creation is not the return to a primordial state of perfection, but the redemption of creation into a new state of being, which includes overcoming death and transience.[3]

The result is that life, or rather new life, becomes a festival without end. I cannot think of anything more awful. Moltmann's fundamental error is his view that we cannot truly love if love is not forever.

> Ought we to accept death as a natural part of life? If so we must do without love, for love desires life, not death.[4]

More on this aspect of his thought in my next chapter on Moltmann. For now, the best thing to say about Moltmann's view of the eschaton is that it is not about a terrible and terrifying end of the world, but the glorious beginning of a new one. It is too bad that we cannot have it all: the intensity of experience that depends on the fact that it will end, and a guarantee that the good stuff will never end. But we cannot. Moltmann brings us too close to immortality. Not just the immortal soul, but human immortality.

---

2. Morrison, *Moltmann*, 632; Moltmann, *Theology of Hope*.
3. Morrison, *Moltmann*, 3314.
4. Moltmann, *Christ for Today*, 900.

The Crucified God

The idea of the crucified God is that God suffers with those who suffer.

> The central concept of *The Crucified God* is love which suffers in solidarity with those who suffer. This is love which meets the involuntary suffering of the godforsaken with another kind of suffering: voluntary fellow-suffering.[5]

From this viewpoint, the theodicy question (the justice and fairness of God) is misplaced. It is not a question of God making the world better. It is a question of his willingness to suffer with us in this world.

> God either causes pain, is indifferent to suffering, or God suffers with us in our suffering. The first and second possibilities result in an apathetic monster-god, but the third is the crucified God, the God revealed in Christ's cross. The suffering God alone is our solace; only the crucified Christ has anything to offer humanity in the midst of suffering and death.[6]

Christ's experience of abandonment on the cross, "My God, my God, why have you forsaken me?" means that no one dies alone. (Matthew 27:46; Mark 15:34)

My Heresy: Many Have Suffered More than Christ

I understand that the suffering of Christ is deeply symbolic. From one perspective, he suffered for humankind. On the other hand, if we view Jesus as both God and man, it seems to me that he suffered less than millions of people. Suffering is not just measured by torture. It is also measured by an understanding of the reason one is being tortured. Christ knew exactly why he was tortured to death. It was, in a real sense, the purpose of his life. Though he felt momentary despair, it was likely less, or at least different, than the despair felt by the inmates of Auschwitz, or the parents of a dying child. What purpose is served by their suffering? Many martyrs have suffered willingly because their suffering had meaning. What is the meaning of a dying child? It has no larger meaning, even if some are able to give it one, such as "it was God's will, which we will never understand." Christ understood God's will perfectly. (John 12:20–33) In that respect, at least, he suffered less than millions of humans throughout history.

---

5. Bauckham, *Theology of Moltmann*, 11; Moltmann, *Crucified God*.
6. Morrison, *Moltmann*, 992.

The Social Trinity

My favorite aspect of Moltmann's thought is his reinterpretation of the trinity so that it becomes a holy family, not simply the three faces of God. If we think about God from the perspective of the New Testament, we encounter the trinity as the narrative history of Jesus, in which God is Abba (father), and Jesus is the son of the father. They are separate beings. John 17:21–24 captures this relationship well. Jesus never calls God "Lord," for Christ is Lord and God is God. Richard Bauckham argues that if we start with the doctrine of the one God, then the trinity is about the different aspects or modes in which God presents himself.[7] But if we start with the New Testament, we get a narrative of a relationship between three divine persons. As usual, the Bible is the best place to start.

For Moltmann, this means that the Trinity is open, leaving space for human participation. Perichoresis is the fancy term that means the participation of each of the three persons of God in one another. It is often represented by a chalice pouring into another chalice which pours again into a third chalice, the circle of wine, or love, continuing forever.

God *is* a community, and within this community, there is a place for humans. The modern Western world thinks of people as separate individuals. The communal trinity reminds us that, as the essence of God is community, so is it the essence of humans to belong with others, including God. Moltmann goes about as far as one can go with the trinity without abandoning monotheism. In so doing, he highlights the communal nature of Christianity at its very core.[8]

Conclusion

In a subsequent chapter, I characterize what the five theologians mentioned above shared, as well as what divides them. It is harder for me to characterize Moltmann, so I think I will just continue to tell you more about him. The next chapter will include a discussion of Moltmann's ecological writings, which grant to this earth its own creaturely perfection.

---

7. Bauckman, *Theology of Moltmann*, 173.
8. Moltmann, *Trinity and the Kingdom*.

11.2

Moltmann's Ecological God

IN *THEOLOGY OF HOPE*, Jürgen Moltmann's most well-known work, he argues that the man who hopes will hope to transcend this earth, including death.

> All this must inevitably mean that the man who thus hopes will never be able to reconcile himself with the laws and constraints of this earth, neither with the inevitability of death.[1]

As I argued in my previous chapter, this means that the eschaton (end of this world and beginning of the next) will be realized on this earth, on which immortal beings will dwell. I find this seriously weird.

More than weird, it denies what it is to be human, which is to be finite and mortal. Heaven there may be, but it will not be here (as if heaven were in time and space), and it will not be populated by immortal earthlings. More than this I do not know, and even about this I cannot be certain.

The Resurrection of Nature

The core of the ecological crisis, says Moltmann, is subject/object thinking, which inevitably leads to the subject (man) dominating the object (nature). Moltmann sounds like the utopian Marxists who founded the Frankfurt School of Critical Theory, but Moltmann's quotation from Karl Marx on the resurrection of nature tells us all we need to know.[2]

---

1. Moltmann, *Theology of Hope*, 272.
2. The leading utopian Marxists of the Frankfurt School were Max Horkheimer and Theodor Adorno, both of whom Moltmann cites. But it was Herbert Marcuse, the most utopian of them all, who imagined that death itself might no longer be a natural necessity (*Eros*). Moltmann says that Ernest Bloch, another utopian Marxist, inspired his *Theology of Hope* (814).

> Karl Marx called this "the true resurrection of nature," and hoped that it would come from a "naturalization of man" and from the "humanization of nature."[3]

The humanization of nature and the naturalization of man is the work of the Holy Spirit, which dwells continuously in nature. God resides not in heaven, but in this world, which he is constantly creating and recreating.

> The inner secret of creation is this *indwelling of God* . . . If we ask about creation's goal and future, we ultimately arrive at the transfiguring indwelling of the triune God in his creation, which through that indwelling becomes a new heaven and a new earth (Rev. 21) . . . in which the whole creation will find bliss.[4]

Here truly is the resurrection of nature.

The Trinitarian Vision and Panentheism

Moltmann's claim is that the open nature of the Trinity, which has room for man, as discussed above, also has room for earth. God not only creates the world, he is in the things of this world. This is not pantheism, because he does not claim that things of the world are deities in themselves. They become holy because God is present in them, the meaning of panentheism.

> An ecological doctrine of creation implies a new kind of thinking about God. The centre of this thinking is no longer the distinction between God and the world. The centre is the recognition of the presence of God *in* the world and the presence of the world *in* God.[5]

The Plague

There is another way of looking at the natural world, and the great utopian ecologist Herbert Marcuse put it this way:

> The world was not made for the sake of the human being and it has not become more human.[6]

---

3. Moltmann, *God in Creation*, 2427.
4. Moltmann, *God in Creation*, 2474.
5. Moltmann, *God in Creation*, 2655.
6. Marcuse, *Aesthetic Dimension*, 69.

We live in a complex relationship to nature: it is an inspiration, a wonder, and the source of life itself. At the same time, nature wants to kill us: the black plague killed between 30 to 60 percent of the population of Europe. Malaria kills about 3,000 children every day, mostly in Africa. Humanizing nature means fighting a nature that would kill us before our time. Nature is wasteful; millions of lives mean nothing to it. Nature is not hostile; it does not care because it cannot care. Only humans and God care.

A doctor friend of mine says health is not the natural condition of man; sickness is. Or as a character in Albert Camus's *The Plague*, puts it, "What's natural is the microbe. All the rest—health, integrity, purity (if you like)—is a product of the human will."[7] An earlier world might have lived closer to nature, but the life span in England at the dawn of the twentieth century was forty years; for the world it was thirty-one years.[8] Modern medicine has done more for the happiness of the average man or woman than most other things. Religion brings meaning, even more important, but there is no conflict between them. We just should not imagine that God is in nature. Nature is in nature.

The Plague, Again

The Plague, a novel by Camus (referred to in chapter 10.1 of this work), is about human courage and cowardice in the face of a fictional plague during the World War II era.[9] In talking to Father Paneloux, a Catholic priest who says we should love what we cannot understand, Dr. Rieux replies that "until my dying day, I shall refuse to love a scheme of things in which children are put to torture."[10] When a child dies a torturous death, another character named Tarrou says a Christian should either lose his faith or consent to having his eyes destroyed. He means that one can hardly look at the heartlessness of this world and still believe in God.

Tarrou is wrong. We can still believe in God, even a benevolent God, but that means a God who shares our suffering. This is the meaning of Christ. What I cannot believe in is a God who is active in nature. God created a beautiful world, but not a tender one.

---

7. Camus, *The Plague*, 235.

8. https://en.wikipedia.org/wiki/Life_expectancy.

9. It has been argued that *The Plague* is a parable about the Nazis. I don't think that works very well. The Nazis were a human catastrophe, not a natural one.

10. Camus, *The Plague*, 235.

Conclusion

Moltmann's deep interest in ecology makes him unique among the modern Protestant theologians. At the same time, it reveals the flaw at the heart of his theology: heaven on earth requires the cooperation of earth, and the earth lives a life of its own, in which humans are just one more species. We serve nature best when we leave it alone. Humans must intervene for the sake of humanity, and at other times for the sake of nature, but we need not draw nature into our plans for salvation.

12.1

Reinhold Niebuhr and the Scandal of the Twentieth Century

AROUND THE MIDDLE OF the twentieth century, Reinhold Niebuhr was the most prominent Protestant theologian in America. He was on the cover of *Time* magazine (March 8, 1948). More recently, Barack Obama called Niebuhr his favorite philosopher. Niebuhr is the author of the well-known serenity prayer.

> God, give us grace to accept with serenity the things that cannot be changed, courage to change the things which *should* be changed, and the Wisdom to distinguish the one from the other.

His daughter, Elisabeth Sifton, says that this is the real version of the prayer, noting the difference between "should be changed" and "can be changed," which is the version usually recited. She thinks the usual version represents a dumbing down of the prayer, for in its original version, it calls us to do the right thing, not what I can do, but what I should do.[1]

The World as Gift and Idolatry

> The difference between science and theology, as I understand it, is one over whether you see the world as a gift or not; and you cannot resolve this just by inspecting the thing any more than you can deduce from examining a porcelain vase that it is a wedding present.[2]

If one sees the world as gift, then humans were created to savor life surely, but also to be responsible stewards of the gift, not only of one's own life, but also a world. Everything is gift. Humans are not just creators, but created.

---

1. Lemert, *Niebuhr Matters*, 195–6.
2. Crouter, *Niebuhr*, 133.

From this perspective, idolatry becomes the gravest and most tempting sin, the worship of our own creations. For Niebuhr, "communal idolatry" is the most common sin of our time, certainly the most damaging in scale and intensity. For Niebuhr, sin, and with it idolatry, is an anxious attempt to hide our finitude, to make ourselves the center of life, and so take the place of God. Each of us can imagine all manner of terrible things that might befall us. And so, humans seek by an act of will what Niebuhr calls "the will-to-power," to overreach the limits of human creatureliness. Since most people lack the ability to do this on their own, they join communities of self-justification and self-assertion.

Niebuhr was never very interested in the details of Christian doctrine. For Niebuhr, original sin had little to do with desire. Original sin stems from a person's fear at being alone and vulnerable in the world, leading him or her to worship the gods of the community, indeed the god that is the community. Nationalism, money, success, fitting in—all this and more become our idols.

The Scandal

In Niebuhr's view, God is not victorious in history, for evil is not defeated. Rather than imposing His goodness upon the world, God suffers the injustices of the powerful. To be sure, Niebuhr holds that God would not allow evil to completely triumph over the face of this earth. But human history is marked by the "scandal of the cross," the willing defeat of God in this world.

> The perfect love which [Christ's] life and death exemplify is defeated, rather than triumphant, in the actual course of history. Thus, according to the Christian belief, history remains morally ambiguous to the end. . . . Suffering innocence, which reveals the problem of moral ambiguity in history, becomes in the Christian faith the answer to the problem at the point when it is seen as a revelation of a divine suffering . . .[3]

In the meantime, all we know, all we *can* know, is that there is a decisive difference between good and bad, right and wrong. Historical outcomes are not merely relative or subjective. History does not "just happen," as Richard Rorty puts it.[4] Consequently, we can know that it is worthwhile fighting for the good, and we need not become overly discouraged when we lose, as we often will.

3. Niebuhr, *Faith and History*, 135.
4. Rorty, *Contingency*, 184.

Worthwhile means that fighting for the good is a meaningful (and not absurd) activity. Neither is it simply an existential choice, receiving its value because I have chosen it. Fighting for the good can be measured by, and receives its value from, a standard of infinite value. We have been given a glimpse of this good and its standard, even if in practice this glimpse is indistinct. The good's basic principles were laid down in the Hebrew and Greek Testaments. Facing the scandal of the cross (Christ's weakness), as Niebuhr calls it, reflects a determination to be utterly realistic about the prevalence of evil in the world, while remaining committed to the belief that history is meaningful because it has been given meaning by the traces of God's presence.

Nonetheless, Niebuhr's theology raises a problem. The knowledge of God in history is not known through the study of history. It is grasped inwardly, by repentance and "the shattering of the self," placing one's trust in divine power and mercy.[5] Niebuhr is referring to the type of knowledge often characterized in terms of revelation or faith.

Where Niebuhr's Biblical Understanding Leads Him Astray

For Niebuhr, as for Bultmann, God wins by losing.

> It is impossible to symbolize the divine goodness in history in any other way than by complete powerlessness, or rather by a consistent refusal to use power in the rivalries of history.[6]

God stays neutral in the conflicts of history, recognizing that no side is without an ego invested in the outcome, that all conflict is rivalry, not good over evil.

> Any participation [by God in the rivalries of history] means the assertion of one ego interest against another.[7]

But Niebuhr's account of the "war of finites" makes no sense when talking about the Holocaust, Hiroshima, Hitler, Mao, Stalin, and the destruction of the Rohingya. In the case of authoritarian annihilatory power, no rivalry is involved, only the slaughter of innocents.

If God can act in history, if his divine grace is occasionally present in history, as Niebuhr asserts, then God's failure to act in the presence of the

---

5. Gilkey, *On Niebuhr*, 193–4.
6. Niebuhr, *Nature and Destiny* 2, 72.
7. Niebuhr, *Nature and Destiny*, 2, 72.

annihilation of innocents preserves no one's freedom. Does it really make a difference to say that God in Christ suffered for them? Perhaps it minimizes the suffering of believers, but I doubt it, especially when one considers that God could have acted, but chose not to.

Gilkey interprets Niebuhr correctly when he says that

> There is the judgment of God in history, which limits and so controls within bounds the inevitable (though not necessary) *misuse* of these creative achievements.[8]

If God's limits are not reached with the deaths of millions of humans, some the result of "creative achievements" like Zyklon B, gas ovens, and hydrogen bombs, then it is hard to know what these limits are.

Human suffering does not testify to God's suffering for us. Human suffering becomes human sacrifice if we insist on a God who acts in history but chooses not to. Christ's suffering is an inspiration; it is not an invitation to suffer. Niebuhr writes

> Suffering innocence, which reveals the problem of moral ambiguity of history, becomes in the Christian faith the answer to the problem at that point, when it is seen as a revelation of a divine suffering which bears and overcomes the sins of the world.[9]

To see human history from the perspective of divine suffering is to view it at a great distance. The twentieth century, and the beginning of the twenty-first, is not just a history of war, it is the history of the annihilation of large groups of people by evil others.

A God who can but does not act in the presence of enormous evil is not a God whom I can understand. The Book of Job concludes that Job will never understand God, and that is OK. (Job 42:1–6) It is Job's path to acceptance. I believe that divine justice must be comprehensible to humans, at least about the big things, or he cannot be a God whom humans worship. The doctrine of process theology, discussed in chapter 37 of this work, makes more sense. God weeps but cannot act. Not *does not*, but cannot. That too is the message of the cross. Jesus could have fled, but he stayed and suffered to convey this message, the infinite sadness of God when faced with human evil.

This is not Niebuhr's view. It is not the view of any Christian denomination that I am aware of. But it is a view that makes the most sense of the world we live in, and Niebuhr was always interested in that.

---

8. Gilkey, *On Niebuhr*, 211, author's emphasis.
9. Niebuhr, *Faith and History*, 135.

Making Sense of Original Sin with Reinhold Niebuhr

The doctrine of original sin is the only empirically verifiable doctrine of the Christian faith.

—Reinhold Niebuhr

I NEVER TOOK THE concept of sin seriously until I read Reinhold Niebuhr. I think this is mostly because I did not read Niebuhr until I was in my sixties, when I began to take a lot of things in life more seriously. If so, then perhaps I should say that Niebuhr is a particularly good interpreter of a concept that hovered just out of range until now.

Communal Idolatry

For Niebuhr, sin is most clearly seen and expressed in communal idolatry. This is the context of the epigraph that opens this chapter. We see sin every day in the actions of groups, and above all, nations. I discussed communal idolatry in the previous chapter, so I will not spend much time on it here.

In sin, we worship the idols of the group, and not just extremist groups or nations. In the midst of World War II, Niebuhr argued that the American idealization of liberty could itself degenerate into a form of idolatry. As Andrew Bacevich puts it in his introduction to a new edition of *The Irony of American History*, Niebuhr

> went so far as to describe the worship of democracy as "a less vicious version of the Nazi creed." He cautioned that "no society, not even a democratic one, is great enough or good enough to make itself the final end of human existence."[1]

---

1. Bacevich, Introduction, *Irony*, xii; Niebuhr, *Light and Darkness*, 133.

If even democracy is at risk of becoming an idol, then what does it take to avoid communal idolatry? Niebuhr argues that only the belief in a providential God can save us. "Modern man's confidence in his power over historical destiny prompted the rejection of every older conception of an overruling providence in history."[2]

Not Exactly a Providential God

In fact, Niebuhr's view of a providential God is a little complicated, for God acts not so much *in* history as *above* it, judging our sins, and offering forgiveness. God judges our sins, while Christ represents the mercy of this judgment, the forgiveness that makes the judgment bearable; that is, knowable and acceptable. This is the gift of the cross to the world.

> ... [j]ustice alone does not move men to repentance. The inner core of their rebellion is not touched until they behold the executor of judgment suffering with and for the victim of punishment.... The fact that justice and mercy are one is symbolically expressed in the idea of the unity of Father and Son.[3]

Any who still worry about the heresy of patripassianism, the belief that God suffers, should worry about something else. The whole point of God the father and son is to say God suffers in the form of Jesus Christ. Christ suffers not only the horror of the cross, but for a moment the doubt of almost all men and women about God's existence, expressed in His dying words according to two of the gospels: "My God, my God, why have you forsaken me?" (Matthew 27:46; Mark 15:34) For a moment, God was forsaken by God, so that we might experience eternity.

It Is Not about Divine Omnipotence

For Niebuhr, God's participation in history has nothing to do with a divine omnipotence that enters into historical events. God's participation takes the form of solidarity with suffering humanity.

> The suffering servant does not impose goodness upon the world by his power. Rather, he suffers, being powerless, from the injustices of the powerful. He suffers most particularly from the

---

2. Niebuhr, *Irony*, 4.
3. Niebuhr, *Essential Niebuhr*, 29–30.

sins of the righteous who do not understand how full of unrighteousness is all human righteousness.[4]

Niebuhr calls this the scandal of the cross, God's strength made perfect in weakness. (2 Corinthians 12:9)

Knowing this is enough to know that history has a meaning, and that we must never abandon our historical responsibility to fight evil where we find it, while remembering that we are not God's righteous avengers, but humans who have made a fallible decision about who and how to fight—and knowing, too, that we might lose. But still we must fight.

When the good lose (or even when they win), millions suffer, but only in the short run. History does not last forever. Trouble is, for those who suffer, the short run can last an awfully long time. The knowledge that Christ suffers with us has been a comfort to many, but to others, it has been cold comfort. Historical events such as Hiroshima and the Holocaust sometimes seem to mock Christ's presence among the suffering of innocents.

---

4. Niebuhr, *Beyond Tragedy*, 181.

12.3

Niebuhr and the Things That Are Not

FOR A PERIOD IN the 1950s, it seems as almost half the State Department was quoting Reinhold Niebuhr. But did they understand the man they were quoting? They had reason to be influenced by Niebuhr. His *Irony of American History* is generally considered among the most important books ever written on American foreign policy. Arthur Schlesinger Jr. spoke for many agnostics in wondering whether Niebuhr's wisdom on human nature had anything to do with his Christian theology.[1]

It is important to understand what Niebuhr's theology brings to his politics. His theology not only adds, it is necessary. Consider "The Things That Are and the Things That Are Not," which takes its title from Corinthians 1:28. The King James Version that Niebuhr uses reads:

> Yea, and things which are not [hath God chosen], to put to nought things that are.

The NIV translation reads:

> God chose the lowly things of this world and the despised things—and the things that are not—to nullify the things that are.

The NIV translation, as far as my weak Greek can tell, is better, for, "things which are not" is in this context not a philosophical term, but a category under which is included things that are despised or contemptible.

Yet perhaps we need both versions. People are always imposing themselves on nature and others, and yet in the end, it all comes to nothing. But this nothing is not just death and the annihilation of all earthly things in the course of time. The oppressed, and as well as nature itself, resist imposition in ways that surprise and check our vanity. Apparently

---

1. Crouter, *Reinhold Niebuhr*, 96.

steadfast regimes can disappear in the space of a few months. People we love can disappear in a moment.

Every order of existence seeks to overcome its fear of insignificance by imposing itself on others. The best remedy against this tendency is belonging to a community that allows us to know how much we need each other, and finds a place of respect for all its members. Only such a community is capable of respecting the integrity of other communities.

> ... [t]hat other unique community is the limit beyond which our ambitions must not run and the boundary beyond which our life must not expand.[2]

Faith

Faith is the recognition that human logic and reason are nothing more than a contingent historical reality that thinks it is more. Or rather, a reality that thinks it is all there is. Some individuals are capable of faith, and communities of faith exist among us, many of which are no doubt self-righteous. But Niebuhr seems correct that "[i]t is not to be assumed that any nation or social order, any civilization or culture will ever be convicted by such a word [faith] so that it would cease from its pretensions."[3]

Why is it so important to remember that the things that are not will one day replace the things that are? Because this is the only remedy for the belief that one's own way of life was destined to be because it is better, or because it just is, the only way things could possibly be. Once one begins to believe that, idolatry cannot be far behind.

Plato and Christ?

Though I have not paid much attention to it, Simone Weil sees a direct connection between the ancient Greek philosophers and Christ.

> Plato describes how man, assisted by the power of grace, passes out of the cavern of this world; but he doesn't say that a whole city can pass out of it. On the contrary, he depicts the collectivity as something animal, which hinders the soul's salvation.[4]

---

2. Niebuhr, *Irony*, 139.
3. Niebuhr, "Things That Are Not," 11093.
4. Weil, *Roots*, 128.

Plato received the gift of grace? But the gift is only given to some? Not only does this make no sense, but it gets history wrong. Christianity arose out of Judaism; Judaism is Christianity's foundation, the Old Testament (as Christians call it) as important as the New.

But if Weil denies the Judaic origins of Christianity, substituting Plato for Moses, she has nonetheless identified the chief problem: the transformation of the state into an idol.

Idolatry

From Niebuhr to Simone Weil, there is shared recognition that idolatry is the sin of our age, more tempting, or at least more widespread, than in other ages, in which men and women knew themselves to be at the mercy of nature and the powerful. There is something about modern life, its scientific and technological achievements, and the relative security available to more people than ever before (while still excluding the majority) that makes idolatry, the worship of one's own, more tempting than ever before.

Sometimes idolatry takes the form of nationalism, sometimes a worship of science and medicine, as though they could save us from suffering and death, while bringing us happiness. Some people cradle their smartphones as though they were tiny golden calves. But often, idolatry is more subtle, people convinced that the beliefs they hold are necessary to existence itself.

> Thus the 'things that are' are persuaded into their vain defiance of the 'things that are not.' The defiance is vain because God is the author of the things that are not. They reveal his creative power as both judgment and mercy upon the things that are.[5]

Without the things that are not, we would be stuck in an endless and static existence.

The Things that Are Not Should Not Be Idealized Either

And yet we should be careful of idealizing the things that are not. Niebuhr is not careful enough. I have listened to and watched hundreds of hours of testimony from Holocaust survivors. For many, the smoke and smell from the crematoria were a constant reminder of the power of the things that are not, the power of annihilation. Many still smelled the smoke of annihilation

---

5. Niebuhr, "Things that are Not," 108.

years later. Some things that are, the values of life, are a condition of respect for all humanity in any era.

God shares these values not because he is humane, but because he is good. However, if his goodness were completely incomprehensible in human terms, we could not worship him.

13

Paul Tillich and Existential Christianity

PAUL TILLICH (1886–1965) WAS a popular theologian who reinterpreted the Bible in terms of existential themes.[1] Existentialism was fashionable in the 1950s, for it addressed the loneliness and absence of meaning that many felt after World War II. We had won the war, the economy was booming, but what was the point of it all, especially when the population of the planet could be annihilated in an hour? For this was the height of the Cold War.

Unusual for a popular author, Tillich was also esteemed by his colleagues for his intellectual rigor, above all, his three-volume masterwork, *Systematic Theology*. There, and in his more popular works, Tillich transformed the language of the Bible into the language of existentialism. God became our "ultimate concern," and sin became estrangement, separation from God, from self, and from neighbor.[2]

Other familiar theological terms were also translated into existential ones. Grace breaks into the darkness of our lives as if a voice were saying, "you are accepted just as you are." In *The Courage to Be*, Tillich describes this as "self-affirmation . . . which presupposes participation in something which transcends the self."[3] Providence, argues Tillich,

> is not a theory about some activities of God; it is the religious symbol of the courage of confidence with respect to fate and death.[4]

In many ways, Tillich continued the project of his postwar contemporaries, Karl Barth, Rudolf Bultmann, and Reinhold Niebuhr. Though not strictly postwar (he was murdered by the Nazis), Dietrich Bonhoeffer's religionless Christianity must be included here. But Tillich was the most

---

1. Tillich was on the cover of *Time* magazine on March 16, 1959.
2. Tillich, *Essential Tillich*, 165–6.
3. Tillich, *Courage to Be*, 165
4. Tillich, *Courage to Be*, 168.

apologetic of the Christian apologists, says Stanley Hauerwas. Apology in this context means defense, but Hauerwas plays off the double meaning of the term. It was not a compliment.

God Above God

Most controversial was Tillich's belief in a "God above God." Actually, it makes sense, more so than some of his other redefinitions, such as sin and grace. Tillich is taking aim at the image of God as the man upstairs, wearing a white cloak and a long beard, and ticking off the sins and good deeds of everyone. Or is it just everyone who believes in God?

God above "God" means that our language of talking about God has become trivialized and bereft. Needed is a way to talk, or at least think, about a God who is above and beyond the limits of our imagination. "How do we talk about eternity" might be another way to put it, for eternity is not endless time. Eternity is beyond time, in the same way God is above the "God" we worship and pray to. God must be rendered unfamiliar, more than we can imagine.

Faith and History

Faith interprets history in terms of man's "ultimate concern," Tillich's synonym for God. But more than that, our ultimate concern is our search for the meaning of it all.

> Faith can say that something of ultimate concern has happened in history because the question of the ultimate in being and meaning is involved. . . . Faith can say that the reality which is manifest in the New Testament picture of Jesus as the Christ has saving power for those who are grasped by it, no matter how much or how little can be traced to the historical figure [who is called Jesus of Nazareth.][5]

In other words, Christ has saving power for those who believe that Christ has saving power. Is this statement redundant and empty? Or is it exactly the way things are: Christ is salvific for those for whom Christ is real. There may be a lot to this actually. In any case, Christ becomes more real in a community of Christians who regard him as real.

The trouble with Tillich's work—and *Dynamics of Faith* is among his most popular—is that he is so abstract. I prefer the approach of Michael

---

5. Tillich, *Dynamics*, 101.

Perry, who argues that the claim of religious faith is the opposite of Albert Camus's claim of absurdity, in which the world is silent in response to our human cry for meaning. Religious faith says that the world is finally hospitable to our deepest human yearnings, because this world was in some way made with the human being and his yearnings in mind.[6]

I do not know that Perry's is the best way to put it, but it has the advantage of substance, for it raises the question of whether, as we look around the world today, it makes sense to say that it was made with the human being in mind, and what that might mean. Tillich's existentialism, on the other hand, is so abstract that the world as it is hardly enters into consideration. In this respect, he was quite unlike his colleague, Reinhold Niebuhr.

Stories and Symbols

What makes religion special, Tillich realizes, is that it is not so much about statements as it is about symbols. Unlike statements, symbols are not right or wrong. Rather, "a symbol *has* truth: it is adequate to the revelation it expresses."[7] But symbols do not live a life of their own. They are originally embedded in a story.

The cross is a powerful symbol. Many people wear a representation of this torture instrument on a chain around their necks. But it is the story behind the cross, of Christ's betrayal, torture, death and resurrection that makes it more than a piece of jewelry. The Bible is filled with stories, from Adam and Eve through Abraham and Isaac to Christ's crucifixion and resurrection, with at least a hundred stories in between, and more that follow.

Tillich has eliminated the stories. The symbols remain, but not the stories in which they are embedded. Or consider Christ's parables, uttered in a spare language as close to the thing itself as language can be. Nothing of this remains in Tillich.

One might respond that this is the difference between theology and religion, and there would be some truth in this claim. Tillich is a theologian, not just a preacher, though evidently, he delivered powerful sermons. But rendering basic religious concepts in the language of existentialism does not bring them closer to existence, but further away. Existentialism is the language of existence per se. The Bible is a series of stories and parables about why we are here, what we should do, how we should love, and where we are going. Like Shakespeare, it can be read at many different levels, from the literal to the abstract.

6. Perry, *Idea of Human Rights*, 14.
7. Tillich, *Systematic Theology*, 1, 240.

Tillich has left the Bible behind. I do not think this is bad in itself, especially if he can find a more compelling way to talk about God. But existentialism is not it. God is the story of God.

14

What Do Niebuhr, Barth, Bultmann, Bonhoeffer, and Tillich Have in Common? More than You Might Imagine

REINHOLD NIEBUHR, KARL BARTH, Rudolf Bultmann, Dietrich Bonhoeffer, and Paul Tillich are the most well-known Protestant theologians of the twentieth century. All downplay the mythical worlds of heaven and hell. The eschaton is now; we have already been saved by Christ's intervention in history; he is already here. What we have to do is live up to what we have been given gratis. Bultmann, Bonhoeffer, and Barth hold this view most strongly, Niebuhr less so, and I am ignoring important differences among them.

Bultmann and Barth come to this view because there is nothing left but faith. If we regard the Bible as a historical document, while at the same time conveying an essential truth, then that truth must be known by faith alone. The Bible provides symbols, such as the cross, to help us discover and express that faith.

There are few references in this chapter; most are found in my original chapters on each man.

Barth beautifully summarizes what God demands of us: allow yourself to be loved by God, and love God in return. That, and just that, is the good. We are all elected. Barth holds this view because he believes that all the action is with God: Jesus Christ is the electing God and the elected man at the same time (chapter 7.1 of this work).

I think there is much truth in this view, but Bonhoeffer's caution about cheap grace is worth remembering. Salvation is a great thing, and at the same time an enormous responsibility. For none of these men is salvation equivalent to eternal life. To be justified in the eyes of God is its own reward.

Notice, by the way, that none of these theologians attempts to prove the existence of God. As the myths that organize Christianity become more transparently mythical, faith remains the only alternative, and it's pointless to argue someone into faith. It is not pointless to talk about it.

Bultmann puts the point most clearly.

> We cannot use electric lights and radios and, in the event of illness, avail ourselves of modern medical and clinical means and at the same time believe in the spirit and wonder world of the New Testament.[1]

Like Barth, he holds that "paradoxically, the community of faith looks ahead to an event that has already happened." What has happened is freedom—freedom from this world. "The Gospel has the power to grant freedom from the world." There is no security but faith in God; the conceits of this world amount to nothing. Like Barth, we are already saved if we would take the time to know it.

Much of what Bultmann says makes sense, particularly his interpretation of the *kerygma*, the message of the gospels. The *kerygma* is not just the "good news." Its purpose is to interrupt our existence, call the meaning of our lives into question, and so free us from the world. One sees here how the core conventions of Protestant faith remain, even as the mythological scaffold is removed.

The main problem with Bultmann is that, while he has updated the Bible, so to speak, he has not updated sin. It remains an individual act. But something we can call "structural sin" also exists: unrestrained capitalism, neo-colonialism, and a way of life in which everything has its price. Just by being a citizen of this world (and not everyone on the planet belongs to this world; many are simply its victims), I have hurt other people. How to think about this, how to make atonement for it, has no place in Bultmann's theology, which is about the relationship between me and my God. That is true, but it is not the whole truth (chapter 8 of this work).

Bonhoeffer's religionless Christianity may seem like a contradiction, but it is not. Christ did not seek to establish a religion, but to speak for the oppressed and downtrodden, as well as to save our souls. Christ and his first followers sought to establish communities in the midst of the Roman empire. Bonhoeffer, along with Barth, and Bultmann, sought to do the same amidst the Nazi empire.

For Bonhoeffer, religion is no longer about redemption. Religionless Christianity, as he called it, is interested in two things: prayer and righteous action.

---

1. Bultmann, *New Testament*, 4.

Bonhoeffer came to admire the Old Testament more and more because it is not a teaching of redemption; that is, the saving significance of Jesus Christ. "Myths of redemption search outside history for an eternity after death." For Bonhoeffer, our job is to care for others in this world.

As for prayer, Bonhoeffer believed it leads to action only when we understand God properly. God's participation in Christ, his identity with Christ, meant for Bonhoeffer that God chose to become weak and powerless so as to identify with and represent the suffering of this world. Bonhoeffer believed, and I think he was right, that this vision of a weak God who depended on humans to do his work in this world was a uniquely valuable aspect of Christianity. God not only speaks for the outcast, he became one.

Sometimes it seems that, for Bonhoeffer, we could get by on prayer and social service agencies. Not so. His alternative to the church was small ecclesiastical communities such as Finkenwalde. There, students and faculty lived together as well as studied and worshiped together. It was closed by the Gestapo in 1937.

Bonhoeffer writes of the "secret discipline" that constitutes prayer and worship in the absence of religion. Some think the secret is the Eucharist. I think the secret is God's weakness. The secret asks the world to hear the screams of its victims, for it is we who must save them (chapter 7.3 of this work).

What happened to God? For Bonhoeffer, the transcendent is not about the infinite, but the neighbor who is within reach in any given situation. The transcendent is here and now in the desperate needs of others. He reminds me of the Jewish philosopher, Emmanuel Levinas, who is discussed in chapter 20 of this work.

Tillich would turn Christianity into existentialism. God becomes our "ultimate concern," and sin becomes estrangement, separation from God, from self, and from neighbor. Some seem to find this language useful. I am not one of them. The most moving parts of the Bible are its stories and parables, and they get lost in an existential approach.

Tillich's concept of a "God above 'God'" makes the most sense. Tillich is taking aim at the image of God as the man upstairs, wearing a white cloak and a long beard, and ticking off the sins and good deeds of everyone. Or is it just everyone who believes in God? The God above "God" means that our language of talking about God has become banal and bereft. Needed is a way to talk, or at least think, about a God who is above and beyond the limits of our imagination. "How do we talk about eternity" might be another way to put it, for eternity is not endless time. Eternity is beyond time. Similarly, God is above the "God" to whom we worship and pray. God must be rendered unfamiliar, more than we can imagine.

Niebuhr is my favorite theologian, but I am not sure why. He is not the most profound. Perhaps it is his worldliness that appeals, not just his belief that Christians must act in the world, but his willingness to recognize that nations exist, and so do limits. That sometimes means choosing the lesser of two evils.

His deepest insight, the one with the most ramifications, is that the greatest ethical and religious danger is communal idolatry. We may talk about God, but science, technology, medicine, and the nation state (nationalism) are our real gods. Even democracy may become an idol. We did not fight the Second World War to destroy evil, though that was one result. We fought it to preserve and extend our power and influence over the world. Not democracy, but God, has the first and last word. I still do not understand what the American flag is doing in church. It seems like idolatry to me. God may take sides, but not the side of nations.

God take sides in the sense that he judges but does not impose. He stands outside of history, but his grace is occasionally a weak force in history. Or so says Niebuhr. The judgment of God preserves the distinction between good and evil in history, but like Bonhoeffer, Niebuhr emphasizes the powerlessness of God. It is a chosen powerlessness, so that he might side with those whom history has cast aside. Niebuhr calls this the "scandal of the cross." Once again, God wins by losing.

> It is impossible to symbolize the divine goodness in history in any other way than by complete powerlessness, or rather by a consistent refusal to use power in the rivalries of history.[2]

God stays neutral in the conflicts of history, recognizing that no side is without an ego invested in the outcome, that all conflict is rivalry, not good over evil.

Trouble is, Niebuhr's account of the "war of finites" makes no sense when talking about the Holocaust, Hiroshima, Hitler, Mao, Stalin, and the murder of the Rohingya. In the case of annihilatory power, no rivalry is involved, only the slaughter of innocents.

Niebuhr was often accused of leaving the Bible behind. He did not. He understands that, while history is a war between good and evil, none of the participants is pure. What he does not seem to understand, and like the others, he wrote after the Holocaust and Hiroshima, is that while no regime is evil incarnate, some regimes practice annihilatory evil. If God could step in to save the lives of millions of children, but does not, then I am not sure I want to worship this God.

---

2. Niebuhr, *Nature and Destiny* 2, 72.

If God can act in history, if his divine grace is occasionally present in history, then God's failure to act in the presence of the annihilation of innocents preserves no one's freedom. If God's limits are not reached with the deaths of millions of humans, some the result of "creative achievements" like Zyklon B, gas ovens, and atomic bombs, then it is hard to know what these limits are.

Human suffering does not testify to God's suffering for us. Human suffering becomes human sacrifice if we insist on a God who acts in history but chooses not to. Christ's suffering is an inspiration; it is not an invitation to suffer.

Conclusion

In one way or another, all four agree with Bultmann that we can no longer believe in the spirit and wonder world of the New Testament. For all, Heaven and Hell are myths. The second coming is relatively unimportant. Important is how we respond to the first coming, when God intervened in history in the form of Jesus Christ. This statement does not apply to Niebuhr. Jesus Christ is God incarnate, and he offers salvation to all. Salvation, though, has little to do with eternal life, and much to do with how we live, care, and worship in this world. In this regard, Niebuhr is as godly as any of the others.

Because the miracle and wonder world of the Bible no longer inspires us, faith becomes central. God cannot be proven, only believed. This is the source of a certain conservatism in the four men's teachings. If we cannot rely on the Bible, except as a source of religious symbols, then faith becomes ever more important. For some, faith becomes more private, but Bonhoeffer particularly recognizes that a "religionless Christianity" requires a new type of community.

All take the God of Israel, the God of the Jews, as foundational for Christianity. Four left Germany to escape Hitler; Bonhoeffer remained and died at the hands of the Gestapo. But it seems to me that given their historical experiences, none address the Holocaust and Hiroshima as marking a new era of annihilatory evil on a mass scale. Doing so would, in my humble opinion, require struggling even more seriously with God's relationship to the world, and what his "grace made perfect in weakness" really means. (2 Corinthians 12:9)

Perhaps God is powerless, but for several of these men, he chooses powerlessness in order to unite himself as Christ with the outcasts and exiles of this world. But somehow, I cannot get past Niebuhr's statement that, while God remains neutral in history, he would prevent the destruction of this world. Could he not do more? Should he not? I suppose that is not up to humans to decide. In any case, it certainly makes the good and decent action of humans in this world more important.

15

Stanley Hauerwas and the End of Socially Responsible Christianity

STANLEY HAUERWAS WAS NAMED "America's best theologian" by *Time* magazine in 2001. (Has *Time* become our theological scorekeeper?). It has been a few years, but was he *ever* America's best theologian? Or does that category even make sense?

Hauerwas's most well-known and popular book is *Resident Aliens*. There he argues that Christians should see themselves as "resident aliens" in a foreign land. Instead of attempting to influence government and society, Christians should live lives that exemplify the love of Christ. The first social task of the church is to be the church.[1] Hauerwas quotes an American Jew in South Carolina.

> It's tough to be a Jew in Greenville. We are forever telling our children, 'that's fine for everyone else, but it's not fine for you. You are special. You are different. You are a Jew. You have a different story. A different set of values.'[2]

Christians should live and think the same way. Serious Christians have become a diaspora community.

How could this be, the reader might ask. An aggressive Christianity is everywhere, from abortion protests to people knocking on your door asking if you have been saved, a recent experience of mine. But this is not what Hauerwas is worried about. He worries that Christianity has been colonized and tamed by American society, so that it no longer stands for much of anything different or separate from the culture at large. Nothing brought this home to me more clearly than Hauerwas's suggestion of what the church he belongs to should say to prospective members.

---

1. Hauerwas, *Peaceable Kingdom*, 235, 2492.
2. Hauerwas, *Peaceable Kingdom*, 293.

> When you join our church, you don't get to decide by yourself when and where you will move. If your company wants to send you to a new town, you first need to ask the church whether it's a good idea. New members, all members, should disclose how much money they make.[3]

Behind this startling idea, at least to individualistic Americans, is Hauerwas's claim that the most important thing the Christian church did was to "create a community whose like had never been seen before."[4]

Truth and Community

Hauerwas's most difficult claim, at least for me, is his assertion that Christian claims must be objectively true. Theology is not a matter of being liberal or conservative, but "a matter of truth."

The reason I had so much trouble with this claim is that Hauerwas insists that the most important thing about the gospels is that they were written in stories. Recent theology is mostly about abstract propositions. Understanding the gospels is making its stories your own. We understand Christianity when we understand its narrative, and our tiny part in it. For all true understanding, as opposed to factually true statements, depends upon the narrative it is embedded in.[5]

Finally, I got it, though Hauerwas does little to make it easier. By "objectively true," Hauerwas means "in accordance with lived narrative." Truth is narrative truth, its story developing over time, its characters rich and real, and the story ending in a way that makes sense of all that has passed. One advantage of this approach is that it supports the Christian view of a linear history, one that will end with the return of Christ. Now that's a story.

I still think that Hauerwas plays off this double meaning of truth: objective truth versus narrative truth. But for the most part, it becomes clear that, when Hauerwas says "truth," he means people making Christianity true by living it every day. This fits with his view that Christianity is itself a narrative.

> The nature of Christian ethics is determined by the fact that Christian convictions take the form of a story, or perhaps better, a set of stories that constitutes a tradition, which in turn creates and forms a community. Christian ethics does not

---

3. https://www.plough.com/en/topics/community/church-community/why-community-is-dangerous

4. Hauerwas, *Reader*, 1563.

5. Hauerwas, *Reader*, 701–6.

begin by emphasizing rules or principles, but by calling our attention to a narrative that tells of God's dealing with creation, gifting it to us.[6]

Church and World

Hauerwas is critical of almost every recent theologian, including Paul Tillich, Reinhold Niebuhr, H. Richard Niebuhr, Karl Barth, and Dietrich Bonhoeffer, because they want to involve the church in the world. The result is to make the church worldlier. Instead, the church must fight to remain free of the world, so that its members can be exemplars of a true Christian life.

I continue to wonder why my Episcopal church has an American flag standing by the altar, something I have noticed at every church I have attended. Isn't that idolatry? The whole point of the church is that it not be loyal to the state (though its members may be), but to the message of the gospels, which is to love others as Christ has loved you. (John 13:34–35) Does anyone really believe that America even pretends to this ethic? Are the Beatitudes on anyone's list of American virtues? (Matthew 5:3–12)

Reinhold Niebuhr says he is quite prepared to admit that his brother Richard's "ethical perfectionism and its apocalyptic note" is closer to the gospel than his. But such an admission simply notes the inability to construct an adequate social ethic out of a pure love ethic.[7]

As I read Hauerwas, it becomes clear that it is impossible to construct a social ethic from a love ethic. The virtue of the gospels is love. The virtue of society is justice. This is why it is important that the church stay out of politics, that the church care for the souls of its members. "The church does not have a social ethic. Rather the church is a social ethic."[8] The church should strengthen its members' resistance to the common culture, not encourage it.

Cells of Joy?

It may be that we must learn to "do nothing" in the face of one nation's invasion of another nation, or the suffering of so many, says Hauerwas.

> Yet we can be a people who witness confidently to the peace that we know is possible in this life, since we have begun to feel its power in our lives. For what hope has the world if there are not

---

6. Hauerwas, *Peaceable Kingdom*, 864.
7. Hauerwas, *Peaceable Kingdom*, 3082.
8. www.*commonwealmagazine.org/bricklayer's-so*

"cells" of people who manifest a joy that otherwise the world would have no means of knowing to be possible in this life?[9]

These cells, he suggests, might coordinate with other cells around the world, but I do not know why. Is coordination going to increase the joy of any of its members, or extend it beyond other cells? Maybe.

It is realistic to hold that the church can do virtually nothing to stop the bloodshed around the world. It need not try to do nothing. It *can* do nothing. But consider the beggar on the street, or the homeless family anywhere in the world. Here the church has a chance to make a difference, one person, one family at a time.

If I were a member of Hauerwas's church, I would ask prospective members if they are willing to donate 10 percent of their income to the poor. Not to the church, but directly to the poor through organizations like Oxfam. I think this is more important than just about anything else, and it follows Christ's pronouncement that whatever you do for the least of men you do for me. (Matthew 25:40) I would also ask if they are willing to donate their time.

The Church and Desegregation in America

The church may not be able to change much about the world, but there was a point beginning about sixty-five years ago when it changed everything. The American civil rights movement was based in the African American church. Without the institutional structure of the church, the civil rights movement would have looked vastly different, and been less effective. Add to this that it brought peace to the struggle via the strategy of nonviolent resistance, and the church enabled America to make a decisive moral breakthrough. The question we must ask Hauerwas, who understands the church as a community unto itself, is whether the church will know when the world needs it once again, and whether the institutional structures will still exist.

---

9. Hauerwas, *Peaceable Kingdom*, 3256.

16.1

Thomas Merton Is Wrong: Christian Mysticism Is a Bad Idea

THOMAS MERTON WAS A great proponent of ecumenism. For Merton, all religions—East and West—seek the same thing: unity with God. He was also a beautiful writer. Nevertheless, it seems to me that he got something fundamental wrong.

The goal of Christian mysticism is to find unity with God. Solitude, contemplation, self-denial, and often silence all aim at the emptying of the self in order that we might be filled with God. But what if the goal of unity is the wrong goal? The proper Christian goal is faith in God and following the teachings of Jesus Christ. Chief among Christ's teachings are loving and caring for other people.

Whatever unity with God that is necessary in order to feel fulfilled is achieved through the Eucharist. We partake of the blood and body of Christ, and in so doing, incorporate his body into ours, and our body into the membership in the church. What else is needed? What else is there?

If this is so, what purpose does the contemplative search for mystical unity with God serve? I think it serves solely the need of the individual, and little to do with a greater unity with God. What if, instead of the word "unity," I substituted "a feeling of belonging to God's world because I am one of his creatures?" Putting it this way is more long-winded, but it says all that need be said. The search for wholeness is a search for self, not God.

The experience of God in this world does not rest on the acceptance of propositions and assertions. Arguments are not important. The experience of God rests on faith in the unseen and unknown, and in this sense, it is not wrong to say that there is a mystical element in Christianity. But faith and feeling are different from mystical unity: they do not require the purging of the self; they depend upon a type of nonrational knowledge.

Zen or No Zen

For Merton, Zen was entirely compatible with Christian mysticism if by Zen we mean "the quest for direct and pure experience on a metaphysical level."[1]

Who says we want or need direct experience of God on a metaphysical level? And what does "metaphysical" mean here anyway, except beyond the physical? It seems to me that this metaphysical experience is designed to soothe or satisfy human longing for completion. That is not God's job.

The right attitude is that of Job, who learns in the end that he knows nothing, that the world is a wonder he can barely comprehend, and that his task is to accept whatever God brings him. In other words, there is a vast distance between Job and God; it was meant to be that way, and it will remain that way. Or as God puts it, "For my thoughts are not your thoughts, neither are your ways my ways." (Isaiah 55:8)

From this perspective, it is impious and foolish to seek unity with God. Not unity, but a vast respectful distance seems to be the attitude of the Bible. Christianity changes things. Jesus shares our humanity, and in the Eucharist, we participate in God. But the basic idea remains, just as the continuity between the Old and New Testaments remains. We experience God most respectfully when we recognize that God's love is premised on the distance between God and man, not their unity. Between creator and created there is always a void. The void may be bridged by love, but it is a human conceit that we can become the void and so be one with God.

The Prophet and the Pope

The prophet delivers a message the world needs, but does not want to hear: that there is something deeply wrong in society, and it can be named. For Merton, the problem was alienation, and his answer was "world consciousness."

The alienation that Merton wrote of was not economic, but spiritual—our estrangement not only from God, but from ourselves.[2] The concept is not very clear, but I am more interested in Merton's solution, "world consciousness." For Merton had come to see the world as a single organism composed of "one human family, one world."[3]

Recently, I saw a film documentary by Wim Wenders, "Pope Francis: A Man of His Word." Though Francis too talked in terms of one human

---

1. Merton, *On Zen*, 102; Moses, *Divine Discontent*, 149.
2. Merton, *Faith and Violence*, 153—4.
3. Merton, *Redeeming Time*, 65; Moses, *Divine Discontent*, 190.

family, he spoke from the ground up. Needed are actual human families in which the parents love each other and their children, while having the leisure to do so. Needed too is meaningful work, communal ties of affection and friendship, and loving care for those in need. For Francis, world consciousness begins not in contemplation, but in those small places where humans meet, greet, and love each other.

Conclusion

Contemplation turns inward in an attempt to find unity and wholeness with God. It is a private pursuit, perhaps even a self-indulgence for those few with the time and resources to pursue it. Pope Francis talks about bringing God into our everyday life with partners, children, neighbors, and the needy. The two paths are not completely incompatible, but I disagree with Merton when he says solitude has its own special work: a deepening of awareness that the world needs, a struggle against alienation. True solitude, says Merton, is deeply aware of the world's needs.[4]

I do not think it is true. "The world is too much with us," and solitude is necessary. But a life of solitude is a retreat, and most important things are learned amid the love and the company of others. Pope Francis said that it was in his work as a parish priest listening to confessions that he came to understand how important leisure and family time is. It is not an experience that can be learned in solitude.

---

4. Merton, *Conjectures*, 136.

16.2

The Unknown Thomas Merton

From the late 1940s through most of the 1960s, Thomas Merton was the most well-known and admired Catholic monk in North America. *The Seven Storey Mountain*, his autobiography written while he was still young, was one of the best-selling books of 1949, going on to sell over four million copies. It has never been out of print. During his lifetime, he published over 70 books. He belonged to the Trappist order, remaining at the Abbey of Gethsemani, in Kentucky, United States, from 1941 until his sudden death in 1968 at age 53. In his later years, he became interested in Zen Buddhism. It was at an ecumenical conference in Bangkok that he was accidentally electrocuted.[1]

A Lonely Man

These facts tell us virtually nothing about who he was, nothing interesting anyway. Merton's mother died when his was six, and his father died when he was sixteen, leaving him well provided for. Even before his father's death, he was raised by a series of relatives and at boarding schools. During his entire life, Merton never worked for wages, but there are more important things in life than money, such as a stable home and loving parents. Merton had neither.

In the previous chapter, I discussed Merton's mystical version of Christianity. This section tries to figure out who he was as a man. The simplest and most important thing to say is that he was terribly lonely, longing for love. His solution, which never really worked, was to abandon himself to God, thus eliminating his needy self. One of his biographers writes that "when the Gethsemani gates closed behind him, Merton tasted freedom

---

1. Some speculate that Merton was killed by the Catholic hierarchy. Others, such as John Cooney, that he committed suicide, but the evidence is slight. Accidents happen; in this case, a faulty electric fan and a wet floor.

even though he was within four walls."[2] If we can understand that, we can understand Merton.

Freedom from Need

For Merton, "freedom" meant freedom from his terrible loneliness and need. He was free at Gethsemani, at least for a while, because he could not act on his need. Merton's close friend and brother monk Father Basil Pennington agreed. He said Merton told him that asking "Am I happy?" was the wrong question, with the real one being, "Am I free?" Pennington concluded Merton meant the freedom from need, whether it was happiness, pleasure, things, or people.[3]

If you do not trust human love, choose a path in which union with God is the highest love. In this union, there is no need and no room for others, who can never disappoint. Fortunately for both Merton and his readers, he could not stick to this path.

Merton kept detailed, almost daily, journals from his years at Columbia University (he was 21) until his death. Evidently, they are lightly censored, unlike *The Seven Storey Mountain*, cut one-third by Catholic censors. Merton stipulated that his journals not be published until twenty-five years after his death. Today they are readily available, and the best source of information about him.

Several entries are particularly striking, such as his self-criticism for wanting to keep his own identity, the source of his misery, or so he believed.[4]

Margie and Having It All

Merton had back surgery in April 1966. He was cared for by a student nurse named Margie. They fell deeply in love, beginning an affair that lasted about six months, and a relationship that lasted about two years.[5] Much ink has been spilt over whether they ever consummated their relationship, whatever that old-fashioned term means exactly.

Merton wrote about Margie in his journals (Journal 6), stating that he wanted their love to be known, for it was an important part of who he became.

2. Shaw, *Beneath the Mask*, 925.
3. Shaw, *Beneath the Mask*, 3459.
4. Journal 4, 323–34
5. Cooney, "Thomas Merton: the hermit who never was, his young lover and mysterious death." The Irish Times, 11/9/2015. https://www.irishtimes.com/culture/books/thomas-merton-the-hermit-who-never-was-his-young-lover-and-mysterious-death-1.2422818

It was, and from the affair, he became a deeper and better man. But it is worth noting Merton's desire to have it all. Merton lived in his hermitage on the grounds of Gethsemani, while entertaining guests such as Joan Baez. His goal, he said, was to have her [Margie] as a kind of mistress while he continued to live as a hermit. Could anything be more dishonest, he asks?[6]

Who would not want such a thing? Many perhaps, but some would. The difference between Merton and the rest of us is that he thought such things were possible. And why should he not? He was the only monk allowed to have his own hermitage (a little private house), and his psychiatrist and friend Dr. Wygal made his office available to Merton and Margie, where Merton and Margie drank champagne, and he remembered "her body, her nakedness the day at Wygal's, and it haunts me."[7] One reason Merton was allowed such liberties is because he was the most famous monk in America. Another is that he turned over his royalties to the abbey. At one point, they accounted for 16% of the abbey's income.

Merton's Symposium, or What Merton Learned

In Plato's *Symposium*, his dialogue on love, Plato has Socrates say that love moves from beautiful bodies to beautiful ideas to beauty in itself (*Symposium* 210a-211b). He calls this the ladder of love (*epanabathmois*). Is it any wonder that centuries of Christian writers have baptized Plato, interpreting his forms, such as beauty in itself, as God's thoughts?

Merton's life can be read as an enactment of this vision. Up to a point. All his life, he desperately wanted and needed love. Not just, he emphasizes, to receive love, but also to give love. Without this experience, he said, we cannot love God as mature men and women. With Margie, he found someone who needed his love as desperately as he needed to give and receive hers.

Eventually, Merton gave up Margie, but rather than being crushed, he seemed to experience life anew. Some speculate that he would not have remained at Gethsemani, but that is unknowable, for he died shortly after. In any case, he seems to have learned Plato's lesson. As Merton put it,

> ... [w]e cannot love [God] *perfectly* if we have not in some way loved [another person] maturely and truly.[8]

---

6. Merton, *Journal* 6, 94.
7. Merton, *Journal* 6, 94.
8. Merton, *Conjectures*, 188.

17.1

C. S. Lewis Is Popular But Wrong: We Are Not Little Christs

C. S. LEWIS (1898-1963) was one of the most popular Christian writers of the twentieth century, and our century as well. Though he would have disliked being called a theologian, that is exactly what he was, even as he had no formal theological training. In fact, this is exactly what makes his works on Christianity so popular. *Mere Christianity*, begun as a series of radio lectures during World War II, is almost conversational in tone. It is still taught in adult Christian education groups. The fact that Lewis had no formal theological training does not imply that he lacked intellectual standing, having taught medieval history at both Oxford and Cambridge. He also wrote the fictional *Chronicles of Narnia*.

Most critics of Lewis as a theologian are Christian evangelicals, and others, who believe he was too loose with doctrine, such as saying that other religions might contain a portion of truth about God. My take is somewhat the opposite. He is too literal about what it means to follow Christ. For Lewis, it means to become "little Christs," which to me makes no sense at all. Nevertheless, there is a charm and simplicity to his religious writing which has no equal, though perhaps G. K. Chesterton comes close.

God, Mad, or Bad: Lewis's Trilemma

Lewis has what he thinks is a fairly simple, almost logical, proof, that Jesus was God incarnate. Jesus was not a lunatic, and he was certainly not a fiend, so the only possibility left over is that he was God in human form.

Some things are best not left to logic, and this is one. Jesus's standing is not a logical question, but a historical and religious one. As Bart Ehrman points out in *How Jesus Became God*, the synoptic gospels (Mark, Matthew, and Luke) never claim that Jesus is God.[1] Only John does, Jesus famously saying "Before Abraham was, I am." (John 8:58) All four gospels came three to four generations after Christ's crucifixion, the letters of Paul only a little earlier. Furthermore, there were lots of people running around at this time claiming to be the son of God. Apollonius of Tyana has a history that runs almost parallel to Jesus, his followers also claiming his divinity after his death at Roman hands.

It is historically naive to claim that Jesus was God, mad, or bad. The idea of a divine human being was widespread, and Jesus Christ its most effective spokesman, due to the content of the message, as well as the missionary efforts of Paul. Whether the Holy Spirit had a role in Christianity's success depends on your religious beliefs, as does Christ's divinity itself. It does not depend on logic chopping.

What Has to Be Believed to Be a Christian

> We are told that Christ was killed for us, that His death has washed out our sins, and that by dying He disabled death itself. That's the formula. That's Christianity. That's what has to be believed.[2]

I would put it differently, which I suppose makes me a lay theologian as well, though a heretical one. At some point a little over 2000 years ago, God entered into world history in human form so that he could suffer as humans do (perhaps the better to know human suffering), and so that we could know him in the way humans do: not as an abstraction, or an idea, but in the form of a human being. Thinking about God in this way is quite the opposite of the teaching of Emmanuel Levinas (chapter 20 of this work), for whom God is nonbeing. Pointing this out does not make Levinas wrong.

My account is heretical, because I do not emphasize Jesus as sacrifice who died so that we might be saved from the wages of sin. Nor do I believe that Jesus disabled death, whatever that means exactly. About doctrines such as the virgin birth, I do not really care. God did something much grander, transforming the historical expectation of our Savior as a mighty prince who would come in glory to vindicate the lowly. Instead, God became a suffering human in order to demonstrate how we should love each other, especially the "least of these my brothers," in this world. (Matthew 25:40)

While I do not believe that Jesus disabled death, Christ put human life under the perspective of eternity. Lewis expresses this view nicely when he

1. Ehrman, *How Jesus Became God*.
2. Lewis, *Mere Christianity*, 55.

says that "there are no *ordinary* people. . . . [i]t is immortals whom we joke with, work with, marry, snub and exploit."³ It is good to think about people this way, whether it is literally true or not, for it makes our transactions more serious.

I am reminded of a very different author, Friedrich Nietzsche, and his doctrine of the eternal return.⁴ Imagine that everything you do, you will do again and again in lifetime after lifetime. Imagine that your worst moments will repeat themselves endlessly. The point of the eternal return is not to take it literally, but to recognize the weight and significance of everything that you do, as if it would be endlessly repeated. Take this life seriously, for it lasts forever.

Nietzsche was a great critic of Christianity, but it seems to me that in different and perhaps even opposite ways, each asks us to live our lives under the aspect of eternity.

Pride

Pride, says Lewis, is the worst sin, the chief cause of misery in every nation and every family since the world began.⁵ Surprisingly, Lewis does not emphasize the denial that makes this sin possible, the denial of our own creatureliness. Pride is best expressed by Milton's Satan in *Paradise Lost*.

> We know no time when we were not as now,
> Know none before us, self-begot, self-raised
> By our own quick'ning power . . . (Milton 5.853–61)

Satan would pull himself from the earth with his own right hand if he could, even his birth an act of self-creation.

The belief in self-creation is so dangerous because it can accept no limits. If I create myself, there can be no place for God. Or rather, I become God by default. How does one rid oneself of this pride, what I would call the arrogance of humanism? The first step is to love or admire anyone or anything outside oneself. With the proviso that we must love this person or thing for itself, in its otherness, not just in terms of what it says about or can do for me.

---

3. Lewis, *Weight of Glory*, 46.
4. Nietzsche, *Gay Science*, para. 341.
5. Lewis, *Mere Christianity*, 123–4.

Every Christian a Little Christ

The part of Lewis that I do not understand (and perhaps my understanding of Christian doctrine is insufficient) is his claim that

> Every Christian is to become a little Christ. The whole purpose of becoming a Christian is simply nothing else.[6]

No, the Christian ideal is to follow Christ's example, insofar as humans can, and to follow his teachings about how to live good human lives. *The Imitation of Christ* is a Christian devotional book from the fifteenth century. Other than the Bible, it is the most widely read devotional work among Christians. It is almost always understood as instruction in following Christ, not imitating him.

Writing about evolution, Lewis says,

> [c]entury by century God has guided nature up to the point of producing creatures which can (if they will) be taken right out of nature, turned into "gods."[7]

The most puzzling part of this sentence does not have to do with Lewis's view of evolution, which is compatible with the scientific view. The puzzle is the quotation marks around "gods." What could this mean? With the introduction of Christ into history, salvation becomes possible, but that does not make us gods, not even potential ones. Lewis has taken the imitation of Christ too literally. Paul's reference to Christians as saints in six of his letters makes sense, for it referred to members of a church he was addressing, and the Greek is readily translated as "holy ones." But gods? Actually, "gods" is a bad translation of *agios*, which is usually translated as "sacred," "pious" or "devout," attributes of a worshipful person, not a little god.

What about the Eucharist, it might be asked? Is that not the oral incorporation of Christ, and so becoming part of him, and Him of us? To some it is; to many others, including Jesus, it is an act of remembrance. Both 1 Corinthians 23–25 and Luke 22:19 refer to Christ's introduction of the ritual as something to be done "in memory of me." The Greek term is *anamnesis*, or remembrance, sometimes translated in this context as "affectionate memory." If Christ did not understand transubstantiation literally, why should we?

Lewis admits that becoming a little Christ is a bit of "fakery," along the lines of the expression "fake it until you make it." I do not believe we should try to fake being Christ-like. We should work to be good human beings who

---

6. Lewis, *Mere Christianity*, 177.
7. Lewis, *Mere Christianity*, 222.

love God, and one another. Jesus is too "other," too radically different from humans, to be someone to imitate. Are we to separate the wheat from the tares, the sheep from the goats? Are we to explain ourselves in parables? The disciples healed others in the name of Christ, but none except a stray evangelist would claim to do so today.

We need not be distant from Christ, but we do not become closer by pretending to be Christ. To be a good human being, a follower of Christ, is hard enough. Understanding ourselves as followers also serves to remind us of our creatureliness, not tempting us with the promise of more. First Corinthians 2:16 refers to having the "mind of Christ" (*nous*), but the context is one of opening the mind so as to understand Christ's teachings. It is not an invitation to become a little Christ.

Final Thoughts

Christians should imitate the mind of Christ in order to come closer to God. But what if someone does not? Lewis's answer is grim.

> Look for yourself, and you will find in the long run only hatred, loneliness, despair, rage, ruin, and decay. But look for Christ and you will find Him, and with Him everything else thrown in.[8]

Not even Thomas Aquinas thought things were so bad. The point of natural law is that one need not believe in God in order to follow it. It is enough to be a decent human being. Aquinas would agree with Lewis that it is not enough to look inside yourself. One becomes a decent human being by living in a community whose members care for each other. I believe that this community is enriched and strengthened when it is a religious community, but life in its absence need not be Hell. More on Aquinas and natural law in chapters 34–36 of this work.

---

8. Lewis, *Mere Christianity*, 227.

17.2

Thoughts While Reading *A Grief Observed,* by C. S. Lewis

C. S. Lewis begins with a well-known line, at least among those who follow him: "No one ever told me that grief felt so like fear."[1] A nervous stomach, constant swallowing—these are some of grief's fear-like symptoms.

The Reason Grief Feels So Much Like Fear

Grief feels so much like fear because it *is* fear. The loss of a beloved person threatens to empty the world of value. Saint Augustine writes about this empty world after the loss of a dear friend.

> My heart was utterly darkened by this grief, and everywhere I looked I saw nothing but death. . . . My eyes looked for him everywhere, but they could not find him. I hated all places because he was not there. . . . I wondered that other men should live when he was dead, for I had loved him as though he would never die. Still more I wondered that he should die and I remain alive, for I was his second self.[2]

Lewis wonders if grief is not selfish. After all, in grief what I really grieve is the loss of someone I held dear. I am not grieving for my beloved; I am grieving for myself. True enough, but consider what I am really grieving: the loss of who I was when I was with this other person. The person who I was with this other person, I can never be again. I can never be this same self even should I love another. That self is gone forever.

---

1. Lewis, *Grief*, 15.
2. Augustine, *Confessions*, 4.4.9

Of course it's easy enough to say that God seems absent at our greatest need because He *is* absent—non-existent.[3]

If God is the source of ultimate value, then the loss of one's beloved threatens everything of value. This is where the fear comes from. In many ways, it resembles the childhood fear of abandonment: that I will be left alone in an empty world. Writing about the death of her husband of 48 years, Joyce Carol Oates felt devoid of worth.

> *Here is a woman utterly alone. Here is a woman utterly unloved. Here is a woman of no more worth than a pail of garbage.*[4]

It is truly terrifying to love deeply, for almost certainly one will die before the other, and there is no such thing as healthy grief. Grief is an illness of the soul.

Grief, Boredom, Nausea

Lewis asks, "Does grief finally subside into boredom tinged by faint nausea?"[5] It might, because the experience of being bored stems from an inability to connect with one's inner world. The boredom of grief is the boredom of a world emptied of value, a world of things that cannot be reanimated. Not just the beloved, but everybody is dead. About this experience, Oates writes that

> the terror of mere things from which meaning has been drained—this is the terror that sweeps over the widow at such times.[6]

In such a world, time no longer flows; it curdles.

God Is the One Who Remembers

One can say that one's beloved is in a better place, but how many people really believe it? I think the basic experience of loss is the experience that Augustine and Lewis describe, the experience of awe that one so loved should no longer exist.

---

3. Lewis, *Grief*, 19.
4. Oates, *Widow's Story*, 324, author's emphasis.
5. Lewis, *Grief*, 48.
6. Oates, *Widow's Story*, 232.

> I look up at the night sky. Is anything more certain than that in all those vast times and spaces, if I were allowed to search them, I should nowhere find her face, her voice, her touch? She died. She is dead. Is the word so difficult to learn?[7]

I like to think about God as the One who remembers (chapter 38 of this work). The person I loved is gone, but the fact that I loved her, and we loved each other, is a fact in time and space, and will remain so even if none remain to remember it. For God is the One who remembers. Throughout all of time and all of space, God remembers the fact that I loved and was loved.

God remembers other things, I imagine, including the terrible truth of the Nazi Holocaust and slavery. One might reply that there is a vast difference between my little life and world historical events like the Holocaust or slavery, and of course there is. But God, if he is to make any sense, remembers everything in its place.

Are Faith and Grief the Same?

Lewis worries that his memory of his dead wife will become more and more his possession, and hence less and less real. His memory of her will become less and less subject to the reality check that was her existence refusing to fit into his idea of her.

I do not think there is any good answer to Lewis's concern. It is why some people seem to prefer their loved ones dead or at least absent, so as not to get in the way of their idealization of the beloved. Absence makes the heart grow fonder because there is no complicated reality to intrude.

But there is another side to this story, told by Joan Didion in her memoir about the death of her husband of forty years, John Gregory Dunne. "Were faith and grief the same thing?" she asks.[8] For, in both, one must believe in someone who is not there, at least not in the usual way that people are present to us. In this sense, grief is good practice for getting in touch with God. Not, I think, a good God, at least in conventional terms, but a God behind the scenes, the creator of all that exists, as well as the One who remembers.

Grief, Mourning, Bereavement

Until now, says Didion,

---

7. Lewis, *Grief*, 28.
8. Didion, *Magical Thinking*, 34.

> ... I had been able only to grieve, not mourn. Grief was passive. Grief happened. Mourning, the act of dealing with grief, required attention.[9]

Lewis does not make a distinction between grief and mourning, but his distinction between grief and bereavement is similar.

This is where Oates' account of her husband's death in *A Widow's Story* fails. It is all about her grief during her first year of widowhood. She says she wanted to capture the hysterical, insane grief into which she was plunged, but in a strange way, this is the easy part. Lewis comments that passionate grief does not so much link us with the dead as cut us off from them. That seems right. Bereavement, as much a social category as a psychological one, finds a place for the dead in the land of the living.

Oates concludes her memoir on grief with these lines:

> Of the widow's countless death-duties there is really just one that matters: on the first anniversary of her husband's death she should think *I kept myself alive*.[10]

There is something small, true, and awful about this conclusion. It is true: the death of one's beloved threatens one's own existence. At the same time, Lewis knows there is a larger world to contend with, and that his late wife now belongs to that world. He concludes with these lines:

> How wicked it would be, if we could, to call the dead back! She [Joy] said not to me but to the chaplain, 'I am at peace with God.' She smiled, but not at me. *Poi si tornò all' eterna fontana*.[11]

The Latin lines are from Dante's Paradiso (canto 31). Beatrice turns to Dante, but her final gaze is directed toward eternity.

What Happens After We Die?

I do not know what happens to us after we die. I think I know that the task of the living is to keep the dead alive in our hearts. That too is faith.

---

9. Didion, *Magical Thinking*, 89.
10. Oates, *Widow's Story*, 416, author's emphasis.
11. Lewis, *Grief*, 88–89.

17.3

Why We Need Pain: A Bad Answer by C. S. Lewis

IF GOD IS ALL good and all powerful, why is there so much pain and evil in the world? It is a classic question, known as theodicy, or the justice of God. The problem starts with the insight that the Lord who loves righteousness is at the same time an awesome and terrible presence. God is not just good. He is terrifying. As Lewis puts it,

> [F]or it was the Jews who fully and unambiguously identified the awful Presence haunting black mountain tops and thunderclouds with "the righteous Lord" who "loveth righteousness."[1]

It is a simple point that sometimes gets lost. We worship God not just because of his goodness, but because of his power, an experience that fills us with awe and dread. Why else is it death to see the face of God? (Exodus 33:20)[2]

God, Goodness, and Power

What we most want in the world, especially as children, is for goodness and power to be one. Many of us never grow up in this regard. A long line of psychological experiments demonstrates this.[3] When forced to choose, abused children generally blame themselves, rather than seeing their powerful parents as bad.

---

1. Lewis, *Problem of Pain*, 13–14.
2. Actually, it's a little more complicated, for elsewhere in the Bible, people see God (Exodus 24:10–11). Much depends on how the Hebrew term *panim* (Strong's *Concordance*, 6440) is translated, for it may be rendered as "presence" as well as "face." In the New Testament, people saw God every day in the presence of Christ. Most just didn't know what they were seeing. Perhaps they still don't.
3. Lerner, *Just World*, 178.

It is for this reason that Jesus Christ is so compelling, an all-powerful God who emptied or poured (*ekenōsen*) himself into a human vessel in order to experience human pain, and perhaps human pleasure as well. This is not how God's identity with Jesus is usually explained, but I like to think that God allowed himself to become human partly so that he might understand us better, and partly so that we would not be so quick to identify power with goodness. "[His] strength made perfect in weakness" is how Paul put it, and that seems about right. (2 Corinthians 12:9) Of course, there are many passages in the Bible where Christ identifies himself with God's power, but what a wonderful idea that God would pour himself into human form in order to experience human weakness and pain.

Our Happiness Is Not God's Goal

Our happiness is not God's goal. His goal is to make us better people, worthier of loving God, and worthier of God's love. This may require pain, says Lewis.

> . . . [l]ove may cause pain to its object, but only on the supposition that that object needs alteration to become fully lovable. Now why do we men need so much alteration? The Christian answer—that we have used our free will to become very bad—is so well known that it hardly needs to be stated.[4]

How Much Pain, and for What?

Let us assume that pain often makes people better, more serious, more dedicated to the things that really matter in this world, including love of God, love of nature, love of family, and love of humanity. But how much suffering is enough? I have viewed hundreds of hours of testimony by survivors of the Holocaust. I curate a blog on psychic trauma, including PTSD.[5] For most people, too much suffering is destructive: of faith, and even of love and goodness. The peculiar quality of PTSD is that it involves suffering that is endless.

Lewis states that people forget their pain relatively quickly once it is over.

---

4. Lewis *Problem of Pain*, 49.
5. Alford, *After the Holocaust*; https://www.traumatheory.com

> ...[p]ain has no tendency, in its own right, to proliferate. When it is over, it is over, and the natural sequel is joy.[6]

It is simply not true. The suffering of many Holocaust survivors lasts forever. Not only because they lost confidence in the basic goodness of the world, but because they frequently lost their entire families, as well as the towns they grew up in. All were obliterated. Having lived in fear and terror for years, it is often impossible to return to everyday life.

Many who suffer PTSD suffer for decades. Indeed, this is what post-traumatic stress disorder means: that the cause of suffering is removed, but the suffering never stops. Sometimes it does. Some find understanding families and good therapists, but many remain forever vigilant, forever unable to relax and enjoy the pleasures of this world.

My conclusion: pain makes some people better, in the sense of deeper and more profound. But too much pain can destroy a life forever. More precisely put, too much pain destroys the ability to experience pleasure in life. For most people have a remarkable capacity to endure.

The Limits of God's Omnipotence

Why does God not take some of the pain away? Lewis says he cannot. God could have created any world, or none. But he is constrained by logic, and evidently by consistency and nonintervention. If humans are to be free, nature must be as it is.

> Try to exclude the possibility of suffering which the order of nature and the existence of free-wills involve, and you find that you have excluded life itself.[7]

Even so, even if free will means pain, suffering, and crimes against humanity, what good or necessity is served by malaria, typhus, or the black plague, which killed almost half of all humans in Europe in the fourteenth century? If God is omnipotent, could there not be some limit on human pain? For there does not seem to be, and Lewis is completely wrong to claim that, when the pain stops, it stops. Sometimes the ending is only the beginning. To watch your child die of a painful and debilitating glioma (a type of brain tumor) is not the end, but only the beginning of suffering.

If we take God's omnipotence seriously, then God need not be constrained by the all-or-nothing logic of human freedom: give humans their freedom, and anything goes, for humans are sinners. I think the explanation

---

6. Lewis, *Problem of Pain*, 118.
7. Lewis, *Problem of Pain*, 26.

of process theology (chapter 37 of this work), makes the most sense: God's power is limited, and God learns and suffers with us. An advantage of this perspective is that it allows us to clearly separate power and goodness, which is the main reason the process perspective is so widely rejected.

Conclusion

Our happiness is not God's goal. His goal is to make us better people, more able to love God, more worthy of being loved. About this, Lewis seems right. The question is the contribution of pain to this process, about which I think Lewis lacks imagination, even as he experienced his share of pain, including the death of his beloved wife.

Another question is Lewis's claim that God could not give men and women their freedom without opening them to a world of pain without limit. Why could He not? At some point, pain degrades the soul, something that the Greek tragedians understood.[8] It is against this tendency that civilization is erected as support against a nature (including perhaps our own nature) that was not made for the human being, and has not become more human.

---

8. Nussbaum, *Fragility of Goodness*; Alford, *Psychoanalytic Theory of Greek Tragedy*.

18.1

Pagels and the Gnostic Gospels

SEVERAL DECADES AGO, THE Gnostic gospels seemed to be making a comeback after a couple of thousand years of loss and neglect. Elaine Pagels' *The Gnostic Gospels* was published in 1979, and for the first time in a long time, people outside the schools of theology began to talk about them—often favorably, as if the Gnostic gospels contained a purer, less institutionalized form of Christianity.

I bought into this in a vague way (most of what I thought about religion then was pretty vague), but recently I read most of *The Nag Hammadi Scriptures*, a collection of forty-six texts that are generally referred to as Gnostic, though not all are. One is a selection from Plato's *Republic*. Most seem to date from the second and third centuries CE, but the Gospel of Thomas, the most well-known Gnostic gospel, may have been written around the same time as the synoptic gospels (Matthew, Mark, and Luke). To make things complicated, the Gospel of Thomas contains both orthodox and Gnostic elements.

After some more reading, I decided that, on the whole, I am glad the Gnostic gospels did not make it into the New Testament, or a new canon.

What Is Gnostic?

Gnostic refers to *gnosis*, the Greek word for knowledge. Not all knowledge, but knowledge by intuition or insight into spiritual truths. It is hard to summarize the Gnostic scriptures. They vary enormously. The death and resurrection of Jesus Christ are not central. They go unmentioned in The Gospel of Thomas. In the Treatise on Resurrection, Jesus is said to come not to save us from our sins, but from our mortality. If there were a single Gnostic take on Jesus, it would be that He came to help us find salvation in ourselves, where gnosis lives. Or as the Testimony of Truth puts it, the

Gnostic becomes a "disciple of his [own] mind," discovering that his own mind "is the father of the truth."[1]

Gnostics are dualistic: matter, including the flesh, is bad. Spirit is good. The goal is to become pure spirit. In The Secret Book of John, a bad god, the creator-god, called Yaldabaoth, took power from his mother, part of the One. Implanting sexual desire in humans, Yaldabaoth spoiled things for Adam and Eve, who were punished by the jealous creator-god when they claimed to know after eating from the tree of knowledge. (In this story, the snake is the good guy.) The creator-god is the one we know as the Judeo-Christian God. Eventually, Jesus Christ tells John that He came to earth to bring light from the higher realm. Those who cast off earthly things will be spared from death and reunited with the luminous One.

Not all the Gnostic gospels are quite so weird. In many, the basic principle is that stated in The Gospel of Mary. The son of man exists within you. Follow it, for you already possess the means to save your soul. In The Gospel of Thomas, the divine light that Jesus embodied is shared by all humanity, since we are all made in the image of god. By encountering the living Jesus within yourself, you may come to recognize yourself as the twin of Jesus. Or as Jesus puts it in Thomas,

> Whoever drinks from my mouth will become like me; I myself shall become that person, and the hidden things will be revealed to that person. (chap. 108)

Pagels remarks,

> This, I believe, is the symbolic meaning of attributing this gospel to Thomas, whose name means "twin." By encountering the "living Jesus," as Thomas suggests, one may come to recognize oneself and Jesus as, so to speak, identical twins.[2]

Many Christians would have no difficulty with the statement that we all contain a spark of divinity within us. The difference is that most Gnostics, like Valentinus, take this insight even further than Thomas, so that after a second (Gnostic) baptism, humans may be reunited with the One. If all this is a little vague, do not blame it on me; blame it on the Gnostics.

---

1. Pagels, *Gnostic*, 131–2.
2. Pagels, *Beyond Belief*, 100.

Why I Am Glad the Gnostics Lost

Gnostic theology rejects the Judeo-Christian belief in the goodness of all creation. Sure, many Christian denominations are hostile to sexuality, but the basic idea remains: it is good that men and women marry, have children, and populate the earth. For many Jews and Christians, this includes being a responsible caretaker of the earth.

If Jesus Christ is the only begotten son of God, then he is fundamentally different from you and me. And if Jesus Christ is different, then we cannot aspire to be gods—always a dangerous idea.

The gospels of the New Testament make caring for the poor and needy the same as caring for Christ. That we would care for the wounded as we would care for a wounded Christ is a fine idea, and a good basis on which to build a community. (Matthew 25:34-46; John 13:15-17) The attitude of the Gnostic gospels is similar to that of Socrates and the Stoics: save your own soul.[3]

Stressing the humanness of Christ, as the synoptic gospels do, expresses the fine idea of a God who would come to understand humanity's suffering by becoming human and sharing our suffering.

The Gnostic mistake that leads to all the rest is taking God out of history, especially the history of the Jewish people. The Gnostic gospels only rarely refer to the Old Testament, and seldom to history. Locating God in history situates God in a human time and place, even as God remains outside of history. This tension is often fruitful. Consider, for example, the role of the African American church in the American civil rights movement, which was both theological and organizational. "Let justice roll down like waters and righteousness like a mighty stream" (Amos 5:24) said Martin Luther King in his "I Have a Dream" speech.

The Canonical Gospels are more interesting because they tell a story, the greatest story ever told, as the cliché has it. God becomes a vulnerable human who suffers, people make decisions, and events happen. Only the Canonical Gospels have plot and character. The Gnostic Gospels are either sayings-gospels (Thomas), or are about the acts of abstract nouns, such as the One and the light. One reason the Canonical Gospels won out, I imagine, is because people always like a good story.

---

3. The early dialogues of Plato seem to reflect the views of his teacher, Socrates. By the time Plato gets to *The Republic*, Plato is concerned with managing the souls (*psyches*) of a city.

Conclusion: the Good Guys Won, But . . .

The suppression of the Gnostic Gospels was not simply due to the spiritual or intellectual superiority of orthodox Christianity. The Roman Emperor Constantine's conversion to orthodox Christianity helped enormously. It was under Constantine's auspices that the Nicene Creed (325 CE) was written. Even so, it was certainly easier to organize a church around a canon that already existed than a variety of scriptures, which is what the Gnostics possessed.

The side that won, the Judeo-Christian tradition, as we now call it, had superior teachings for human beings living mortal lives in this world, which is what I really care about. Nevertheless, certain Gnostic teachings make much sense, then as well as now.

Heracleon, a follower of Valentinus, wrote that most Christians tend to take literally the images they find in Scripture, such as the God who gave Moses the Ten Commandments on two tablets, or the divine father who begot Jesus. It is not necessary, he continues, to reject such stories, for that is how we express what we know but are otherwise unable to say. However, the story may come to stand as a barrier to further understanding if we do not recognize its human purpose.[4] I think that many Jews and Christians today would agree.

Beyond this, there is something about certain Gnostic images that is widely appealing. In *Proof of Heaven: A Neurosurgeon's Journey into the Afterlife*, Eben Alexander tells of being in a coma for a week, the result of a serious illness. While dead (do not ask me why being in a coma is the same thing as being dead), Alexander says he went to heaven, where he communicated with God directly, becoming one with the orb of light that is the source of all life, and which unites humanity.[5]

It is a silly book, but it suggests that the basic human experience that gives rise to Gnosticism, the desire to be one with the luminous All, remains attractive even in our modern scientific world. Perhaps it even seems more plausible today than organized religion, for today's gnosticism is unmediated by ancient ritual and canon. But it is not an experience we should fall in love with and forget to think.

---

4. Pagels, *Beyond Belief*, 291–2.
5. Alexander, *Proof of Heaven*, 160–161.

18.2

Elaine Pagels: *Why Religion?* A Fine But Flawed Book

A RECENT (2018) BOOK by Elaine Pagels, *Why Religion?*, has garnered great reviews. It is a brave book, telling the story of the death of her six-year-old son from a long illness, and then her husband in a hiking accident, both in the space of about a year. It has been almost thirty years since these tragedies, and the reader gets the sense that it took her this long to tell the story. Or rather, to weave her story of loss together with the place of religion in her life, and our collective lives.

I admire the book, but I have a problem with it. She seems unaware that people who are not well-off and famous might have a different experience of loss. She aims to be realistic about the politics of religious belief, but perhaps there is also a politics of loss, or better, a political economy of loss. About this she says not a word.

Beginnings

Pagels grew up in the upscale suburbs of Palo Alto, California. Hers was an angry, sterile family, hostile to religion. At fifteen, she went with some religious friends to a Billy Graham Crusade for Christ. Why was this irreligious teenager so overwhelmed that when Graham called members of the audience forth, she went to the front of a huge stadium to dedicate herself to Christ? Thinking back on it, Pagels says the answer is all about meaning.

> First, the language spoken in that Crusade for Christ was not spoken in my home—an evocative, emotionally charged language that opened up worlds of possibility, to include legions of angels and archangels, armies of demons, Jesus's bloody

sacrifice, a divine someone who heard and understood even the secrets I ferociously protected.[1]

In all its permutations, this remains the appeal of religion: it makes the world richer, fuller, and more meaningful than the world of everyday life, the world of science, technology, commerce, and the isolated nuclear family. Obviously, this statement applies to some societies and cultures more than others, but only because other societies have already integrated religion into everyday life. This is the attraction not of any particular religion, but all religion.

First Practice, then Belief

Pagels went on to study religion at Harvard, and came to recognize that the question "What do you believe?" is actually a political question. What most Protestants believe, or are supposed to believe, is laid down in the Nicene Creed, which was enforced by the political power of the emperor Constantine and his successors in the fourth century. What you believe is the result of the political power of bishops and rulers to suppress other Christian doctrines, often summarized as Gnostic.

At Harvard, says Pagels, they had been told that controversies over heresy were arguments over conflicting ideas. Pagels figured out—and this is her great contribution—that behavior and tradition come first, beliefs second. Beliefs are not the cause of what people believe, but a way of maintaining traditional social and political practices.

> From now on, instead of writing primarily about ideas, I'd have to show how ideas are inseparably woven into actual social codes, and so into behavior. Although no one, so far as I knew, had ever read these sources that way, now I had to, and so began the research that eventually would lead to the book I wanted to write.[2]

What so many people, including her father, had dismissed as "science for dummies," stories that primitives tell to explain the creation of the world did not have a scientific purpose. Instead, creation stories create the cultural world, by transmitting traditional values.

Creation stories, such as found in Genesis, or the Book of Job, claim to tell how the world was meant to be, or how it should be, how it was in the

---

1. Pagels, *Why Religion?* 18.
2. Pagels, *Why Religion?* 46.

beginning. The practice and the tradition come first, then the myth or story in order to justify it. Myth is the theory of the practice, enforced by power.[3]

Is There a Moral Order?

Pagels tells us little about her religious beliefs, but it is clear her experiences of loss changed her. Realizing she still wanted to believe in a morally ordered universe, she understands that this remains the purpose of religion, "like those old Bible stories I'd heard, that suggest that doing good ensures well-being and doing wrong brings disaster." She wonders if she herself is "a relic of Western cultural tradition that moralizes history."[4]

The manifest unfairness of life and death should make us immune to such stories. For many, these experiences only strengthen belief, often along the lines of, "It's part of God's plan that humans simply can't understand." This is what Job concluded after all his sufferings (Job 42:1–5), but it is not what Pagels concludes.

And by the way, it is not just the Western tradition that moralizes history. The Buddhist concept of karma—what goes around, comes around in this life or the next—is also a moral balancing act.

But it is not Pagels's view, and not Pagels's path. Her husband Heinz was a physicist studying chaos theory. There is a fundamental randomness to the universe, he told her, and it is in this direction that she turned. In a word, there is no moral order to the universe. Pagels is a fine scholar of religion, but neither her studies of how people come to believe nor her life seem to have made her more religious, but less.

The Political Economy of Loss

Pagels writes that once, when her husband saw her in anguish over her son's deadly diagnosis, he said, "Everyone's life has something like this in it." Angrily, she snapped back, "No, not this, a child with a terminal illness." "No," replied Heinz, "not this, but something like it."[5]

I do not know if Heinz was right or not, but I think there is something less dramatic but no less bad: the slow-moving horror of a dreadful way of life, such as never knowing where the next meal is coming from, or if you are going to be thrown out of your crummy motel apartment because you

---

3. Pagels, *Why Religion?* 52, 54.
4. Pagels, *Why Religion?* 167.
5. Pagels, *Why Religion?* 208.

cannot make the weekly rent. For some, this becomes a way of life. Perhaps they get used to it, but it is no less horrible for that reason.

It is really impossible to compare sufferings like this, and I will not. I will only say that Pagels had more resources than most, such as a five-year MacArthur "genius award" that came at the time of Mark's original diagnosis, giving her extra time to be with Mark during the five years it took for him to die.

At the time Heinz died, she was teaching at Princeton, and was readily given a paid leave from teaching to help her recover.

There is no reason Pagels should not have had these advantages. I think everyone should, but most do not, and she shows no awareness of how religion might play a different role in the lives of those without these and other advantages. I am sorry she had to sell her second home in Aspen after her husband died, but I am sorrier for those who lose their only home, or never have one to begin with.

Pagels had the time, wealth, and support to contemplate the randomness of the universe in the years after her losses. Perhaps religion plays a different role in the lives of those who lack these advantages. Perhaps meaning itself takes on a different meaning when there is no leisure to think thoughts like these. Perhaps traditional religion is a comfort, and for this reason, no less real.

For all her brilliant work on the politics of religious belief at the beginning of the Christian era, she has not a moment for the political economy of belief in today's world.

19

Huston Smith: Does Religion Matter Anymore?

WHY DOES RELIGION MATTER? Should we even take it seriously? The modern scientific worldview does not, so why should we?

Huston Smith's *Why Religion Matters* is not a defense of Christianity. It is a defense of the very idea of religion, which he defines as a belief in transcendence: that there is something beyond this material world, and it matters whether you let this other world into your life.

It is a good book, but Smith gets off to a bad start when he argues for what he calls the traditional worldview (this world is *not* all there is) by saying that "the finitude of mundane existence cannot satisfy the human heart completely."[1] All this shows is that we are needy creatures who want more than there is. The human desire for transcendence does not prove that something beyond the material world exists, but only that we wish it so.

Myth and Truth

Smith gets serious when he argues that belief in the traditional, nonscientific worldview, in which we experience this world, as well as another that transcends it, leads to a better life. In other words, we fulfill our human nature most fully when we recognize that, while the traditional religious stories are myths, the truth beyond words that these myths express allows us to feel at home in the world. We can feel that we belong here. The alternative view, that each of us is but a tiny bit of matter in an endless universe, is not only hard to bear, it makes life less interesting, exciting, and fulfilling. We are creatures of narrative, and telling stories (myths) is how we make ourselves at home. The God story is a much better story than the story that this is all there is.

---

1. Smith, *Why Religion Matters*, 3.

Some days I am tempted by agnosticism. If God exists, how could we ever know for sure? Similarly, if God does not exist, how could we ever know that? This is the point of the two-world doctrine. Similarly, if there is another better world that transcends ours, God's world, then science is not going to find it. That would be like the old joke about looking for your lost keys under the streetlight because that is the only place you can see.

Who knows what the darkness of transcendence conceals? Many men and women think they know; perhaps some are right, but since we have not even a candle to light the way, how do we know? Faith is the usual answer, but is there really much difference between hope and faith? And if you say there is a big difference, then why do a large group of Christians commit the dead "in sure and certain hope of the resurrection to eternal life"?[2] What is the difference between a sure and certain hope and just a hope?

Making the Transcendent Real

We make the transcendent real by acting as though it is, and living accordingly. In this way, it becomes truly real, for humans make real almost everything they subsequently discover. We could not find it any other way.

Let me explain. Humans could not have discovered that the earth is round, and rotates on its axis, unless they were prepared to find it. I do not mean they expected to find it, but only that people were open to the possibility. Eventually it becomes common knowledge, and any other view becomes antiquated or silly, like that of The Flat Earth Society, which actually exists. But you have to believe something is possible before you can see it. It is the same thing with a transcendent God. When you believe it is possible, you will be more likely to have experiences that support it. And that is really all there is to it. Science does not disprove it, and the Bible does not prove it. We have a choice.

Does Choice Spoil Everything?

Once, say, five hundred years ago (and in many places even today), most people didn't have a choice. It was settled that there exists this world and the next—the mundane everyday world, and the transcendent world, which some saw more clearly than others. Of course, not everyone believed in the two-world doctrine, but for the most part, disbelievers kept quiet.

Now we know we have a choice, even if some people, especially in traditional societies, do not recognize the choice. In a way, choice spoils

---

2. Burial Rite II, *Book of Common Prayer*.

everything, for it makes it seem like we create the second world, the transcendent world. The best answer, the only answer, is that we create every world that humans have ever inhabited. Humans created the scientific worldview; it wasn't given to us at creation, but came along around five hundred years ago, part of the Enlightenment. For many purposes, it is a better worldview, allowing us to do things like cure people from previously deadly diseases. And if we look to the cosmos, there is something awesome in the scientific hypothesis that the universe is about 14 billion years old, and will last perhaps another 5 billion years, from big bang to the big chill, as the universe stops expanding. I do not know that this is correct; probably no one knows for sure, but I am confident that scientists will continue to try to figure it out.

What I do know is that all this has nothing to do with whether God exists, whether he/she is called Yahweh, God, Christ, Lord, or a dozen other names. God exists in another universe, the transcendent universe, and for many religions God cares for each one of us. Each one of us is loved by God, which is why we should love each other. I believe this because I want to believe it, and because science has nothing to say about it.

I want to live in a God's world because it is a more caring place for humans to live and die. We should care for each other because God cares for us all. That is not the best argument; it is really the only argument. Any other argument, such as, "It is a humane value to care for others" runs up against the Why? question, such as "Why is it a humane value?", "Why are humane values good?", and so forth, a pattern that can go on indefinitely, as anyone with small children knows.

Conclusion

I choose to live in God's world. It is an act of faith but not ignorance. I know other worlds exist. The scientific worldview (not science itself, but those who use it to justify a strictly materialistic worldview) is its major competitor today. As for me, it is not as meaningful. I do not have to choose between science and God, only between science as universal worldview and God.

20

Emmanuel Levinas Says We Cannot Talk to God, Only Each Other

EMMANUEL LEVINAS SAYS WE cannot talk to God, only each other. When we care for others in words and deeds, we come as close as we can to God.

Emmanuel Levinas is popular among philosophers because "he introduces God into the scene without making so much ontological noise," as Ryan Urbano puts it.[1] In other words, Levinas lets us talk about God without talking about God. It is true, but it is not because he is shy about using the "G" word.

For Levinas, God is experienced in the ethical encounter with the other. Religion is Levinas's term for this ethical relationship. For Levinas, there is no direct relationship with the Divine. The Divine can only be approached through the other human to whom the self is infinitely responsible. We know God when we act ethically toward another person. We do not keep God alive by trying to prove his existence—a waste of time. Everything I can ever know about God is experienced in caring for others.

No Theology, and a Face with No Face

Levinas is not fond of theology. Theology is too abstract and metaphysical, as though it could grasp God by an act of thought. We can never know God, but only his presence in the face of the other, who asks all I have to give and more. Through giving we make religion live.

Levinas writes a lot about the face as bearing the trace of God. This has led many to believe that he is referring to the actual human face. He is not.

---

1. Urbano, *Approaching the Divine*, 75.

> It would be a radical misunderstanding of the transcendence of the face to construe it as a visible instantiation of the sacred. Such an interpretation confers upon the face the status of an idol.[2]

"The best way of encountering the Other is not even to notice the colour of his eyes," says Levinas.[3]

Levinas has it wrong here, not about religion, but about the face. One thing he has wrong is his focus on the face at the expense of the body. Levinas explains that the face is the most exposed, particular, and vulnerable aspect of the other person. But if one does not even notice the color of the other's eyes, how unique can the other be?

The most intimate way in which we care for others is to care for their bodies, whether it is through erotic love, or caring for someone who is ill. Sometimes all it takes to care for another is a touch.

The problem is that Levinas wants the face to do double duty: as the sign of the particular other, and as the trace of God. The situation does not get any better if we talk about bodies, not just faces. Bodies are vulnerable, particular, and expressive. We experience ourselves and others as embodied, not enfaced.

The Holocaust and God

Levinas survived the Holocaust in a prison camp for French officers. His wife and daughter were hidden in a monastery. The rest of his family was murdered. Levinas has spent much time and energy trying to understand a world seemingly abandoned by God. His answer is that:

> God renounces any manifestation of himself that would give succor, and calls on man in his maturity to recognize his full responsibility.[4]

As opposed to a religion that promises magic, marvels, and salvation, Levinas calls Judaism a religion for adults.[5]

An interesting comparison with Christianity emerges when one considers Levinas's keen response to a short story by Zvi Kolitz, "Yosl Rakover talks to God." In his letter, written shortly before his death in the Warsaw ghetto, Yosl says that while he loves God, he loves the Torah more.

---

2. Wyschogrod, *Levinas: Ethical Metaphysics*, xii.
3. Levinas, *Ethics*, 85.
4. Levinas, *A Religion for Adults*, 82–83.
5. Levinas, *Difficult Freedom*, 11–23.

> I love Him. But I love His Torah more. Even if I were disappointed in Him, I would still cherish His Torah. God commands religion, but His Torah commands a way of life . . .[6]

Kolitz's story fascinates Levinas because it puts our proper relationship with each other before our relationship to God.[7] Yosl can be angry at God, but that does not change how we should treat each other. How we care for others is almost always partly within our control. Even if we are about to be murdered by evil men, as Yosl was, we can often care for those among us who share our fate, perhaps with a word, touch, glance, or gesture.

But who am I to talk about what the victims of the Holocaust could or could not do? I have listened to hundreds of hours of survivor testimony, and many talked about the value of the smallest gesture. I doubt I could care for others in such a desperate and terrifying situation, but some did. Fortunately, most situations are not so desperate.

Properly approached, Jesus Christ plays much the same role as the Torah in Judaism. If Christ is the word made flesh (John 1:14), then we learn how to treat each other by attending to Christ's teachings, as well as his example, insofar as humans can.

> For I was hungry and you gave me something to eat, I was thirsty and you gave me something to drink, I was a stranger and you invited me in, I needed clothes and you clothed me, I was sick and you looked after me, I was in prison and you came to visit me.
>
> Then the righteous will answer him, "Lord, when did we see you hungry and feed you, or thirsty and give you something to drink? When did we see you a stranger and invite you in, or needing clothes and clothe you? When did we see you sick or in prison and go to visit you?"
>
> Jesus will reply, "Truly I tell you, whatever you did for one of the least of these brothers and sisters of mine, you did for me." (Matthew 25:35–40)

God is refractory to thought, as Urbano puts it.[8] To think about God almost always results in confining him within our concepts. Christ is easier to think about than God, the Torah easier to follow. Neither is easy to obey, but both can be thought about without trying to constrain the infinite. Jesus Christ is

---

6. Kolitz, *Yosl Rakover*, 18.
7. Levinas, *Difficult Freedom*, 142–3.
8. Urbano, *Approaching the Divine*, 65.

God constraining himself so humans might know him. Not everything we learn is comforting.

God, Nature, and the Book of Job

Levinas seems mistaken in his assertion that had the Israelites refused the Torah, this "would have been the signal for the annihilation of the entire universe."[9] This assumes that humans are the center and meaning of the universe.

Consider the Book of Job. God is proud of his creation, which he talks about in terms of the grandeur and power of nature, from the oceans to the stars to the horse and antelope. The point of the Book seems to me that humans are part of this creation, but not its reason for being. We are not quite so important as all that. God's speech from the whirlwind is essentially nature poetry. (Job 38:1–41:25)

A Jewish friend tells me that seeing God in nature is a Christian thing. Maybe. I suspect it is more complicated. In any case, nature plays almost no role in Levinas's account. It should. Understood as God's creation, not as something to be exploited, nature puts humans in our place. We have a purpose and a place in this world, but the world is not made for the human being, certainly not exclusively for the human.

As for me, I experience the feeling of God's presence in the wind on the waters when I am kayaking. I think this fits the Book of Job, where we are asked to marvel not at God, but at the wonders of his creation. People come first, as Levinas reminds us, but the grandeur of nature is not far behind.

---

9. Levinas, *Nine Talmudic Readings*, 41.

21

Martin Buber: *I and Thou*, Dialogue or Touch?

I and Thou is Martin Buber's most well-known book, originally published in German in 1923. Its aim is to make everyday life a sacred experience. I am not sure that anyone has fully understood the book; perhaps that explains its hold after so many years. In many places, it reads more like poetry than theology or philosophy.

We do not exist in any important human way except as part of a relationship. "In the beginning is the relationship," says Buber.[1] Trees and animals can be part of a I-thou pair, and a human can be a part of an I-it pair. Buber would perhaps reject the term "pair." It is just I-thou, or I-you, more than one, less than two, as the Tao puts it.

Buber's Horse

Buber's childhood encounter with his favorite horse best explains the I-thou relationship for me. Horses can be thous, and as anyone who has been around horses knows, they are massive animals. As such, the horse is intensely other: other than me, other than human.

> When I stroked the mighty mane, sometimes marvellously smooth-combed, at other times just as astonishingly wild, and felt the life beneath my hand, it was as though the element of vitality itself bordered on my skin, something that was not I, was certainly not akin to me, palpably the other, not just another, really the Other itself; and yet it let me approach, confided itself to me, placed itself elementally in the relation of *Thou* and *Thou* with me.[2]

1. Buber, *I and Thou*, 69.
2. Buber, *Between Man and Man*, 11.

It is almost as if an exchange of vitality took place, Buber absorbing the horse's strength without subtracting anything from the horse. That is an I-thou relationship, and about it there is always something sad, "the melancholy of man," as Buber puts it.[3] Why? Because any response to the experience, such as Buber's awareness of his hand on the horse's mane, causes the experience to vanish. You cannot have your cake and eat it too. You can have the experience, but you cannot think about it and have it at the same time. Thinking is the enemy of experience. But there is no alternative. Just as one enters an I-thou experience, so must one leave it. Only God remains.

Touching is Like Talking . . . Sort Of

Most people think about Buber as the man who made dialogue central. We are not just subjects, but subjects who engage other subjects in dialogue. Before Buber, most philosophers emphasized vision over speech, and subject over object. In a sense, Buber goes back to Plato, who also made dialogue central.

I do not disagree with this dialogic interpretation of Buber, but few have noticed that several of his leading examples are about touch, not speech. Not just Buber's account of the physicality of thou when stroking his horse, but even his view of redemption is accounted for in terms of touch. Consider Buber's account of a particular Baal-Shem (a legendary Hasidic rabbi).

> The man was here and everywhere, possessed of manifold being and overspanning presence. Now his arm clasped round the body of the trees, the animals clung to his knees and the birds to his shoulders. Then lo, comfort had come into the world.[4]

Touch Is in Between, and It Is Not

As a philosopher of dialogue, Buber is a philosopher of the in between: the space between I and thou. What resides in that space is separateness and relatedness at the same time. Touch is a little more complicated. What lies between touch? Does touch lessen the boundary between you and me, or does it heighten it, for it is the last stop between beings? And the first stop too. When we are very young, our capacity for dialogue is minimal, and

---

3. Buber, *I and Thou*, 89.
4. Buber, *Legend*, 70.

most relationships are experienced in terms of being held, cuddled, lifted up, nursed, and so forth.

More die from the lack of touch than the lack of words. Not just babies, but all of us. Touch is the medium through which we reach out, console, love, and are loved in return. Touch is also a medium of aggression, including the obliteration of otherness.

Nothing I have just said is new. But philosophers have become so caught up in subject-object language that an entire aspect of Buber's work has gone missing. Touching and being touched are the creation and restoration of "betweenness," the residence of God.

"Sick Ages"

Buber writes less about individual I-thou relationships than one might imagine. His primary aim is to analyze certain tendencies in modern society, particularly the tendency to turn I-thou relationships into I-it relationships. Consider, says Buber, the language of so-called primitive people, meaning those who are poor in objects, and whose life develops in face-to-face relationships of strong presence. The result is that "man becomes an I through a Thou."[5] This was and is always true, but the thou is becoming weaker, less present, in the contemporary world, as the it becomes more.

> In sick ages [like our own] it happens that the it-world, no longer irrigated and fertilized by the living currents of the thou-world, severed and stagnant, becomes a gigantic swamp phantom and overpowers man.[6]

People want certainty, which leads men to flee from everything "unreliable, unsolid, unlasting, unpredictable, and dangerous" to a world marked by possessing things. You may treat your smartphone as a thou, but it will always remain an it, and you will become more it-like if you forget this.

God and Redemption

Buber does not write much about God until part 3 of *I and Thou*, where he refers to God as the eternal Thou. The basic idea seems to be that every I-thou relationship is mediated by God, who is everywhere, the eternal in-between. Recognizing the importance of touch does not change this much, except to remind us that God is not just pure spirit. Buber is not

---

5. Buber, *I and Thou*, 80.
6. Buber, *I and Thou*, 102.

writing about a traditional God when he says that whenever an atheist lovingly addresses the most important human thou in his life, he or she is addressing God.

Conclusion

Many who write about Buber's I-thou relationship render it almost as a spiritual encounter, a tendency made stronger by the use of thou to translate the German "du."[7] Thou has a biblical connotation, a legacy of the King James translation. Of course, the I-thou relationship is spiritual, but it is an embodied spirituality in which touch is as important as prayer.

If this is so, then we should be especially troubled by the rise of I-it relationships, for the world is doubly impoverished by the loss of both God and thou. You might respond that, for Buber, they are essentially the same. I would not argue with you.

---

7. I-Thou, or I-you? The problem starts with the book's title. *I and Thou* is how the book has been known since its 1937 translation into English, but the title is misleading. *Ich und Du* is the original German title. *Ich* is almost always translated as I, and presents no problem. Trouble is, we have no English equivalent of *du*, which is the German familiar for you. I would say *du* to my friends and family, *Sie* or you to everyone else, though the language is changing—less Sie, more du.

The problem, as Walter Kaufmann (1970) argues in the introduction to his translation, is that thou has religious connotations, and Buber is not writing about religion, at least as it is conventionally understood. Instead of thou, Kaufmann translates *du* as you. But that does not really work either, for the *Ich/du* relationship *is* an intimate one, and "hey you" is hardly an invitation to friendship. There is no good solution to the problem. I am going to continue using "thou" to render *du*, but otherwise rely on Kaufmann's translation, which uses "you." Curiously, Kaufmann's translation uses "Thou" in the title, but nowhere else, presumably because *I and You* is both off-putting and unfamiliar.

Generally, I render "thou" in lower case in order to work against the tendency to elevate the term in translation.

22.1

Simone Weil Is Not a Christian Mystic

OFTEN CALLED A CHRISTIAN mystic, nothing could be further from the truth. Wikipedia labels Weil's "school" as "modern Platonism," which is only slightly less misleading. Weil developed a post-Christian, post-Western theology in her later work. Lissa McCullough argues that Weil's universalism can be characterized as religious pragmatism, and that seems about right.

> ... religious conceptions prove their value by their effectiveness in bringing about an attitude of *amor fati*—perfect humility, obedience, longing for justice, and action that is consistent with the ineluctable truth of finitude and death.[1]

Weil was particularly interested in Buddhism. She is a harsh critic of the institutionalized church, likening it to the Great Beast, a collection of egos bent on the sanctification of their satisfaction.

Not Your Ordinary Christian

The crucifixion of Christ is where force meets submission to force, and submission is made holy. Weil shares this view with several contemporary theologians, such as Niebuhr. God wins by losing, Christ's power made perfect in weakness. (2 Corinthians 12:9) The incarnation and crucifixion are enough for Weil. Resurrection spoils it; sacrifice, not salvation, is what religion is all about.

For Weil, heaven and hell are essentially the same. Both are a cover for nothingness. We come from the void and we return to the void. Heaven is the nothingness of consent to the void. Hell is the refusal to accept nothingness as the destiny of the soul. The only difference is whether we accept or refuse this nothingness. In consenting to die, we share in the transcendent value of God.

---

1. McCullough, *Religious Philosophy of Weil*, 236.

Absence

Absence is Weil's key theological category. God is perfect goodness, like Plato's form of the Good (Republic 505a–509c). Trouble is, in a universe filled with perfect goodness, there would be no room for humans, no room for anything else. God did not create the world so much as depart from it, so that the world could be.

> On God's part creation is not an act of self-expansion but of restraint and renunciation. . . . God accepted this diminution. He emptied a part of his being from himself. . . . God permitted the existence of things distinct from himself and worth infinitely less than himself. By this creative act he denied himself, as Christ has told us to deny ourselves.[2]

Force and Affliction

The result of God's withdrawal is that we live in a world of force and affliction. But this can be good if we let it. War, oppression, severe illness, extreme poverty, and much more besides creates affliction. With the term "affliction" (*malheur*), Weil means a state in which we question all we had previously believed: that life is good, that life is worth living, that the pursuit of happiness is possible. McCullough puts it well:

> Human thought is unable to acknowledge the reality of affliction. To acknowledge the reality of affliction means saying to oneself: "I may lose at any moment, through the play of circumstance over which I have no control, anything whatsoever that I possess, including those things that are so intimately mine that I consider them as being myself. There is nothing that I might not lose. It could happen at any moment that what I am might be abolished . . .[3]

Weil puts it simply. "Human life is impossible. But affliction alone causes this to be felt."[4] The world is necessity, not purpose, and the function of society—including most religion, and virtually every church—is to conceal this fact from us.

---

2. Weil, *Waiting for God*, 89.
3. McCullough, *Religious Philosophy of Weil*, 25.
4. Weil, *Notebooks*, 311.

The Nail of Necessity

For Weil, affliction is good, for it nails us to the wall of necessity.

> Extreme affliction, which means physical pain, distress of soul, and social degradation, all together, is the nail. The point of the nail is applied to the very center of the soul, and its head is the whole of necessity throughout all space and time. Affliction is a marvel of divine technique. It is a simple and ingenious device to introduce into the soul of a finite creature this immensity of force, blind, brutal, and cold.[5]

Affliction has done you a favor because it compels you to consent to a universe you do not control, forcing you to bend your knee to it. Like Job, you are no longer the center of even your own life. You belong to the void. The only question is whether you accept this fact.

Attention and Decreation

"Attention, taken to its highest degree, is the same thing as prayer."[6] Through attention, we learn that others exist. Our ego no longer gets in the way, and we learn what is otherwise almost impossible to grasp: that other people and things exist.

Attention is the way we decreate ourselves. Decreation means that the ego is no longer present. Another way of saying the same thing is that we consent to the void.

> We possess nothing in the world—a mere chance can strip us of everything—except the power to say "I." That is what we have to give to God, in other words, to destroy. There is absolutely no other free act which is given us to accomplish, only the destruction of the "I."[7]

God withdrew from the world so that we might be. Decreation is the human complement; I withdraw my I, my ego, so that God's goodness can take its place.

Weil gives good quote, but we should think seriously about whether we want to sign on. Most of us cannot in any case, and that is probably a good thing.

---

5. Weil, *Love of God and Affliction*, 452.
6. Weil, *Notebooks*, 205.
7. Weil, *Gravity and Grace*, 26.

> The ego is only the shadow projected by sin and error which blocks God's light and which I mistake for being.[8]

"May I disappear in order that those things that I see may become more perfect in their beauty from the very fact that they are no longer things that I see."[9]

Conclusion: Politics or Purity?

Some say Weil turned to religion later in life because of her disappointment with radical politics. I think her religious views were implicit all along, but her religious views are incompatible with radical politics; indeed, with any politics at all.

No one works for a just cause (or any cause) without the involvement of the ego. The ego is what brings energy to the cause. Otherwise expressed, helping people requires other people who pay not just sensitive attention to the other, but bring their own agenda of what help means, such as food, water, security, opportunity. While perhaps unfortunate, action and the suppression of the ego are an impossible combination. Even if the ego is identified with a just cause, it is still ego, still a commitment of the self. Not all ego is bad; it depends on the values it identifies with. Levinas uses a similar argument. The self cannot abandon itself to the other; the self must stay in existence to help the other.[10]

Weil's religious view is so anti-ego that it deprives just causes of the energy and people they need to succeed. In Weil's late work, the goal of decreation is to disappear. Weil did so at the age of 34, starving herself to death in sympathy with the occupied French, or whomever. That did not do anyone any good.

Weil became increasingly interested in personal purity, understood as liberation from the burden of the ego. But this is an individual goal, not a social one. One might even say it was self-ish.

---

8. Weil, *Notebooks*, 409.
9. Weil, *Gravity and Grace*, 42.
10. Levinas, *Totality and Infinity*, 21.

22.2

Simone Weil and the Need for Roots

BECAUSE SHE CONCENTRATES ON the relationship between the individual and the universal, man and God, Weil generally regards the collectivity, society, as an idol. Whether we know it or not, most of us worship this idol, which means thinking and acting the way people in our position in society are supposed to think and act. The world begins and ends with the society in which we live.

The Need for Roots

It comes as a surprise, then, to see how important the community is to Weil. *The Need for Roots* was written during the early months of 1943; she would be dead by the end of that summer. Weil argues that "to be rooted is perhaps the most important and least recognized need of the human soul." The damage that springs from rootlessness is the curse of contemporary life. Perhaps the worst thing about "unrootness": the unrooted go on to uproot others.

Though she spent a lifetime arguing against "the collective," the Great Beast that is society, she recognizes that the collectivity is "the sole agency for preserving these spiritual treasures accumulated by the dead . . ."[1]

Between Earth and Eternity

Weil faces a dilemma. We cannot survive without the horizontal, the familiar, the institutions of everyday life. We need protection from criminals, as well as foreign enemies. In *The Need for Roots*, Weil recognizes that the nation is really the only collective that remains that can fulfill this function. Written when the outcome of World War II was still in doubt, she writes that our obligation to our country co-exists with other obligations.

---

1. Weil, *Roots*, 8, 41, 45.

> It does not require that we should give everything always; but that we should give everything sometimes.[2]

In other words, we should be prepared to die for our country, our heritage, our traditions. Getting carried away, she imagines all sorts of demeaning rituals for cowards. Whatever else one may say, Weil was always ready to die for something.

> But why, then, is patriotism itself necessary? In the opening sections of *The Need for Roots* Weil . . . makes the point that "we owe respect to a collectivity, of whatever kind—country, family, or any other—not for itself, but because it is food for a certain number of human souls", and that "the food which a collectivity supplies . . . has no equivalent in the entire universe."[3]

The community is not a supreme value, but it is an ultimate value, in the sense that no other entity can replace it. Nevertheless, "it is certainly forbidden to love one's country, using the world 'love' in a certain sense. For the proper object of love is goodness, and 'God alone is good.'"[4]

Always the Beast

However much society is necessary, for Weil it always remains the Great Beast, an image from Plato's Republic (493a-e).

> The real sin of idolatry is always committed on behalf of something similar to the State.[5]

There is and should be a chasm between the social order and God. It is helpful to compare Weil with Václav Havel. Weil says,

> It is only by entering the transcendental, the supernatural, the authentically spiritual order that man rises above the social. Until then, whatever he may do, the social is transcendent in relation to him.[6]

Havel says,

> The relativization of all moral norms, the crisis of authority, the reduction of life to the pursuit of immediate material gain

---

2. Weil, *Roots*, 155.
3. Weil, *Roots*, 76.
4. Weil, *Roots*, 129.
5. Weil, *Roots*, 112.
6. Weil, *Simone Weil Reader*, 166.

without regard for its general consequences . . . do not originate in democracy but in that which modern man has lost: his transcendental anchor, and along with it the only genuine source of his responsibility and self-respect. . . . Given its fatal incorrigibility, humanity probably will have to go through many more Rwandas and Chernobyls before it understands how unbelievably shortsighted a human being can be who has forgotten that he is not God.[7]

For Weil, we must enter into the transcendent. For Havel, remembering the transcendent is the way we protect ourselves from the idolatry of humanism—the worship of humanity and its creations. In many ways, his is the more acute observation. The danger is not the State; the danger is ourselves. We need not, and perhaps cannot, enter the transcendent, but we can respect it as a barrier to human ambition and folly.

Weil is both right and wrong. Idolatry is the great human flaw, but we need not enter into a transcendent (whatever that means exactly) relationship with God to overcome it. We need only remember—and it is no small thing—that we are not gods. Perhaps that is the single most important reason to believe in God.

---

7. Havel, *Forgetting*, 49–50.

22.3

Paying Attention with Simone Weil

WELL KNOWN, AT LEAST among those who study Weil (perhaps a few thousand), is her concept of attention. Less well known is the way in which Iris Murdoch, Oxford don and novelist, adapted the term. The idea is a good one, but Weil gets it mixed up with self-denial, her desire to be nothing more than "a certain intersection of nature and God."[1]

For Weil, "attention" means to suspend thinking, leaving one's mind detached, empty, ready to be entered by the other. Attention means not always trying to know, not categorizing, but waiting, as though the other could participate in forming the idea we have of it. "Attention is the highest and purest form of generosity."[2] Attention is the opposite of a thought that has seized upon some idea too hastily, and thinks it knows. For Weil, attention requires self-emptying. In attention,

> the soul empties itself of all its contents in order to receive into itself the being it is looking at, just as he is, in all its truth.[3]

Weil is mistaken. I have no other way of knowing another's suffering (or joy) except by trying to find comparable experiences in myself. It is the only way we can know: to be open but not empty. I know others not by knowing myself, but by feeling myself resonating with the experiences of others. The more in touch with my feelings, the better I can experience the feelings of others.

Iris Murdoch

The term "attention" was adapted and adopted by Iris Murdoch, who was deeply influenced by Weil, more so than by any other woman.

1. Weil, *Love of God and Affliction*, 462–3.
2. Weil, *Reflections*, 48–49.
3. Weil, *Reflections*, 51.

> The enemies of art and of morals, that is the enemies of love, are the same: social convention and neurosis.[4]

With the term "neurosis," Murdoch refers to fantasies that "inflate the importance of the self and obscure the reality of others." Convention refers to the tendency of the individual to become "sunk in a social whole which we allow uncritically to determine our reactions, or because we see each other exclusively as so determined."[5]

Both obscure our vision of the particular other, what Murdoch calls "attention," a term she draws from Weil "to express the idea of a just and loving gaze directed upon an individual reality."[6]

> Love is the perception of individuals. Love is the extremely difficult realisation that something other than oneself is real.[7]

The goal is to see the other person justly, honestly, and compassionately. Doing so means moving away from universality and principles, and toward increasing depth, privacy, and particularity. "The central concept of morality," says Murdoch, "is 'the individual' thought of as knowable by love."[8] That is attention.

Is Murdoch just borrowing a term from Weil, or is she borrowing a way of thinking? For Weil, attention is preparation for an encounter with God. For Murdoch, attention is the way we open ourselves to the experiences of other humans. But perhaps these are not so different after all. In the legend of the Holy Grail, the vessel belongs to the seeker who first asks its guardian, a king paralyzed by a painful wound, "What are you going through?"[9] That's paying attention. Attention turns us from ourselves, opening us to the experiences of other people. Attention is love.

But what kind of love? Surely not *eros*, which loves the other for the pleasure he or she brings. The Latin *caritas* seems the best way to think about attention as love. Defined as affection, love, or esteem, the term connotes the value of the object loved rather than the intensity of desire.

An attitude of *caritas* toward the particulars of this world—what Weil and Murdoch call "attention"—is one that renders this world sacred, holy, not necessarily that it belongs to God, but in the sense that humans become capable of taking their everyday experiences with the things and people of

---

4. Murdoch, *The Sublime and the Good*, 216.
5. Murdoch, *Sublime*, 216.
6. Murdoch, *Sovereignty*, 30.
7. Murdoch, *Sublime*, 215.
8. Murdoch, *Sovereignty*, 30.
9. Weil, *Reflections*, 51.

this world and lifting them out of the mundane by an act of attention, or lucid concentration. In doing so, everyday experiences become, for a moment, numinous, set apart and special, worthy of our wonder and our awe. Paying attention renders the world we live in sacred, holy, ablaze with meaning.

And What about Weil?

And what about Weil? In many respects, she is admirable. There should not be the least discrepancy between one's philosophy and way of life, she once said, and she tried her hardest, working in factories, fighting in the Spanish Civil War, eating no more than the ration she believed people in occupied France received, refusing to heat her apartment because the workers she taught could not afford to heat theirs. Though she never formally converted to Catholicism, she was in many respects a saint. But like many saints, she seemed more interested in the suffering of others in general, rather than particular people. In other words, she paid more attention to the experience of suffering than the people who suffer, which is really not attention at all.

22.4

Weil: "The great mystery of life is not suffering, but affliction"

SIMONE WEIL (1909-1943), BORN Jewish, stood on the edge of converting to Christianity for most of her adult life. Perhaps she was baptized, perhaps not; the evidence is unclear. She is best known as a Christian mystic, though that ignores her very down-to-earth work, such as her involvement in the trade union movement, and with the international volunteers in Spain. Weil starved herself to death in sympathy with the occupied French. If you think that makes sense, you may stand closer to Weil than you think, closer than you should.

If philosophy were biography, we could dismiss Weil as emotionally disturbed. Disturbed or not, she wrote brilliant essays on a variety of topics. As she grew older, most were about God. It is her essay on "The Love of God and Affliction" that I am concerned with. It is a brilliant essay, and it is quite wrong.

The Mystery of Affliction

What does Weil mean by the mystery of affliction (*malheur*)? It is not surprising, she says, that the innocent are killed, or that people suffer from disease. Criminals and germs (nature) account for that. But it is surprising that God would have given affliction the power to seize the souls of the innocent and possess them as though they were the worst people on earth.

Affliction is the infinite distance between self and God. Affliction is an awareness that the world was not made for the human being and has not become more human. Affliction is the feeling that we are strangers in this world.

Affliction can only be experienced when we are subject to an immense force—blind, brutal, and cold—that separates us from all that is human and divine: the rape victim, the subject of a ravaging disease, the victim of extreme social injustice. All this and more constitute the type of force that first makes affliction knowable as the infinite distance between God and man, between ourselves and others.

Short Story about Affliction

Imagine you are walking down the street, talking animatedly with a dear friend, devoting all your attention to your conversation. Suddenly you step out into the street, where you are run over by a car and almost killed. It takes months to recover, and not only your body, but your mind (*psyche*, or soul) is affected. Only slowly do your memories return, but never quite in the same way. Forever after, there is something about your friend and your family that is a little strange. Not that you love them less; on the contrary, you love them more. Just thinking about them makes you cry. But they occupy a different place in your mind. For you know (not just think, or imagine, but know) that you, or they, can be snatched away in an instant, that they are not yours, and never were, nor are you theirs. First of all, everyone belongs to eternity. When you finally do recover, it is as though you have returned to a different world. You have.

You have experienced affliction, though one would have to say that you were fortunate, for throughout much of the experience you were unconscious, or not fully aware, as though a protective fog had descended over you. Had you been lucid, you would have experienced a world in which all goodness had fled, in which everything you valued—not just your health, but your family and all your attachments—can be snatched from you in a moment. Henceforth, you live in a world in which force and fate cast its shadow over all goodness. As it is, you have experienced that world in retrospect, which makes it a little easier to bear. As you return to the light, you discover that who and what you value still lives. But their position in your personal universe is forever changed.

Affliction has done you a favor, says Weil, because it compels you to consent to a universe you do not control, forcing you to bend your knee to it.

Mine is not a great story, because it omits the social degradation that generally accompanies affliction. It is set in a limited time, whereas the affliction that many suffer begins almost at birth and continues their whole life long. Mine is a middle-class story about affliction. Nevertheless, it raises the issue addressed by Weil—that necessity and tragedy teach us all that we need to know as humans: that we are at the mercy of circumstances at every moment of our lives.

Why Weil Likes Affliction, and Why She Is Wrong

Weil thinks this is good. Affliction kills the psyche, the self, all that is selfish in us. It kills almost all of the soul, and almost all of the body. All that is left of what used to be the person is "a certain intersection of nature and God." That is good, what Weil calls decreation. God's glory is not diminished by affliction. But our attitude changes. "It is our function in this world to consent to the existence of the universe."[1]

I truly do not know what this means. What other choice do we have? Nietzsche wrote that we must embrace our suffering, and wish that it happens again and again. In that way, we might become its master. Theodor Adorno called this "ignominious adaptation" to one's prison.[2] Adorno was right. Many of us must accept affliction at some point in our lives. Millions, perhaps billions, accept it daily. And Weil is correct that there is something to learn from the experience, and that it has to do with the smallness of the self.

Many of the world's problems are caused by people who seek to expand their egos so that there is no room left for anybody else. Accepting the truth of affliction means accepting human limits. This was the lesson of Greek tragedy. It is a lesson that devotion to God teaches. But to wish affliction upon oneself in order to learn this lesson again and again makes no sense. There is quite enough suffering in this world. There is no reason to go looking for more, and no reason to idealize this suffering as divine.

---

1. Weil, *Affliction*, 458–63.
2. Nietzsche, *The Gay Science*, sections 285, 341; Adorno, *Minima Moralia*, 97–98.

23

Peter Berger: A Sociologist Who Turned to God But Never Understood Faith

When I was in graduate school many years ago, *The Social Construction of Reality*, by Peter Berger and Thomas Luckmann, published in 1966, was my bible, and I was not alone. Berger and Luckmann argued that what we experience as reality is socially constructed by men and women. Over time, this construction is forgotten, and the reality taken as given. It is a good argument, but it does not work very well with God. Berger acknowledged as much in a book written just a few years later, *A Rumor of Angels: Modern Society and the Rediscovery of the Supernatural*, published in 1970.

Where Berger Was Right

Berger seems right that what has failed in modernity is not a belief in God, but belief in "another reality." Some theologians seem to have gone along with this. Paul Tillich understood the task of theology in terms of the "method of correlation," by which he meant the interpretation of Christianity in the language of philosophical and psychological thought.[1]

Rudolf Bultmann exaggerates, but has the right idea when he says that no one who uses electricity and listens to the radio can any longer believe in the miracle and wonder world of the New Testament (chapter 8 of this work). Tillich's response was to translate the Christian tradition into the contemporary language of existentialism (chapter 13 of this work).

Bultmann's definition of the disease has proven fruitful. Today many of us are enthralled with the things humans have made, like smartphones. (Confession: I bought my first smartphone recently, and something about it *is* compelling.) So how should religion respond?

---

1. Berger, *Rumor* 11.

Berger's answer is that we should not capitulate to modernity, but anchor belief in God in human experience. Good diagnosis, poor remedy.

Anthropology Is Not the Answer

Berger argues we should anchor belief in human experience.

> The suggestion that theological thought revert to an anthropological starting point is motivated by the belief that such an anchorage in fundamental human experience might offer some protection against the constantly changing winds of cultural moods.[2]

If we begin by assuming that God is an expression of human experience, then God becomes a reflection of human need. God loses his otherness. By the way, Berger is not arguing that we create God from our need. He is arguing that the best way to know God is through basic human needs, what he calls "signals of transcendence."

Good Example, Poor Conclusion

Consider, says Berger, a mother's consoling gesture to a child, holding him or her, and saying that everything is going to be all right.

> This common scene raises a far from ordinary question, which immediately introduces a religious dimension: Is the mother lying to the child? The answer, in the most profound sense, can be "no" only if there is some truth in the religious interpretation of human existence.[3]

This is not right. A mother's reassurance that everything is going to be all right need not be a lie, nor must it rest in a transcendent, and beneficent, reality. Instead it can be interpreted along the following lines: "You are not old enough to be allowed to see the harshness of reality, and I will protect you from it until you are." It is not a question of truth, but love.

What Jesus Christ Adds to this Story

Christ adds love, not just for one's own child, but love for all men and women, especially the lowly, those poor in spirit as well as money. It is easy (for most

---

2. Berger, *Rumor*, 52.
3. Berger, *Rumor*, 55.

people) to love their own children. Harder is seeing a beggar on the street and doing something for him, even if it is just a smile and a few dollars. Harder still is caring for the children (and adults, for we are all children of God) in Yemen, or Syria, or some other Hell on earth. But we must try.

Berger, like so many others, believes that it is important to prove the existence of God, or transcendent reality. I think what is important is to act as Jesus Christ would act, insofar as humans are able to do so. Jesus tells us how to act toward the poor, as does the Hebrew Bible, which tells us to care for the widow, the orphan, and the stranger. (Deuteronomy 10:18)

Mine is not a faith versus works argument. On the contrary, faith in God is revealed not by "proving" his existence, but following the teachings of Christ, captured in the Sermon on the Mount and elsewhere. Faith leads to works, and it probably acts the other way around too, at least sometimes.

The Mystery of the Completely Other

> Put simply, inductive faith moves from human experience to statements about God, deductive faith from statements about God to interpretations of human experience.[4]

Berger is still beholden to sociology. Inductive faith means we model God on human experience. This is the last thing we should want to do. God is the great mystery, the mystery of the absolutely other. The task of theology is to find ways to talk about God that preserve this otherness. "Inductive faith" models God on man.

Inductive and deductive are sociological (and scientific) terms. They have nothing to do with faith. Berger believes that modern life makes God less plausible, and so he would argue for his existence in more practical, down to earth ways. But proving the existence of God is not nearly so important as following Christ's teachings. And faith is a different way of knowing, a subjective experience that is irrelevant to science, as science is irrelevant to faith.

Faith

Faith is an experience independent of reason and logic, because it concerns truths that can only be subjectively experienced. This is what Kierkegaard meant when he said "the truth is subjectivity," and "subjectivity is truth."[5] Faith is subjective knowledge that cannot be made objective without

---

4. Berger, *Rumor*, 57.
5. Kierkegaard, *Postscript*, 203–17.

destroying it. Faith can be exemplified in a person's life, but it cannot be known, only experienced. Not every religious person experiences faith, but all can live as the Bible teaches us to.

Narrative Is Better than Argument

The principle benefit of religion, says Berger, is that it permits a confrontation with the age in which one lives by providing a perspective that transcends history. That is good. Trouble is, Berger turns religion into a series of abstract claims about how we can and should know. What makes the Bible so compelling is that it is a series of stories, a narrative about humans in darkness and in light. Stories are always more compelling than philosophy, especially where faith is concerned.

Part III: On Some Books of the Bible

24

The Book of Job Is the Most Puzzling Book in the Bible

THE BOOK OF JOB is one of the most puzzling books of the Hebrew Bible. If we take Yahweh's speeches from the whirlwind seriously, then there is no humanly comprehensible reason for the suffering of innocents and the righteous. The good suffer, the bad flourish, and we must accept this without question.

One way out of this puzzle, generally called the problem of theodicy (if God is all good, all powerful, and all knowing, then why do the innocent suffer?), is to read the Book of Job from the perspective of the New Testament. This is what G. K. Chesterton does, seeing the suffering of the most innocent and righteous of men as a preface to Christ.[1]

Though God rewards Job at the Book's conclusion with seven new sons and three new daughters even more beautiful than before, as well as doubling his flocks and oxen, most scholars agree that Job 42:10–17 was an addition by later redactors to encourage the faithful. The Book really ends with Job despising himself for his arrogance in questioning God. (Job 42:6) Or at least that is one translation. Another is that Job says God is wrong to make him suffer for no reason.

1. Chesterton, *Introduction to Job*.

The Patience of Job?

To read the Book of Job from the perspective of the New Testament is to miss what is so challenging about it. Job's harsh criticism of God is not answered by God, at least not in any way the pious reader might expect. Says Job,

> The good and the guilty He destroys alike.
> If some scourge brings sudden death,
> He mocks the guiltless for their melting hearts;
> some land falls under a tyrant's sway—
> He veils its judges' faces,
> if not He, then who? (Job 9:22–24)

Job goes on like this chapter after chapter. Whoever wrote about the patience of Job was crazy. Job wants to take God to court and find him guilty. (Job 9:32–10:5)

From a human perspective, God *is* guilty. He punishes a good man for no sufficient reason that humans can understand. If one takes the opening prose frame scene seriously, in which God is making bets with the satan (who at this stage in the Bible's development is still an agent of God, God's accuser), then Job is the victim of God's pride.

What We Learn

One thing we learn by the time God is finished speaking to Job from the whirlwind is that God is not angry at Job for saying these terrible things about Him. God is angry at Job's friends, Eliphaz, Bildad, and Zophar, who think they know God's modus operandi. They think that God rewards the righteous and punishes the guilty, what is sometimes called Deuteronomic theology, a world of moral balance. Not anger at God, but the self-righteous belief that humans can know God, is the real sin. If Job does not pray for his friends, they seem not long for this world. (Job 42:7–9)

Job prays, and the friends survive, but it is worth asking what Job has learned from the Lord who speaks to him from the whirlwind, the last time the Lord makes an appearance in the Hebrew Scriptures. Job learns that the world was not made for the sake of the human being. The world is a sublime creation in which humans participate, but it was not established with humans in mind. It was made to be an expression of God's creative powers. Of His creation, God is proud; if He were human, we might call him haughty. To Job he says,

> Who dares speak darkly words with no sense?
> Cinch your waist like a fighter, and I will put questions, and you will inform me.
> Where were you when I founded the earth?
> Speak, if you have any wisdom. . . . Who barred the sea behind double gates
> as it was gushing out of the womb? . . .
> When did you ever give dawn his orders,
> assign the rising sun his post?
> Can you loose the lightning, and have it say, as it goes, "Your servant!"?
> (Job 38:2–35)

The point is that the universe was not made for man, and human standards of justice and fairness simply do not apply. God is playing in a different game. Or as God puts it elsewhere,

> For my thoughts are not your thoughts, neither are your ways my ways, declares the Lord. (Isaiah 55:8)

To be sure, there are brief references to what we might call "social justice," except that God seems more interested in humbling the proud than punishing the wicked. (Job 40:10–2) In this, He is not unlike the Greek gods. Human pride and arrogance are the sins God takes most seriously, as his anger at Job's friends reveals.

Job's Puzzling Response

Here we come to the real puzzle. Did Job learn his lesson, and what was it? Job learns that the universe is ordered and purposeful, only in a way that seems to have little to do with human justice or fairness. These do not seem to be God's categories, but humanity's. And so in a spirit of true humility, Jobs final words are simply

> Therefore I despise myself and repent in dust and ashes. (RSV, 42.6)

Only It is Not So Simple

In Hebrew, there is no object to the verb "despise." It is the English translation that adds the object "myself." Other translations are similar to the RSV. Job might equally well despise, or regret, or abhor, his situation, or the situation of the world, or even the kind of God he has learned about: one who has little care to offer humans, and even less justice. Furthermore, the word "repent" (*nacham*) is more commonly used in the Hebrew Bible to mean "to change one's mind" or "regret," rather than repent. God does that several times. (Exodus 32:14; Genesis 6:6)[2]

Raymond Scheindlin, whose translation I have frequently relied upon, says that Job has resigned himself to the lot of being merely human, and the terrible losses that go with it.[3] Job regrets the "dust and ashes" of human mortality more than ever, for it is not compensated for by the care or justice of God, at least not in a manner that humans can comprehend. In any case, Job ends up where he began, sitting on an ash heap scratching himself. It is not entirely clear, by any means, what he has learned.

The Moral of the Story

My NIV Study Bible says that the moral of the Book of Job is that,

> God does not allow us to suffer for no reason, and even though the reason may be hidden in the mystery of his divine purpose—never for us to know in this life—we must trust in him as the God who does only what is right.[4]

I suppose this interpretation makes sense when taken in the context of the Bible as a whole, but the Bible was not written as a whole. It was written by hundreds of men over hundreds of years, and redacted by many more. The translation of the Hebrew Bible that we use today is heavily influenced by the Masoretic Text, referring to a group of Jews living between the seventh and tenth centuries CE, who decided, among other things, where the vowels in words should go, and so what they mean.

The advantage of this perspective is that it leaves us free to interpret the Book of Job. Not in every respect, but certainly its message or moral. I think the moral of the story is that God has created a universe of sublime beauty and given humans a place in it. The universe is not random or chaotic.

On the other hand, God is not particularly concerned with justice as humans understand it. Justice, fairness, and the like are strictly human concerns. We should be inspired by the knowledge that we are creatures of God to treat each other with care and respect, but it is up to humans to work out the details, and it is up to humans to promote the natural law (part V), as

---

2. Strong, *Concordance*, 5162.
3. Scheindlin, *Book of Job*.
4. Barker, 723.

God is not going to do it for us—not now, and not necessarily ever. Whether this is something to regret, or a source of inspiration, is up to you.[5]

---

5. A lecture by Amy-Jill Levine influenced my interpretation of Job. A longer discussion of the Book of Job is found in my *After the Holocaust*.

25

Ecclesiastes Is a Dark Book

ECCLESIASTES IS A DARK book whose message can easily be taken to be that everything is meaningless, so what is the point of anything, including living? We read in the Babylonian Talmud (Shabbath 30b) that the rabbis tried to keep the Book of Ecclesiastes out of the Hebrew Bible, what Christians call the Old Testament. I can see why.

The popular parts are taken out of context. Growing up in the 1960s, I remember when "Turn! Turn! Turn! (To Everything There Is a Season)" by the Byrds was a big hit. Written by Pete Seeger, the song is a musical recitation of Ecclesiastes 3:1–8. Sung at too many weddings by young men and women with daisies in their hair, it might just as well have been sung at funerals, but as far as I know, it was not. But I did not go to many funerals in those days.

Grand Mimetic Incoherence

Ecclesiastes has been called a work of "grand mimetic incoherence." The incoherence of the style mimics (mimetic) a fundamentally incoherent reality.[1] One moment the author, conventionally called the Teacher (Kohelet), tells us that

> Meaningless! Meaningless, says the Teacher
> Utterly meaningless! Everything is meaningless. (1.2)

Nice way to begin a book, saying that everything is wearisome; whatever has been done will be done again, there is nothing new under the sun, and all a man's wisdom and acts come to nothing in the end, for soon he will be dead and forgotten, his achievements eclipsed by another who will soon go the same way.

---

1. Berger, "Qohelet" 163.

A few verses later, we find the author, who purports to teach the wisdom of Solomon, arguing that God will bring the righteous and the wicked to proper judgment (3.17). And back and forth it goes for twelve chapters: all is meaningless, but God has everything in hand, we just do not know his plan.

Hevel

Some people, including me, think that a lot depends on how the Hebrew term *hevel* is translated. Its original meaning is "air," "vapor," or "breath." If so, then the best translation would be transience.[2] All is transience. It is with this that Ecclesiastes begins and ends (1:2, 12:8). The word appears thirty-eight times in the chapter.

It makes a difference. If life is vain or meaningless, then it is hard to make sense of how to live. But if life is transient, then Ecclesiastes is not just a reflection of grand mimetic incoherence. Ecclesiastes is about how to appreciate what God has given us in creating a world in which there is a possibility for meaningful work, wine, friends, and love. (3:11–13, 9:7–10) Wisdom is, all in all, a good thing (7:11–12), but it too will not save us from extinction.

In some ways, Ecclesiastes is like the Book of Job, only this time it is written not by a man afflicted, but by a man of abundant wealth, everything his heart could desire: Solomon in his old age, or so the story goes. But he faces the same problem as Job: the meaning of it all. Only, unlike Job, he must find the answer for himself. God is no longer there to tell him.

Solomon does not rely on his nation, its traditions, and rituals. On the contrary, Solomon is remarkably unsituated in time and space, the history of his people irrelevant. He looks on life under the sun for himself, and what he sees is this incredible opportunity that he and others like him have been given to be fulfilled in work, friends, wine, and love, coupled with the realization that, in some sense, it does not add up to anything; it just is. He has lived well, which is better than living poorly, but in the end, we are all just dead.

Sometimes this leads to despair. It would have been better never to have been born, says the Teacher (4.3). At other times, the Teacher is grateful to have been given the life that he has lived, a life that is a gift from God, he has no doubt. Life's worth is what the Teacher questions, almost always within the framework of Eugene Ionesco's question, "Why was I born if it was not forever?" Because forever would be as meaningless as

---

2. Strong, *Concordance*, 1892; Dor-Shav, "Ecclesiastes, Fleeting and Timeless"

transience. The Teacher is already troubled about the presence of "nothing new under the sun." (1.9) Would he not despair even more deeply facing an infinity of years?

Once one gives up the ideal of a reward in the hereafter, but still believes in the presence of a God who has created an ordered (but far from ideal) universe, the Teacher's question is inevitable to any thinking person: what does it all mean, what is the purpose of life? The answer is to enjoy life as much as possible, for life is all there is.

I would add "care for the welfare of others, for it will give your life a sense of meaning by involving you in a world larger than yourself."

Solomon is remarkably self-absorbed. This does not make him admirable. It does make the question he poses starker, for he cannot enmesh himself in the fabric and fate of humanity.

Olam

It is scary that so much can depend upon the translation of a word. And while I can manage a bit of Greek, I know no Hebrew. *Olam* is the Hebrew word for eternity in 3.11. "He has set eternity in the human heart." (Ecclesiastes 10-11)

Trouble is, my NIV Study Bible has a footnote to this passage saying that it can also be read as "God has placed ignorance in the human heart."[3] Well, it makes a difference, does it not? If God has placed eternity in the human heart, then we long for transcendence, a glimmer of hope that we might understand the beginning from the end. If God has placed ignorance in the human heart, then there is no hope. The argument about finding pleasure in the midst of transience still stands, but we shall never long for more. The result is that man is the anxious animal.

In circumstances like these, context is everything, but that is the problem: the context is itself contradictory. So, I turn to Strong's *Concordance* (5769), and find that the term *olam* and its variants are used hundreds of times in the Hebrew Bible to refer to "everlasting," "forever," "eternity," and similar terms. *Olam* is used to refer to ignorance and its cognates hardly at all.

I prefer to interpret 3.11 as meaning that there exists a forever unfulfillable longing for transcendence in the human heart, a longing that gives our lives depth and dimensionality, a sense of somehow participating in eternity. Even so, transience remains the order of the day, and night falls swiftly.

3. Barker, *NIV Study Bible*, 988.

26

Book of Mark: Apocalypse Now

Today almost all scholars agree that Mark was the first Gospel, written around 60-70 AD. Mark was not a witness to the events he recounts. No one knows who Mark was, and his Greek is not elegant. But there is a simplicity and power to the Gospel missing in the longer and more elaborated gospels of Matthew and Luke, both of whom draw on Mark. The Gospel of John is unique, and I will discuss it in another chapter.

I do not think anyone can understand Mark without understanding the world he lived in, a world full of demons. Both mental and physical illness were attributed to demonic power. Jesus demonstrated his power by casting out demons. Demons were the first to recognize Jesus as the son of God. (Mark1:21–28; 5:1–20; 9:14–29)

How are we to make sense of Mark today? For most of us do not live in a world infested by demons. Brendan Byrne argues that the demons represent powers humans are unable to master.[1] If so, then we too are captive to demons: the demons of social, economic, and technological change beyond our control. We do not call them demons (at least not usually), but what else are these changes but forces unleashed by human ambition that sometimes seem to take on a life of their own? The comic version is Walt Disney's "Sorcerer's Apprentice," a tale for our times.

From the demonic to the social forces of science, technology, and economics seems a bit of a stretch, and I am not as convinced as Byrne that it is a good analogy. Nevertheless, it is important to grasp that while Jesus's message is universal, its historical context was particular. It was an apocalyptic era, in which the overthrow of world order seemed not far away. Most contemporary science fiction is apocalyptic in this sense. So are some Christians.

---

1. Byrne, *Costly Freedom*, xii.

What I Like about Mark: the Suffering Humanity of Jesus

I like the simplicity of Mark's story, particularly the way in which Christ's human side is portrayed. As Edwards puts it,

> Mark is most ready of the four Evangelists to portray the humanness of Jesus, including his sorrow (Mark 14:34), disappointment (Mark 8:12), displeasure (Mark 10:14), anger (Mark 11:15–17), amazement (Mark 6:6), fatigue (Mark 4:38), and even ignorance. (Mark 13:32)[2]

Particularly powerful is the portrayal of Christ's suffering. As he awaits his arrest and crucifixion in Gethsemane, "we see him go to pieces before our eyes ... Nowhere else in the gospels do we see Jesus so humanly presented."[3]

Many historical figures go to their deaths with equanimity. Socrates goes serenely to his execution, even as he is unsure about the afterlife (*Crito, Phaedo*). Socrates is not certain of much, but he knows that no evil can befall a truly good man (*Apology* 41d).

Christ is different, because Christ despairs. His disciples have fled in fear; the last supper was attended by traitors and cowards. At the moment of his death on the cross, Jesus fears that he is abandoned by God. "My God, my God, why have you forsaken me?" (Mark 15:34) It may be of interest to Sunday school teachers that this is a quote from the twenty-second Psalm (v 1), but Jesus was not just quoting scripture.

As fully human, Jesus experienced every feeling and fear that humans experience. Not everyone fears death, but all humans fear torture. At least as much, all humans fear a humiliating death marked by the abandonment of friends, followers (three women, including Mary Magdalene stood watch at a distance), and God. Who would not despair? The son of God, you might answer, and you would be right, except that in Mark, as nowhere else, Jesus Christ is so fully human that not even this is a comfort at the end.

The End and the Beginning

Jesus dies alone, and Mark tells us that, after the Sabbath, the three women went to his tomb in order to prepare his body properly for burial. There they met a young man dressed in white who says that Jesus has risen, and gone

---

2. Edwards, *Gospel According to Mark*, 13.
3. Byrne, *Costly Freedom*, 224.

on before them to the Galilee. Tell his disciples, says the young man, that he can be found there.

> Trembling and bewildered, the women went out and fled from the tomb. They said nothing to anyone, because they were afraid. (Mark 16:8)

And that is where the gospel ends. Almost all authorities agree that verses 9–20 were a later editorial addition in order to give Mark an ending more in tune with the other gospels.

We can debate endlessly whether Mark intended to end so abruptly. Some say it is a sign of literary artistry, leaving us to fill in the gaps. Others say ancient writers did not do this; this is a post-modern reading. I do not care, at least not directly. What I care about is that it makes Christ's return on clouds of glory even more important, for he is never encountered as the resurrected Lord.

"His Strength Made Perfect in Weakness"

Christ's disciples expected, as all observant Jews expected, that the Messiah (Christ means "Messiah") would appear as a mighty king with an army of angels ready to avenge the suffering of the pious and the pure. It was inconceivable that the Messiah would appear as the son of a carpenter who lacked even the power to prevent his own crucifixion. Not even Christ's disciples can grasp the idea that he must die in order that we should live.

The Great Idea of Christianity

The great idea of Christianity is that God would take human form so that he might know what it was like to suffer and die as humans do. God did this for two reasons: to know his creatures better, from the inside out so to speak, and so that humans might have an idea of God that is within our comprehension. As we are made in his image, so God can be encountered as human. The trinity is a good, if puzzling, idea.

Whoever God truly is, his son is flesh and blood. James Edwards puts it nicely.

> God is therein precisely God in that he can do what humanity cannot do: God can allow himself to be rejected, to be made low and small, without thereby being driven into an inferiority complex.[4]

4. Edwards, *Gospel According to Mark*, 253, quoting Eduard Schweizer.

Certainly, God does not suffer from an inferiority complex. But humans do, and so we look to a supreme being who combines power and glory with goodness. The idea that God became man in order to experience our inferiority is unbearable and inconceivable.

Where Mark Gets It Wrong

Especially because the risen Lord does not appear in Mark, his return is even more important. Not only that, but the second coming is the opposite of the first. His second coming will fit the conventional view of the Messiah, appearing on clouds of glory.

> And you will see the Son of Man seated in the place of power at God's right hand and coming on the clouds of heaven. (Mark 14:62)

In other words, you will get your traditional Messiah; you just have to wait a little longer, until the apocalypse arrives.

I think this spoils it. It spoils the message of the gospels, which is that goodness, truth, and power will always be sundered. That is what Jesus represents. We should be good and true because these are good things to be, not because we will be rewarded at some grand time in the future, and the bad guys punished. In saying this, I recognize that I am possibly an apostate.

Byrne argues that the second coming

> is what alone gives meaning to both the historical life of Jesus and the lives of those who follow him in discipleship and suffering, and who in that constitute the community of the Kingdom, the final establishment of which this scene [of clouds and glory] proclaims.[5]

In other words, Jesus may not have come as a glorious Messiah this time around, but just wait until the next, which, many of Christ's followers believed, was just around the corner. Christ himself was not quite so sure. (Mark 13:32)

History and Myth

Jesus Christ's life on earth is history. How "historical" the gospels really are is subject to debate. The Jesus Seminar finds much to doubt, but also

---

5. Byrne, *Costly Freedom*, 205–6.

much to accept in the gospels' account of Christ as history.[6] The Apocalypse and Christ's return are not history. They are myth—Biblical myth, but still myth—as they had not happened at the time the gospels were written, and have not happened yet.

Myths are fine; we live and die by myths. My argument is that Christ's return on clouds of glory is a bad myth, for it reinstates a false idea of the Messiah, simply pushing it down the road. This is particularly the case in Mark, which contains no account of the resurrected Jesus. Only the second coming completes this gospel. For many Christians, the second coming is what makes this life worthwhile.

I think *life* makes life worthwhile, especially if it is a life of charity and self-giving. About this life, Jesus showed us the way. One might argue that I have overlooked the role of faith, and perhaps I have. On the other hand, to engage the Gospel of Mark (or any gospel) in a serious way as making a solemn claim on the way we live our lives is itself an act of faith.

---

6. The search for the historical Jesus gathered about fifty Biblical scholars and about one hundred laymen to vote on the historicity of the deeds and sayings of Jesus. They produced a color-coded New Testament with different colors representing the likelihood that Jesus actually did or said what the Bible relates. There are many objections to this project, but at least it took the historical reality of Jesus seriously. Jesus is not just a literary or mythical figure, though he is that too. See Funk, *Five Gospels*.

27

Gospel of John: Christ's Return Is Now

THIS CHAPTER COVERS A number of different aspects of John's gospel. I especially like what is called John's "realized eschatology," his theory of the end time. We should not and need not wait for Advent. It appeared when Christ appeared. There is no need for a second coming. The first is the last.

Almost everyone agrees that John is unique among the gospels. While the other three gospels indirectly refer to each other or a common source, often using almost identical language, John does not. For this reason, the gospels are often divided into the three synoptic gospels (Mark, Matthew, Luke), and John. The opening of John's gospel resembles none of the other gospels. Nor does John's Jesus speak in parables. There are other differences.

John's gospel was written no later than 90 AD, and possibly a decade or two before. It is sometimes argued that the apostle John was the author, but while this is possible (Christ was crucified around 30 AD), the main argument against it is that there is an intellectual complexity to John that seems unlikely in a fisherman with no formal education, even if he had learned to read and write Greek. John's Greek is simple, but his story is not. It is also argued that the gospel was written in layers, an approach called "form criticism." It is probably true, but I am not going to go into that.

God's Relationship with Jesus

God is identical with Jesus, but Jesus stands in a relationship to God, in which case, they cannot be identical. I think this summarizes chapter 1, verses 1–14 well. And it is confusing.

> In the beginning [*en arche*] was the word [*Logos*], and the word was with [*pros*] God [*Theon*], and God [*Theon*] was the word [*Logos*]. He was with God in the beginning. (John 1:1–2)

Some people seem to believe that the word (*Logos*) was separate from God. But *pros* can be translated as "because," or "according," so that the first verse could be translated as "the word was according to God." This would be an unconventional translation, but it is worth remembering how much depends on translation from the ancient Greek.

The tough question is Jesus's relationship to God. Both his unity with God and his relationship with God (there is no relationship without difference) are asserted in the same verse.

> No one has ever seen God, but the one and only Son, who is himself God and is in closest relationship with the Father, has made him known. (John 1:18)

I like Carson's explication.

> In the beginning God expressed himself. . . . And that Self-Expression, God's own Word [*Logos*], identified with God yet distinguishable from him, has now become flesh, the culmination of the prophetic hope.[1]

As in Genesis, where everything that came into being because of God's word, so in John.

High and Low Christology

The Gospel of John is generally seen as a work of "high Christology," which means one in which the similarity, sometimes the virtual identity, of Jesus and God is emphasized. Certainly, that is present in chapter 1, as Carson's explication reveals.

Less emphasized is the "low Christology," which means the closeness of Jesus to all that is human. One sees this most clearly in Mark's gospel, yet it is in John's gospel that Jesus's soul is troubled at the prospect of the cross (John 12:27), his spirit is distressed at the prospect of betrayal (John 13:21), and Jesus is thirsty on the cross. (John 19:28) Together, the high and low Christology seem a full and fair representation of Christian thought.

Realized Eschatology

Eschatology refers to the end times, when Christ makes his reappearance. Realized eschatology, the teaching of John's gospel, argues that Christ's

---

1. Carson, *Gospel According to John*, 96.

appearance has already happened.² Believers already have eternal life (John 3:36; 4:14; 5:24; 6:47, 54); they have passed from death to life (John 5:24), have received the promised Spirit (John 7:39; 14:16–18, 26; 16:13), and have escaped condemnation/judgment. (John 3:18; 5:24)

Rudolf Bultmann, whom I wrote about in chapter 8 of this work, puts it this way:

> This conclusion [the future is now] is drawn most radically by John, who eliminates apocalyptic eschatology altogether. The judgment of the world is not a cosmic event that is still to happen but is the fact that Jesus has come into the world and issued the call to faith. (John 3:19; 9:39; 12:31)³

Add to Bultmann's list John 12:32. In a way, it is simple. The Book of Revelation (which some mistakenly attribute to John) is a dream, or nightmare. Advent is now.

> Faith sees the birth of Jesus as the advent of the eschatological Lord, who comes to judge the living and the dead.⁴

Advent is not something to anticipate, but something to live up to. The first coming is already the second coming, though history will have its end.

To be sure, there are traces of futurist eschatology. For example, Jesus refers to the "last day," when all who believe in him will rise up. (John 6:39–40) The concept is not absent, just undeveloped in comparison to the thesis that Advent is now.

The Holy Spirit

John develops the doctrine of the Holy Spirit more thoroughly than the other three gospels. John calls the Holy Spirit the "paraclete," meaning companion and counselor. The other gospels generally call the Holy Spirit "pneuma," or breath, the usual translation of spirit. John's term is more down to earth. The Holy Spirit is the living spirit of Christ, which remains to guide his followers (you and me) after Jesus left. John 14:16 quotes Jesus as saying "another paraclete" will come to help his disciples after his departure. The only conclusion to be drawn is that Christ is the first paraclete. Since then, the paraclete is the presence of Jesus in his absence. (John 14:26)

---

2. Kruse, *John*, 41–3.
3. Bultmann, *New Testament and Mythology*, 19.
4. Congdon, *Bultmann Companion*, 148.

Emphasizing the Holy Spirit enables John to claim that the end of the age is now, for Christ will always be with us, guiding those who are receptive to his silent voice. John does not develop the doctrine of the Trinity. That comes later, in post-Biblical theology. But he puts all the pieces in their place: God the father, God the son, and God the Holy Spirit, or companion. John is not the first to put them together; but he is the first to make the Holy Spirit a developed stand-in for Christ.

A New Commandment

The synoptic gospels refer to loving God with all your heart, and loving your neighbor as yourself. (Matthew 22:35–40; Mark 12:28–31; Luke 10:25–28) This is often referred to as the Great Commandment. John, as usual, is different. Says Jesus,

> A new command I give you: Love one another. As I have loved you, so you must love one another. By this everyone will know that you are my disciples, if you love one another. (John 12:34–35)

The other three gospels say to love others as you love yourself. John says to love others as Christ has loved you. Not only does this set the bar infinitely higher, but it is impossible. Nevertheless, it remains the goal. Kruse comments wisely,

> Knowing the truth about Jesus is vital, but so also is believers' love for one another. This love is not sentimental, but self-sacrificing love by which they place other believers' needs above their own. Lovelessness among believers nullifies their witness to the world, and reveals them as hypocrites.[5]

This perfects the Book of John. High Christology has its place, but in the end, we are measured by how we love each other.

John is the most simply written but intellectually ambitious of the four gospels. But in the end, intellectual ambition falls before this simple statement: Love one another with a self-sacrificing love, as I have loved you. It is not really as simple as that. Or is it?

---

5. Kruse, *John*, 289.

28.1

Paul: The First Jew for Jesus

THE APOSTLE PAUL HAS gotten a bad rap. He is supposedly anti-Semitic, anti-woman, anti-gay, and anti-sex. This reputation is undeserved. In some ways, Paul was more socially revolutionary than Jesus. Not more revolutionary than Christ in terms of thought, word, and deed, but more concerned with social revolution as the beginning of a new age. Contrary to his reputation, Paul does not want people to stay in their places, or at least it is a lot more complex than that.

The main reason for this misunderstanding is that almost half of Paul's letters are now considered forgeries of varying quality.

- Genuine letters: 1 Thessalonians, Galatians, Philippians, Philemon, 1 Corinthians, 2 Corinthians, Romans
- Fake letters: Colossians, Ephesians, Titus, 1 Timothy, 2 Timothy, 2 Thessalonians

Several legitimate letters are probably composites of additional Pauline letters. Furthermore, later scribes seemed to have felt free to make additions, especially concerning Paul's attitude toward women.[1] Finding the real Paul is a task in itself. Twenty-eight percent of the New Testament is composed of letters attributed to Paul. I am not counting Acts, as it is about just what it says: the acts of Paul and others. The content of Paul's teaching and thought are addressed, but they are not the focus.

Closer to Christ

Paul's letters stand closer to Jesus than any other words in the New Testament. They were the first to be written, the first to be saved. The gospels, beginning with Mark, were written from a quarter to a half century later.

---

1. Wright, *Paul a Biography*, 80–81, 424–5; Wills, *What Paul Meant*, 89–104.

Often Christians talk and write as if the gospels were the primary source. Paul is primary. Born only a few years after Jesus, Paul could have spoken with those who had directly encountered Jesus.

Paul does not tell many good stories, with the exception of his own conversion, and Luke-Acts has a better (if not more accurate) version. Overall, I agree with Marcus Borg and John Dominic Crossan, who argue that Paul most accurately captures the message of Jesus.[2] His letters are not a fascinating read: no parables, no stories, just teachings, anger, and love. Lots of love. His first letter to the Thessalonians starts off almost like a love letter.

Paul's Misogyny

Almost all of Paul's fear and hatred of women is in the fake letters. One notable exception is his statement that, while in church, women should shut up and listen to their husbands if they have questions. (1 Corinthians 14:34–35) The problem is that, in many manuscripts, these two verses come at the very end of 1 Corinthians, a sure sign that they were added by an overenthusiastic (and misogynistic) scribe, for they lack context.

The only other place in 1 Corinthians where Paul mentions women is where he says that women who want to speak or prophesy in church should keep their heads covered. (1 Corinthians 1:2–16) Evidently, Paul considered it usual for women to speak in church; the only question is how they were to be dressed.

Before going further, I should mention that the term "church" is misleading. There were no churches, just as there were no Christians in Paul's time. "Church" was held in the homes of leading members of the community. Many of these were women, such as Lydia of Philippi.

The household basis of the church made it especially attractive to older, wealthy women who were given positions of status in the church in return for making their homes available.[3] Paul took advantage of this from the beginning, including not just women but married couples, such as Priscilla and Aquila among his "fellow workers in Christ Jesus." (Romans 16:3) Gary Wills says that the early church was the most egalitarian group of the day. "There would be a concerted effort, over entire centuries, to hide or diminish this fact."[4]

---

2. Borg and Crossan, *The First Paul*, 19.
3. Fiorenza, *In Memory of Her*.
4. Wills, *What Paul Meant*, 90.

The First Jew for Jesus

The most important thing to understand about Paul is that he was a Jew first, last, and always. Christianity did not exist yet, and so he could hardly have converted to Christianity. Jesus was the Jewish Messiah, and Paul follows Christ (John 4:22) in holding that salvation comes from the Jews. As Paul put it,

> It is the power of God that brings salvation to everyone who believes: first to the Jew, then to the Gentile. (Romans 1:16)

Almost all Paul's anti-Semitism comes from the fake letters. In one genuine letter, Paul complains about the Jews, referring to Jewish leaders angry at his missionary work among the Gentiles who attended their synagogues, a common practice among God-fearers, as they were called. Paul was poaching gentiles for his new churches. (1 Thessalonians 2:14–16)

The Risen Body

As I mentioned previously, I find the Christian doctrine of the risen body seriously weird, as though we were to become revivified corpses. (John 5:25–29) John has the sensible idea that the risen body will be different, more akin to Christ's body.

> He will transfigure our body's lowliness into the pattern of his dazzling body. (Philippians 3:21)

All the objections one might have against risen corpses are addressed in this response. The body raised is not a human body, but a heavenly one.

Critique of Domination

It is Paul's critique of domination, as it is called in political theory, that is most impressive. As Paul puts it,

> Do not conform to the pattern of this world but be transformed by the renewing of your mind. Then you will be able to test and approve what God's will is—his good, pleasing and perfect will. (Romans 12:2)

Borg and Crossan put it best:

> "This world," to which we are not to be conformed, is not the divinely created world of nature. That world is good. . . . "This world" is the world organized in accord with the "wisdom of this

> world"—the humanly created world of imperial normalcy with its conventions of domination, injustice, division, and violence.[5]

When Paul says "renew your mind," he is not just talking about our intellect, but about how we see the present world. We should see it, then and now, as a world opposed to everything Christ stood for.

In "The Grand Inquisitor," Dostoevsky imagines that Christ returned to earth during the Spanish Inquisition. Christ, we learn, must die, for he offers a freedom that is unbearable to the mass of men, who want only to be led. Were Christ to return today, reminding us that the way we treat the sick, the poor, and the stranger is a measure of our love for Christ (Matthew 25:31–46), he would likely be subject to rendition.

Getting Paul Out of the Protestant Reformation

Many discussions of Paul seem to assume that he wrote about things with which the Reformation was concerned, primarily with the priority of faith over works. Not only does this get Martin Luther wrong (chapter 6 of this work), but it misunderstands the Roman context of Paul. Paul wrote about the transformation of ourselves and of life in this world. He wrote about a broken world, in which injustice was enforced by violence. Faith in itself is good. Far better is it to heal the world through faith. In the space of just a few verses, Paul uses the word for reconciliation (*strepho* in Greek, which means to turn back to God) five times. (2 Corinthians 5:16–21)

> All this is from God, who reconciled us to Himself through Messiah and gave us the ministry of reconciliation, that God was reconciling the world to Himself in Messiah, not counting people's sins against them. And He has committed to us the message of reconciliation. (2 Corinthians 5:18–19)

It is with the work of reconciliation that Paul is most concerned.

Religion Is Communal for Paul

Religion was always a communal matter for Paul. His passion was to create communities that embodied an alternative to the "wisdom of this world," the wisdom of domination. Paul's interest in the communal church was not primarily political. With the resurrection of Christ, God's plan for the new world had already begun, and the communal churches were part of a "new

---

5. Borg and Crossan, *The First Paul*, 139.

creation" of the world as it was meant to be.[6] The new church was proleptic; it anticipated the eschaton, Christ's return to earth.

An aspect of this new world is that the new churches were "share communities." Not communism, but the simple assumption that help could be expected from others in troubled times.

> For Paul, love had (for want of a better word) a social meaning as well. The social form of love for Paul was distributive justice and nonviolence, bread and peace.[7]

Love was a critique of empire, as well as church communities like Corinth, reluctant to share their wealth with the poor churches in Jerusalem.

Love Many Others

Paul's poetic praise of love in 1 Corinthians 13:1–13 is well known. It begins

> Were I to speak the languages of all men and all angels, without having love, I were as a resonating gong or jangling cymbal. Were I to prophesy and know all secrets and every truth, were I to have faith strong enough to move mountains, without having love, I were as nothing. Were I to give away all my possessions, or give my body to be burned, without having love, it would avail me nothing. . . .

While only individuals can love, communities can be organized around such people. This was Paul's ideal. His is not just, or even primarily, praise of the love of one person for another, but about churches based on demonstrative love, expressed in sharing and caring.

---

6. Borg and Crossan, *The First Paul*, 186–8.
7. Borg and Crossan, *The First Paul*, p. 204

28.2

Martin Luther King's Letter from the Apostle Paul: Two Revolutionaries

APRIL 4, 2018, WAS the fiftieth anniversary of the assassination of Martin Luther King. This chapter is written in memory of an American martyr.[1] The apostle Paul was also a peaceful social revolutionary, who likely died a martyr's death at the hands of the Romans. For many people, Paul was an uptight social conformist who encouraged slaves to remain with their masters. Martin Luther King knew better. One thing he probably knew is that Ephesians is one of the many forged letters. Martin Luther King's letter from Paul is the focus of this chapter, but first, a few comments on Paul, and why he fits so well with MLK.

Paul

Today, many people think about salvation as a private act. "Christ is my personal savior" is how it is sometimes put. But that is an individualistic way of thinking, Christ rendering a service like any other, dry cleaner for the soul. For Paul, salvation is achieved in and through groups. On the last night of his life, King said he had seen the promised land even if he was not to enter it. The promised land was freedom, but not *just* freedom, it was freedom under God. For King too, salvation was a collective as well as an individual act.

Paul recognized that Christ had broken through all the old distinctions, such as between pure and impure, circumcised and uncircumcised, rich and poor, and even male and female. (Galatians 3:28) This is always threatening to the established order. Paul's goal was the establishment

---

1. I heard one of MLK's last sermons and spoke with him briefly. He knew his death would come soon.

of religious communities, sometimes called *ekklesia*, often translated as church. That is misleading.

What Paul sought to establish was *koinonia*, the fellowship and unity that should exist within the community that worshiped Messiah (it was not a Christian community, for Christianity did not exist at the time Paul wrote). *Koinonias* were share communities; each taking what he or she needed, each contributing what he or she could. Though most reject the term "communism" to describe these communities, it seems the correct term, as long as we remember that we are not talking about Marx, but about communism as communion.

"Do not be conformed to this world," wrote Paul. (Romans 12:2) For the "wisdom of the world" is based on domination, injustice, division, and violence. (1 Corinthians 2:6–16) This order is best rejected in communities based on love and sharing. Perhaps the best contemporary examples are the Christian base communities associated with Liberation Theology. The fate of these communities (most failed) testifies only to the dominance of power, including church power.

Paul believed that the eschaton, God's dream for the world, had begun with Christ and was already underway. Paul's communities were part of the "new creation" of the world the way it was meant to be.[2] When Paul writes of love, as he does a lot, he means *agape*, caring love for others, first in the community, then throughout the world.

"Justification By Faith" Is Not about Belief; It Is about a Way of Life

When Paul wrote about justification by faith (Romans 5:1; Galatians 3:24), he was not writing about the forgiveness of sins, or that the believer would become like Christ. This interpretation came 1,600 years later with the Protestant Reformation. For Paul, justification was the awareness of those who believed in Messiah that they were part of a worldwide family promised to Abraham (Genesis 17:1–8), a community that shared a common table, despite all differences: neither Jew nor Greek, neither black, brown, or white, since "all are one in the Messiah, Jesus." (Galatians 3:28)

An interpretation of Paul that sees him first and foremost as the creator of *koinonias* changes everything we think we know about Paul. While much attention is paid to Paul's transformation on the road to Damascus, more attention should be paid to what he said, and what it meant in its original Roman context, not because Paul was a Roman citizen (that is debatable),

---

2. Borg and Crossan, *The First Paul*, 187–8.

but because Rome was the center of domination, and *koinonias* the alternative. Like Christ, Paul did not oppose Roman taxes, but the Roman way of thinking, what he called with less than subtle irony the "wisdom of the world." This opposition could only be lived out with others.

MLK's Letter from Paul

I, an apostle of Jesus Christ by the will of God, to you who are in America, Grace be unto you, and peace from God our Father, through our Lord and Savior, Jesus Christ.

For many years I have longed to be able to come to see you. I have heard so much of you and of what you are doing. I have heard of the fascinating and astounding advances that you have made in the scientific realm. I have heard of your dashing subways and flashing airplanes. Through your scientific genius you have been able to dwarf distance and place time in chains. . . . All of that is marvelous. You can do so many things in your day that I could not do in the Greco-Roman world of my day. In your age you can travel distances in one day that took me three months to travel. That is wonderful. You have made tremendous strides in the area of scientific and technological development.

But America, as I look at you from afar, I wonder whether your moral and spiritual progress has been commensurate with your scientific progress. It seems to me that your moral progress lags behind your scientific progress. Your poet Thoreau used to talk about "improved means to an unimproved end." How often this is true. You have allowed the material means by which you live to outdistance the spiritual ends for which you live. You have allowed your mentality to outrun your morality. You have allowed your civilization to outdistance your culture. Through your scientific genius you have made of the world a neighborhood, but through your moral and spiritual genius you have failed to make of it a brotherhood. So, America, I would urge you to keep your moral advances abreast with your scientific advances. . . .

American Christians, I must say to you as I said to the Roman Christians years ago, "Be not conformed to this world, but be ye transformed by the renewing of your mind." Or, as I said to the Philippian Christians, "Ye are a colony of heaven." This means that although you live in the colony of time, your ultimate allegiance is to the empire of eternity. You have a dual citizenry. You live both in time and eternity; both in heaven and earth. Therefore, your ultimate allegiance is not to the government, not to the state, not to nation, not to any man-made institution. The Christian owes his ultimate allegiance to God, and if any earthly institution conflicts with God's will it is your Christian duty to take a stand against it. You must never allow the transitory evanescent demands of man-made institutions to take precedence over the eternal demands of the Almighty God. . . .

The misuse of capitalism can also lead to tragic exploitation. . . . God never intended for one group of people to live in superfluous inordinate wealth, while others live in abject deadening poverty. God intends for all of his children to have the basic necessities of life, and he has left in this universe "enough and to spare" for that purpose. So, I call upon you to bridge the gulf between abject poverty and superfluous wealth.

I would that I could be with you in person, so that I could say to you face to face what I am forced to say to you in writing. Oh, how I long to share your fellowship. But I must bring my writing to a close now. Timothy is waiting to deliver this letter, and I must take leave for another church.

But just before leaving, I must say to you, as I said to the church at Corinth, that I still believe that love is the most durable power in the world. Over the centuries men have sought to discover the highest good. This has been the chief quest of ethical philosophy. This was one of the big questions of Greek philosophy. The Epicurean and the Stoics sought to answer it; Plato and Aristotle sought to answer it. What is the [summon] bonum of life? I think I have an answer America. I think I have discovered the highest good. It is love. This principle stands at the center of the cosmos. As John says, "God is love." He who loves is a participant in the being of God. He who hates does not know God. . . .

So, American Christians you may master the intricacies of the English language. You may possess all of the eloquence of articulate speech. But even if you "speak with the tongues of men and angels, and have not love, you have become as sounding brass, or a tinkling cymbal."

So the greatest of all virtues is love. It is here that we find the true meaning of the Christian faith. This is at bottom the meaning of the cross. . . . It is an eternal reminder to a power-drunk generation that love is [the] most durable power in the world, and that it is at bottom the heartbeat of the moral cosmos. . . .

I must say goodbye now. I hope this letter will find you strong in the faith. It is probable that I will not get to see you in America, but I will meet you in God's eternity. And now unto him who is able to keep us from falling, and lift us from the fatigue of despair to the buoyancy of hope, from the midnight of desperation to the daybreak of joy, to him be power and authority, forever and ever. Amen.[3]

What would Paul's love look like today? Or MLK's? We are a mass society, not a *koinonia*. The love we need is social love: housing for the homeless, food for the hungry, education for all who long to know, health care for every American (no, for every person in America), protection from racists and bullies. I could go on, but you get the idea: love can be a guideline for social policy if we let it.

---

3. https://kinginstitute.stanford.edu/king-papers/publications/knock-midnight-inspiration-great-sermons-reverend-martin-luther-king-jr-1

29

The Book of James: Simply Right and Simply Wrong

THE LETTER OF JAMES is one of the shorter books in the New Testament, five chapters, none very long. It does not have any great stories. It does not have any stories period. Yet it is popular, many readers seeming to regard it as a "sayings" source, like Proverbs. But it is not so simple. James has a thesis: good deeds are the substance of faith. He also makes a big mistake. Every horror is not a test of human faith. God should respect human limits in the tests he imposes. God explained himself to Job, but no more.

Who Wrote It?

James, brother of Christ, probably wrote it, though some disagree. When it was written is equally contentious. Probably around 47–50 CE, but some set it as much as 150 years later. Why was it written? Probably to help Jewish Christians get through a losing struggle with Rome, one that would destroy Jerusalem, from where the letter was probably written. I do not think I have ever written a paragraph using the term "probably" so many times, but that is the way it is.

What It Does and Does not Say

Not one reference does James make to the death, resurrection, or the divine sonship of Jesus. Nevertheless, the book is conventional in its belief structure, referring to "the Lord Jesus Christ," and "our glorious Lord Jesus Christ." (James 1:1, 2:1) Whatever it is, the book is not a challenge to doctrine. While it barely mentions Jesus, there are many unattributed references to the Sermon on the Mount, and particularly to the "Q source," as it is called. The content of James is directly parallel, in many cases, to the sayings of Jesus found in the gospels of Luke and Matthew; in other words, parallel to the hypothetical Q source.[1]

Ethics and Deeds

"No other book of the New Testament concentrates so exclusively on ethical questions."[2] By "ethics," the author means doing good deeds. James puts it this way:

> Suppose a brother or a sister is without clothes and daily food. If one of you says to them, "Go in peace; keep warm and well fed," but does nothing about their physical needs, what good is it? In the same way, faith by itself, if it is not accompanied by action, is dead. (James 2:14–17)

The issue is as relevant today. How can anyone call himself a Christian if he or she does not contribute enough to charity until it hurts? Not so much that you go bankrupt, or your children unfed, but enough so that it makes a real difference in your lifestyle, your standard of living. Nine hundred million people in the world today lack the food to lead an active healthy life. Forty-one million of these are in the United States.[3] Here is the appeal of *James*. The book takes us directly to practical issues like these, mostly avoiding arcane theological disputes.

Works and Faith

Speaking of arcane theological disputes, a distinction is often made between James's focus on deeds, and Paul's focus on faith. This is why Luther at first rejected James. But the distinction is false. Paul says, it is "faith expressing itself through love" that counts in God's eyes. (Galatians, 5:6) James says "faith without deeds is dead." (James 2:17) Once one recognizes that Pauline love, all love, is about doing good things for the beloved, the contradiction disappears.

> At the theological level, then, we think that Paul and James are complementary rather than contradictory. Faith alone brings

---

1. The Q source is a hypothetical written collection of Jesus's sayings found in Matthew and Luke, but not Mark. Most people think it represents the earliest written collection of Jesus's sayings; it would be without interpretation or commentary. It is called "Q" for the German "Quelle," or source. "Q" itself does not exist, or at least it has not been found.

2. Moo, *James*, 67.

3. https://www.foodaidfoundation.org/world-hunger-statistics.html

one into relationship with God in Christ—but true faith inevitably generates the works that God will take into account in his final decision about the fate of men and women.⁴

The differences between Paul and James do not disappear. For Paul (and Kierkegaard), Abraham's willingness to sacrifice Isaac is based on his faith in the Lord. For James, the sacrifice is about doing the work (deeds) of offering up his son. (James 2:21–26) But these are the disputes that occupy theologians.

Testing Faith

Remember that James is writing to a Jewish-Christian diaspora that is suffering under the rule of Rome. Testing faith refers to how to think about hard times: they test our character, and our faith. Figuring out why God allows life to be so difficult is important, but how much testing do you need? Furthermore, would not an omniscient God know how deep your faith is in advance? He knows everything. The only argument for testing people's faith is in order to strengthen it.

> This is probably the meaning intended by James: suffering is a means by which faith, tested in the fires of adversity, can be purified of any dross and thereby strengthened.⁵

Believers are expected to embrace hardship and loss, because they know it works to produce a deeper, stronger faith. This is the same view held by Epictetus, the Roman stoic, who wrote about the same time as James. Do not complain if circumstances have set before you a terrible trial. The trial is like a wrestler. If he is strong, and you take him on, you will become stronger.⁶

A Great Mistake

Such a view, whether held by a Christian or a stoic, is seriously mistaken. Even people with a strong faith can be broken by a stronger adversity. I have witnessed interviews with about 200 Holocaust survivors. Many lost their faith, and why not? The Holocaust was not a test; it was obliteration of family, home, and any remaining belief in humanity.

Whether a test weaken or destroys you depends on your experience. Were you a victim of years-long sexual abuse by your father as a child? Or

---

4. Moo, *James*, 64.
5. Moo, *James*, 81.
6. Epictetus, *Discourses*, 1:24.1–2.

did you struggle against an adult cancer? The latter may make you stronger; the former rarely. *The Sweet Hereafter* is a story about a small town that loses almost all its children in a catastrophic school bus accident.[7] Many families never recovered; some lost their religion. A naked man facing a steamroller is not David against Goliath. It is man versus a machine of remorseless obliteration. Sometimes life is like that steamroller.

Conclusion

Simone Weil, who knew a thing or two about adversity, wrote that the great mystery of human life is not suffering but affliction (chapter 22.4 of this work). Affliction is not just suffering that persists over time. Affliction is pointless, meaningless suffering that overwhelms our ability to cope, which means our ability to make sense of the experience, including religious sense. Why would God allow a young child to be tormented by a terrible disease before dying a painful death? Some people can find a reason, usually of the "God has his ways" variety. Many cannot find a reason. Some are strengthened, some not. But those who are strengthened are no better than those who are not.

If the purpose of God's testing is to strengthen our faith, then the ordeal must be within the ability of humans to cope. Humans are just humans after all. That too is the point of James.

---

7. Banks, *Sweet Hereafter*.

30

The Book of Revelation Subverts the Spirit of Christianity

For years, I thought the Book of Revelation was insane. After reading what several scholars have written about it, I no longer believe that. The Book of Revelation makes sense as a coded attack on Rome, among other things. While I understand its place at the end of the Bible, finishing a journey begun in Genesis, I still do not believe Revelation belongs in the Bible, for it subverts the message of Jesus and the Gospels.

Just to remind you of how strange the Book of Revelation is, I will quote from Revelation 12:1–6. Revelation has many such passages.

> A great sign appeared in heaven: a woman clothed with the sun, with the moon under her feet and a crown of twelve stars on her head. She was pregnant and cried out in pain as she was about to give birth. Then another sign appeared in heaven: an enormous red dragon with seven heads and ten horns and seven crowns on its heads. Its tail swept a third of the stars out of the sky and flung them to the earth. The dragon stood in front of the woman who was about to give birth, so that it might devour her child the moment he was born. She gave birth to a son, a male child, who "will rule all the nations with an iron scepter." [Psalm 2:9] And her child was snatched up to God and to his throne. The woman fled into the wilderness to a place prepared for her by God, where she might be taken care of for 1,260 days.

Background of Revelation

Revelation was written by John of Patmos at the end of the first century CE. While some think it was written by the same John who wrote the gospel that bears his name, he would almost certainly have been too old. There were many Johns running around in those days, as there are today. No one seems to know anything about John of Patmos, other than that he identifies himself as the author. G. K. Beale and David Campbell believe that his knowledge of the Hebrew text of the Old Testament demonstrates that he was originally a Jew from Palestine.[1]

Revelation is written in symbolic code as a way of talking about life under repressive Roman rule. A number of 7's appear in the Book, and among other things, they refer to the seven hills of Rome. There are more references in Revelation to the Old Testament, as many as 278 of the 404 verses, than in all the rest of the New Testament. The reason the number of references is inexact is that many are allusions, and so sometimes it becomes a matter of judgment.

In the passage quoted above, Israel is a woman, and the dragon monster refers to the nations that threaten her. The meaning of the number 666, the number of the beast, is unknown, though such number-letter codes were common. (Revelation 13:18) Most likely it refers to Nero, possibly to the nations surrounding Israel.

Everything Changes . . . Only It Does Not

During the reign of Constantine (306–337 CE), the Roman empire became, in effect, a Christian empire. No longer was there a Roman enemy, and one might expect that the Book of Revelation would fade into obscurity. It did not. Instead, it found a new enemy. God's enemies became Christians who had been deceived by the Antichrist (another term that does not appear in Revelation). Athanasius, roughly a contemporary of Constantine, interpreted the whore of Babylon (Revelation 17) as Arian Christians; that is, Christians who had a different interpretation of the Trinity. The beast and the whore were within those Christians who did not accept the Nicene Creed.

More fundamentally, Athanasius opposed those who held that one could learn about Christ directly, through communion with the living Jesus, a view associated with gnosticism. A view like this has always driven the authorities crazy (the Protestant Reformation was the next big act), and Athanasius interpreted Revelation as condemning all heretics.

> Like Bishop Irenaeus two centuries earlier, Athanasius turned John's visions of cosmic war into a weapon against those he called heretics.[2]

1. Beale and Campbell, *Revelation*, 2.
2. Pagels, *Revelations*, 144.

Like paranoids at all times and all places, the enemy without is all too likely to become the enemy within, in this case from pagan Rome to Christians who believed differently about some really fine distinctions, such as whether Christ was begotten or made; that is, was Jesus a mode of God, or God himself in a different aspect? Paranoids need their enemies and will find (or create) them almost anywhere. Sigmund Freud called it the "narcissism of small differences."[3] The less substantive the dispute, the greater the hatred.

Plugged in

Pagels is right. The Book of Revelation wrapped up our worst fears into a horrific nightmare.

> ... [f]ears of violence, plague, wild animals, unimaginable horrors emerging from the abyss below the earth, lightning, thunder, hail, earthquakes, erupting volcanoes, and the atrocities of torture and war. ... John's visions speak to what one historian calls the Christian movement's most powerful catalyst—the conviction that death is not simply annihilation.[4]

I do not understand the last sentence. Are not the Gospels, above all, a story about a God-man who died so that we might live forever? Are not the Gospels a claim that we are partners in eternity? If so, then what does Revelation add?

It adds a story that can be "plugged into any conflict," as Pagels puts it. But if Revelation provides a ready-made explanation of almost any conflict, it lacks the most important lesson of the gospels, "his strength made perfect in weakness." (2 Corinthians 12:9) There are many stories of powerful gods and heroes vanquishing our oppressors. What is different about the gospels is that they teach not power, but the power of weakness. Instead of a God conquering our enemies, the gospels are a story about God becoming weak, allowing himself to be tortured to death, so that he might know human pain and teach us how to live.

> For I was hungry and you gave me food; I was thirsty and you gave me something to drink; I was a stranger and you welcomed me; I was naked, and you gave me clothing; I was sick and you took care of me; I was in prison and you visited me. (Matthew 25:35–36)

---

3. Freud, *Civilization*, 72.
4. Pagels, *Revelations*, 171.

Nothing of this teaching, absolutely nothing, remains in the Book of Revelation. To be sure, Christ's teaching about love and care for all humanity comes with eternal punishment for those who do not. (Matthew 25:40–46) Nevertheless, the tone of the gospels is primarily one of love and care for those in need, taught by a God-man who gave his life to save humanity. Revelation, on the other hand, is about a powerful God who will destroy Christ's enemies in one final battle, returning to earth to establish his kingdom in power and glory. The tone and the lesson are entirely different.

This Is Why Revelation Does Not Belong

The Book of Revelation brings the beginning and the end of the Bible together, from Adam, Eve, and the serpent to God's final victory over evil. Revelation also brings together the Old Testament with the New, connecting them with its hundreds of references to the Old Testament. "Apocalyptic" comes from the Greek word for "revelation," and there is little difference between revelation and prophecy. Though we do not usually think about it this way, Revelation is a work of prophecy in the Old Testament tradition, once again linking the Old Testament with the New.[5]

There was great dispute over whether Revelation should be admitted into the canon we call the Bible. This fellow Eusebius, a bishop, was so ambivalent about the Book of Revelation that he placed it both on the list of books he calls "universally accepted" and on the list of books he calls "illegitimate"; this as late as 325–340.[6]

I can understand Eusebius's confusion. We can understand why the Book of Revelation makes a fitting ending to the Bible, but the concept of God as supreme victor over the Antichrist spoils the tone and tenor of the gospels, which teach a subtler lesson.

---

5. Beale and Campbell, *Revelation*, 4.
6. Pagels, *Revelations*, 161.

Part IV: Psychology and God

31

"Do You Believe in God?" Is the Wrong Question

"*How* do you believe in God?" comes closer to the mark. The founder of psychoanalysis, Sigmund Freud, saw religion as an infantile illusion, one in which God would comfort and protect us from the harshness of the world as our parents once did.[1] But this is not all psychoanalysis has to say about religion.

Jung and Myth

For Carl Jung, a follower of Freud in his younger years, a rebel in his later years, religious myth is a great achievement. As myth, religion is neither true nor false. The categories do not apply. A myth is generally the story of an epic hero sent on a journey to found or save a people, either by defeating an enemy or solving a problem. Moses did both. So did Jesus Christ: the enemy is sin and death; the solution is belief that Christ is the son of God.

It is no repudiation of God to reject him, because almost all of what we know about God and Jesus comes through stories. We live by and through narrative. Stories are how we make sense of our lives, and our world. The Bible is a series of stories; one reason it prospered while the gnostic gospels failed. The Gnostics did not have enough stories. About religious myths, Jung says,

---

1. Freud, *Future of Illusion*, 30–31, 43.

> The religious myth is one of man's greatest and most significant achievements, giving him the security and inner strength not to be crushed by the monstrousness of the universe.[2]

Winnicott

D. W. Winnicott, a psychoanalyst writing a generation after Freud, had the deepest insight into religion. For reality to be real to us, says Winnicott, we must participate in the illusion of having created it. Otherwise, it will be a dead reality, the husk of reality, but never the living thing.

Winnicott distinguishes between objective and subjective objects. Objective objects are things that exist external to us, without reference to us and our needs. They are "not-me-objects," objectively real, but "out there," in the world. Subjective objects reflect back to us our own aliveness. They participate in our needs and wishes. They correspond to our sense of being alive.[3]

> Our . . . Mozart arias, our religious rituals contain in themselves both the subjective and objective poles and hence function as true symbols.[4]

By psychologically investing in the ritual object, such as the cross or Torah, the objective object becomes subjectively real, without reducing the objective to the subjective, which would be mad. The same may be said about the Bible. Read creatively, we help make it true.

I have friends who are simply transported when they hear beautiful music. This experience is transitional experience. The music is real, but it becomes meaningful only when those who listen help create the experience by finding in their minds' desire the actual music. Religious faith works in the same way. We have faith only when we have a hand in creating what we experience as sacred.

But if God were just an internal reality, he would be no more than our fantasy. The God who feels real, the God who excites us, is the God whom we discover because we help to make him real.

> For reality to be real to us, it must partake of illusion . . . meaning that we must contribute to its construction or it will possess no sense of the real for us.[5]

2. Jung, *Collected Works*, v 5, para. 343.
3. Winnicott, *Use of an Object*.
4. Ulanov, *Finding Space*, 11.
5. Ulanov, *Finding Space*, 11.

Transitional Space, Babies, and God

The area between objective and subjective objects is called "transitional space." From the perspective of transitional space, the question becomes not does God exist, but do we experience him in a lively or dead way? If experienced in a dead way, God feels added on, something we are forced to adopt lest something worse befall us. Such a God is not likely to be very helpful when we are faced with limit experiences, such as loss of a loved one, serious illness, and death.

We should not feel insulted that Winnicott compares knowledge of God with a baby's experience of the world. It is a compliment, for lived religion opens us to the wonder of the world, a wonder that many of us have not experienced since childhood. About babies, Winnicott said:

> A baby [man] creates an object [God], but the object [God] would not have been created as such if it had not already been there.[6]

I have inserted "God" and "man" in the brackets above to show that the point is the same whether we are talking about babies or adults: we create what we discover, but what we discover had to have been there in order to be created. Winnicott was aware that this paradoxical insight had theological implications.

From Church to Grace

Generally, church is a ritual in which I am not emotionally involved. The ritual is not dead, but the relationship between worshiper and religion is. Sometimes, however, the service (or just stepping into the church for a few minutes) is just what I needed and did not even know I needed. I help create and make real what is already there. Having a similar experience with God is called belief. It is the only way God gets inside—when we discover to our surprise that he was already there. To do this, we cannot be desperate about our faith and whether we have it or not; instead, we must give ourselves over to the experience.

Consider a traditional account of grace, in which God implants in us the faith to know and believe in him. John Wesley (1738) writes in his sermon "Salvation by Faith," "Grace is the source, faith the condition, of salvation."[7] (see too Ephesians 2:8) Or as Winnicott puts it,

---

6. Winnicott, *Creativity*, 71.

7. http://wesley.nnu.edu/john-wesley/the-sermons-of-john-wesley-1872-edition/sermon-1-salvation-by-faith/

> For me paradox is inherent . . . Although the object was there to be found it was created . . . and in theology the same thing appears . . . around the question: is there a God? If God is a projection [of our needs and desires], even so is there a God who created me in such a way that I have the material in me for such a projection? The important thing for me must be, have I got in in me to have the idea of God—if not, then the idea of God is of no value to me (except superstitiously).[8]

Whether or not we require God's gift of grace to have faith in God, we do not make ourselves. The ability to accept the gift of grace may be implanted by God. What can we do to receive this gift? The most important thing is to relax and not force it. Let it happen in its own time and in its own way. It is like music. You cannot make yourself enjoy music, but you can relax and let the music in.

A culture without God is a culture that has lost its imagination and is afraid to let the God-experience happen. One consequence of this insight is that the God-experience need not be conventional. It need not be Christian. It can stand outside the Abrahamic tradition (Judaism, Christianity, and Islam). It is sometimes argued that Buddhism is not a religion, because it lacks a supreme being. But any belief system that renounces the craving for things, while encouraging self-emptying meditation, all the while fostering kindness and compassion fits the God-experience. The real issue, as Winnicott recognizes, is whether people have enough confidence in themselves to let go of their material certainty and imagine that the world is not all that it seems.

This is why ritual and doctrine are so important: so that we have enough God in common to share. Not because each of us has to believe the same thing, but so that we know the outlines, at least, of what we do not believe. Doctrine defines us whether we adhere to it or not, perhaps especially when we do not.

The Dead Hand of Tradition

Without tradition, religion would have to be remade every generation, which is both impossible and undesirable. At the same time, tradition is the great enemy of faith, as routine substitutes for lived experience, by which I mean an experience we participate in by making it in our minds even as it is happening. The balance between tradition and creativity is delicate. Too

---

8. Winnicott, *Psychoanalytic Explorations*, 205.

rigid a tradition is deadening. Too little tradition and religion lacks gravitas, the Bible just a collection of myths.

A Living Religion

Winnicott's view of a living religion is captured by his account of attending a play.

> This is the exciting thing about the curtain in a theatre. When it goes up, each one of us will create the play that is going to be enacted, and afterwards we may even find that the overlap of what we have created . . . provides material for a discussion about the play that was enacted.[9]

Because religious doctrine and ritual is often pretty well defined, there will be significant overlap in the God each of us helps create. We will find ourselves talking about the "same" God. In fact, God is special and different for each of us, for we have helped make him. "Helped" make him; because if someone simply imagined that his beliefs created God, he would be mad. Or intensely cynical.

Why "Do you believe in God?" Is a Stupid Question

This is why the question "Do you believe in God?" is stupid. How you believe—or disbelieve—in God is what is important. About atheism, Simone Weil said,

> An atheist may be simply one whose faith and love are concentrated on the impersonal aspects of God.[10]

It is harder than it seems not to believe in God. The question is always, how? And, of course, how do you put your beliefs into practice in everyday life?

By putting our beliefs into practice, we not only bring our beliefs to life, but we share this life with others, even if they do not always know what we are sharing with them. Often, we ourselves do not know. Perhaps it is just our goodness that we share, but sometimes it feels like more; almost like we were sharing God. It does not have to feel this way, and generally does not. That is OK too. The gift of paying attention to the other person is enough, at least as far as human relations are concerned.

9. Winnicott, "Child in the Family Group," 133.
10. quoted in Auden, *A Certain World*.

32

Psychology, God and Death

I AM GOING TO look at some psychological reasons for belief in God. Whatever I uncover will say nothing whatsoever about the existence of God. Referring to the human need for God helps us understand our need for transcendence. But the need does not prove or disprove God, which is impossible, in any case. Good psychology is not the same as good theology. Theology is concerned with how we should talk about God, and to God, especially in times of trial and pain. Psychology is about the need for transcendence.

The inspiration for this section is the fear of death experienced by many Christians. The website www.billygraham.org is filled with emails like the following: "I'm a good Christian, but as I get older I'm terrified of death." That is OK, I want to say to the woman who sent the email; everyone is afraid of death. Christianity does not take away that fear; it just makes death meaningful. For what people fear most is not death, but meaningless death, in which one lived and died for nothing. Seen from this perspective, it is not just religion that gives meaning to death, and hence to a life lived toward death, as all lives do. Participation in great art or music (enjoying as well as making it) gives life meaning, a meaning that will continue after my death in the ennobling activities I give myself to. So too does love of natural beauty.

Unfortunately, people can give themselves to wicked activities; for example, terrorism or neo-Nazism. Once we understand that it is not about the goal, but the way the goal gives meaning to life, it becomes easier to understand the attraction of such fraudulent activities. They are fraudulent because they serve the call of death, the destruction and devaluation of other humans, and so bring not more natality and vitality into the world, but less.

Robert Jay Lifton: Death Is More Important than Sex

The psychiatrist I turn to is Robert Jay Lifton. The most important thing to say about him is that he is not a Freudian. He thinks death is a lot more important in human life than sex (actually, so did the later Freud). Indeed, most of our symbolic life is about coming to terms with death. The book I focus on is *The Broken Connection: On Death and the Continuity of Life*.

Some, like Freud, argue that religion is a childish defense against the reality of annihilation.[1] Culture, particularly religion, is a defense against that reality. Lifton argues that culture does not deny death. Culture, especially religion, gives us a sense of continuity between life and death. A part of me lives on, in heaven some believe, in the great works of art and literature that I have cherished. Living up to high values, and knowing and appreciating great art, such as that of Shakespeare, or (one of my favorites) Evelyn Waugh, are two ways almost any person can participate in values and beauty greater than themselves. One does not even have to be literate to participate in high values.

> Lifton is concerned foremost with the psychic process of symbolization, in particular the way we negotiate the finality of death by creating, symbolically, a counter-sense of continuity.[2]

Symbolic Death Equivalents

Freud argued that people cannot imagine their own deaths; unconsciously, they believe they will live forever.[3] Freud was mistaken. It may in some logical sense be impossible to imagine being dead; that is, not existing. But it is quite possible to imagine the world going on without me, and I have imagined my own death many times, even wondering where I will take my last breath. I may not be quite normal, but I do not think I am that strange, either. People have better imaginations than Freud credits. And even if they do not imagine their own deaths, almost everyone is afraid of symbolic death equivalents, as Lifton calls them.[4] Some examples are loneliness, isolation, enforced stasis (immobility), and separation from those we love.

---

1. Freud, *Thoughts for the Times*, 289.
2. Des Pres, "Review of Lifton," 3.
3. Freud, *Thoughts for the Times*, 289.
4. Lifton, *Broken Connection*, 53.

In one way or another, all death equivalents are images of separation: from others, from familiar worlds and objects, to separation from this world itself. We fear death in terms of images of death. As Charles Ryder puts it in Evelyn Waugh's *Brideshead Revisited*,

> Next to death, perhaps because they are like death, he feared darkness and loneliness.[5]

For Lord Marchmain, and perhaps for us all, darkness and loneliness represent the unthinkable, but not the unimaginable.

The Symbols Are Breaking Down

The quality, richness, and depth of our symbols connecting life and death are breaking down. From a religious connection to a medicalized one is probably the biggest and most disruptive change. Doctors have become the new priests, medicine a religion all its own, to which some are admitted to its inner sanctum, such as a clinical trial of a new drug. Trouble is, the replacement of religion by medicine only heightens the terror of death, for it renders death hidden and meaningless. (I suppose that participating in a drug trial could give one a sense of contributing to the march of medical progress. But this would only show how desperately we all need to connect to something larger and longer lasting than ourselves.)

Death, says Kurt Eissler, is "the process of terminal, maximum individualization."[6] We may live for others and their expectations, but we die our own deaths. Individualization is good, the goal of psychic development in the Western industrial nations. But when individualization becomes isolated individualism, that is bad, as psychic investment in a world that continues in my absence becomes impossible. The psychic investment need not be in heaven or the eschaton. A simple example of psychic investment in the future is love for one's children and grandchildren, and hope for their futures.

Religion

Religion is probably the best symbolic connection between life and death. Around the world, it remains the most common image linking the worlds of the living and the dead, even as religion is on the wane in Europe and North America. It need not be a religion of the personal afterlife, such as

---

5. Waugh, *Brideshead*, 331.
6. Eisler, *Psychiatrist and Dying Patient*, 55.

Christianity. Observant Jews, who frequently do not believe in a personal afterlife, understand that they are participating in a millennia-long tradition based on a historical covenant with God. That is more than enough.

"If God did not exist, it would be necessary to invent him," Voltaire famously stated. I do not think that is quite true. What is true is that man invents religion, and cannot help himself, for that is how we give meaning to life: by symbolically connecting ourselves to another world that lives on. But religion requires a deep well of symbolism to draw on, and the well is drying up, replaced by a desert of a zillion images, each no deeper than a pixel.

33

Psychology and the New Atheists

RATHER THAN WRITING ABOUT the puzzling anger directed at the idea of God by the new atheists, as they are often called, I am going to consider one of the best among them; certainly, he is among the less extreme. In *Inventing God: Psychology of Belief and the Rise of Secular Spirituality*, Jon Mills tries to do three things. First, to demonstrate that God does not exist. In this, he joins a long line of aggressive atheists, such as Christopher Hitchens, Sam Harris, and Richard Dawkins. Mills says he is not a "vociferous atheist," but he could have fooled me with his remarks about "the believing masses [who] cannot accept the fact that we are ultimately alone."[1]

The second thing Mills tries to do is construct a defense of a humanistic spirituality. He says a lot of good things about finding "intrinsic worth and meaning in living our lives for the present," but the foundation of this claim was laid down by Albert Camus and Jean-Paul Sartre, and I do not see where Mills adds a great deal to this argument.

The third thing Mills tries to do is construct a psychoanalytic argument explaining the need for God. He begins with Freud, who argued that God is an infantile delusion of an enormously powerful father figure.[2] Along the way, Mills offers some useful insight, such as his observation that religion is related to a failure to mourn.

> The idea or notion of God is the manifestation of our denial and response to our being-in-relation-to-lack, and hence the longing to replace natural absence with divine presence. As a result, God remains a deposit of humanity's failure to mourn natural deprivation or lack in favor of the delusional belief in an ultimate hypostatized object of idealized value.[3]

1. Mills, *Inventing God*, 104.
2. Freud, *Civilization and Discontents*.
3. Mills, *Inventing God*, 2.

Mills appreciates the psychological contribution of the God posit, as it calls it, but only for the disadvantaged.

> There is no need to obliterate peoples' proclivity for religion let alone deracinate their need to believe, only that we need to understand *why* humanity is inclined to think this way in order to introduce an intervening reflective level of self-conscious awareness that points toward the truth of being in a world that does not require God to function or give meaning to existence.[4]

Unfortunately, there is little in the book's tone or substance that reflects this psychological and pedagogical understanding. The primary problem with the book is that the first part, demonstrating that God does not exist, gets in the way of the second part.

In the Beginning

God, Mills argues, is only a thought. Rather than being an ontological subject or supreme being responsible for the coming into being of the universe, God is "merely a psychological creation signifying ultimate ideality."[5] In response, one wants to say, of course, God is only a thought. What else could he be as far as humans are concerned? God may or may not have His own independent existence, but all we can know are our thoughts and feelings about Him. Wrap a good story around an "ultimate ideality," and you have both God and a religion.

Narratives are always more interesting than logic. And does this ultimate ideality exist? Here we should take a prompt from D. W. Winnicott. Don't ask. God, at least for adults, is a transitional object, primarily between being and nonbeing, life and death. Religious experience is about resting in this riddle, neither needing nor demanding proof.

> Of the transitional object it can be said that it is a matter of agreement between us . . . that we will never ask the question "Did you conceive of this or was it presented to you from without?" The important point is that no decision on this point is expected. The decision is not to be formulated.[6]

The most puzzling thing about the new atheists, and Mills has to be considered among them, is their insistence on asking the question in such a way as to assume that there is an answer. Mills, like so many new atheists,

4. Mills, *Inventing God*, 10.
5. Mills, *Inventing God*, 1.
6. Winnicott, "Morals and Education," 93.

misunderstands the issue of scientific meaning. "[t]he God question is not a legitimate scientific topic because it does not meet the basic requisite of falsifiability through testability." In support of this claim, he cites Karl Popper's *The Logic of Scientific Discovery*. But this was never what Popper was up to. Popper was a critic of the Vienna Circle, a group of logical positivists in the years before World War II. Their claim was that a statement had meaning only if it could be verified.

Popper argued that falsifiability is not about the distinction between meaning and nonmeaning, but between scientific statements and nonscientific statements. Many statements are meaningful but not scientific. "That's a beautiful picture because of the way it employs chiaroscuro" is a perfectly meaningful statement, but not a scientific one. Statements about God have roughly the same status. Or should.

Mills struggles to uphold a standard something like this, but in the end, the need to falsify religion wins the day. "There is no evidentiary or verifiable proof for believing that God is *anything but* an idea."[7]

I can say the same thing about goodness, beauty, or love. Relatively few statements in everyday life are falsifiable, including "I love my children." How different is this from "I love my God"? The question is not whether my children exist. The question is whether and in what way I love them, and is it a way conducive to their growth, and secondarily to my own? But your children really exist, the reader might reply. Yes, but the most important thing about God is not his existence (the point of a transitional object) but the way we relate to him. Mills believes the "God posit" is not conducive to human growth. I do not agree, but this is something we could sensibly argue about.

Evidence is relevant. Mills cites studies that show that countries with the highest proportion of unbelievers, particularly the Scandinavian countries, are the happiest. It is a relevant piece of evidence, but of course it could have less to do with atheism than with living in a wealthy social welfare state. In any case, this is the way something like this can be argued.

Winnicott, God, and Transitional Objects

Winnicott seems to have followed his own advice about how best to think about God—by not grasping at either certainty or denial. On what basis does Winnicott give this advice? On grounds that Mills would appreciate, at least in the abstract. The ability to move around in transitional space between self and world, subject and object.

---

7. Mills, *Inventing God*, 75.

Mills reads Winnicott differently. Rather than seeing subjective reality as enlivening objective reality, Mills argues that doing so is a confusion, at least as far as God is concerned.

> Here we may say that the God concept as object representation is a form of inner reality superimposed on externality that is conflated to be an actual, factual extrinsic entity, the experience of which is believed to be objectively real.[8]

Mills seems terribly attached to objective reality, what he sometimes calls a "preordained objective fulcrum."[9] I am not so sure there is any such thing, or that I want there to be.

A consequence of viewing not just religion, but liveliness, as the ability to move around in subjective space is that it explains what happens when we become true-believers, whether it is of the theist or atheist variety. It affects what Mills refers to as "qualia," the qualitative vitality of experience. Winnicott seeks the same thing.

Vitality

Does God-belief contribute to the vitality of experience? Mills seems to think so, but only for those societies without the economic, social, and political resources to live without belief. There is, he says, nothing to be gained from taking away God-belief from people whose daily lives are so difficult and miserable to begin with.

It is worth remembering that many religions, such as Buddhism, lack a belief in a personal heavenly afterlife. And what the religion defines as its doctrine is often held piecemeal by its members. Large numbers of Judeo-Christians no longer believe in a personal afterlife, including some of my friends who go to church, as well as my Jewish relatives.

As long as I am writing about personal experience, I should mention a trip to my local shopping mall. Inside was a store named "True Religion," which turns out to be the brand of blue jeans sold by the store. The true believers to whom Mills frequently refers exist in smaller and smaller numbers in Western Europe and North America. When a clothing store is called "True Religion," are not the days of real religion numbered?

I taught undergraduate students for forty years at a large state university, and it is the rare student who is a true believer. Of course, North American university students are not the "common masses" to whom Mills

---

8. Mills, *Inventing God*, 115.
9. Mills, *Inventing God*, 119.

refers, but they are not so different either. It puzzles me that the rise of the "new atheism" occurs at just that point where true belief is an endangered species, at least in Western Europe and North America.[10]

Does Religion Dictate?

> This is why to this day and in most parts of the world, including developing democratic countries, religion (either explicitly or implicitly) dictates the way we think and largely determines the social roles people play in human interactions and communal life.[11]

This just is not true anymore, if it ever was. People may still act in the name of their god, but if hypocrisy is the tribute that vice pays to virtue, then religion was never so important as people make out. Thucydides's *History of the Peloponnesian War*, written during the last third of the fifth century BCE, explains men's motives in terms of fear, honor, and interest. For Thucydides, evidently an atheist, belief in the sacred is always a sign of weakness and fear. Much has changed since then, but to think that religion dictates behavior is almost always to confuse the justification with the cause. I estimate that this is true even for those who murder in the name of religion.

Deciding What God Must Be

> If one's definition of God does not include or imply a personal (individualistic or subjective) element as divine agent or agency, then what is the point of calling it God? Here God merely becomes an abstraction, impersonality, or category of values one aspires to attain or fulfill.[12]

If I were Mills, I would be more careful about telling people how to believe about God, or even if they qualify as believers. Consider Simone Weil's line, "an atheist may be simply one whose faith and love are concentrated on the impersonal aspects of God." A wise atheist might reply "a theist is simply one whose sense of justice or power requires a face."[13] There are so many different ways to think about God. To decide that some ways are not really thinking about God at all is a philosopher's conceit.

---

10. https://www.pewforum.org/2018/06/13/why-do-levels-of-religious-observance-vary-by-age-and-country
11. *Inventing God*, 121.
12. *Inventing God*, 76.
13. Samuelson, *Deepest Human Life*, 22.

> It may be generally said that our encounter with the numinous often involves a form of unitive experience with the collective, namely, a greater feeling of unity or connectedness to humanity and cosmos as a whole. We may view this experience solely from the vantage point of naturalized psychology or human phenomenology without importing [theology].[14]

Surely this is true, but for many people, God adds a narrative and ritualistic dimension that enriches this experience. Instead of asking why anyone would add God to this story, one might equally well ask, why not add God to this story if it makes it more appealing? Certainly, much damage has been done by people under the name of God, but if the experience of National Socialism (Nazis) taught us anything, it is that monstrous evil can be done in the absence of the "God posit." The same may be said for Stalin, and Mao's cultural revolution.

Conclusion

The trouble with *Inventing God* is that its atheist agenda gets in the way of sustained psychoanalytic argument. It is an agenda that is in many ways already eclipsed by history. By the end of the nineteenth century, Nietzsche had done all the intellectual ground-clearing. The rest of the story belongs to modernity, characterized by Weberian rationalization of the lifeworld.[15]

Another way to put much the same point is that if religion is a necessary panacea in the less developed world, but bad in the Western European and North American democracies, then Mills and the new atheists have carved out an area for critique that is rapidly shrinking. If atheism should be wisdom, then once again, Minerva's owl flies at dusk. I do not believe that atheism is wisdom, but that should be clear by now.

---

14. Mills, *Inventing God*, 177.
15. Mitzman, *Iron Cage*.

Part V: Natural Law

34

Does Natural Law Exist? What Is It?

NATURAL LAW IS NOT something talked about very much these days, except in Catholic theology, which has kept the teaching alive. In this section, I write about Saint Thomas Aquinas, the founder of modern natural law theory. By the way, Aquinas is often just called Thomas; when I refer to Thomas, I am not being familiar.

Not only is natural law not talked about these days, it runs against the cultural current of the age: you cannot judge other people's values. You cannot judge because, for many people, no one culture is intrinsically better than another. The same goes for values. As discussed in the next chapter, I taught natural law to undergraduates at a large state university, and most were natural law relativists. Natural law does not accept this relativity. Some things are good for all people, and other things are bad for all people. Not just good or bad just for others, but for yourself.

Thomas Aquinas

Thomas (ca. 1225–1274) is the exemplary natural law theorist. Not the first, but the one who first fully developed its implications. Thomas believes that natural law is given to us by God, but Hugo Grotius coming along four centuries later is closer to the mark when he says:

> What we have been saying [about natural law] would have a degree of validity even if we should concede that which cannot be

conceded without the utmost wickedness, that there is no God, or that the affairs of men are of no concern to Him.[1]

I can make the same point another way by saying that Thomas would disagree with Dostoevsky's Kirillov, who said in effect, that if God does not exist, everything is permissible. Just by being human, we know some things are right and some things are wrong. Of course, many people do wrong knowingly, and some do wrong and think it is right. Thomas allows room for what he calls

> a perverted reason due to passion or due to evil habit or due to an evil disposition of nature.[2]

What Does the Natural Law Say?

Do good, avoid evil, but since that is a little vague (a lot vague), Thomas gets down to specifics. Above all, doing good means preserving and fostering human life. It is easy to see how Thomas would be led to the conclusion that humans seek to preserve their own lives, because our own lives are good. But how does Aquinas so quickly reach the conclusion that it is equally good to preserve the lives of others? Because for Aquinas, the good is not just my life. The good is life, because life is not merely a private possession, but a shared good.[3]

We are not just isolated individuals. We belong to a community of others to whom we owe our lives, from parents to farmers to soldiers, and by extension to teachers and so forth, all who help make our lives more worth living. At least that is the ideal. Thomas lived in a simpler society, but you get the idea: from birth to death we owe each other almost everything, even if we do not often think of it that way. There are no self-made men or women. Jeff Bezos got rich off of the work of thousands, from warehouse workers to mailmen.

One can reduce Aquinas's teachings to three lessons, even if that is not the whole story:

1. Preserve life
2. Parental responsibility for rearing and educating children
3. Pursue knowledge and sociability

---

1. Grotius, *Prolegomena, II, On the Law of War and Peace*.
2. Aquinas, *Summa*, I-II, 76, 1
3. Aquinas, *Summa*, I-II, 94, 2.

About the last lesson, Kainz says that "this might be interpreted minimally as social consciousness, maximally as love."[4] Love not only of others, but of the knowledge of what others are going through. In one version of the legend of the Holy Grail,[5] the vessel belongs to the seeker who first asks its guardian, a king paralyzed by a painful wound, "What are you going through?" That knowledge requires paying attention to others. Attention turns us from ourselves, opening us to the experiences of other people. One might almost call that love. Certainly, it is a form of knowledge too little practiced.

The Most Important Virtue

If we know what the good is, then what is the most important thing to have? Something that will get you closer to the good. For Thomas, that is pity (*misericordia* in Latin). Pity, says Aquinas, is grief or sorrow over someone else's distress, precisely insofar as one understands the other's distress as similar to one's own. "Among the virtues that relate us to our neighbor pity is the greatest."[6]

Today, pity is generally looked down on. Sometimes it is an insult, such as, "I pity you," said with a tone of contempt. Thomas understood that only in communities of mutual need can the care we extend toward others stem from a genuine distress at their suffering, what is called pity or compassion. It might even be called love of neighbor. This works, of course, only when people recognize their dependency on others. Almost everything in American society and culture works against this recognition.

One other thing about pity is worth noticing. To live in a community of recognized mutual need is generally the most satisfying life for those who give as well as receive. We learn this in that first community, the family, but the principle is universal.

The Limits of Pity

Trouble is, many of us do not live in communities, and many of those most in need of pity live half a world away. This is what makes imagination so important; imagination and a little bit of effort to inform oneself. Today, pursuing knowledge and sociability, as Thomas puts it, includes informing oneself about the lives of others, so pity might have something to work

---

4. Kainz, *Natural Law*, 22.

5. The Holy Grail is traditionally the cup from which Jesus drank the wine at the last supper.

6. Aquinas, *Summa*, II-II, 30, 4.

with. There is enough suffering around that it does not take much work to find worthy objects of our compassion, which is probably a better translation of *misericordia*.

35

Three Stories About Natural Law

THIS CHAPTER CONSISTS OF three stories about the natural law. The first is about an experience of mine, the second is a look at the Nuremberg Trials. The third is a story I told my students who do not believe in the natural law. What connects them is my belief that most of us assume the natural law exists; we just do not know we know it. The other chapters deal more with the foundations of the natural law. This section is more about practice than theory.

First Story: The County School Board Ethics Committee, or "Keep Your Body Parts to Yourself"

A number of years ago, I was invited to serve on the ethics curriculum advisory panel of a local county school board. The goal was to develop an ethics curriculum for the lower grades. Our advisory panel had representatives of all the "good" people in the community: ministers, rabbis, a few concerned parents, some concerned teachers, and me, a university professor of ancient Greek ethics. What should an ideal ethics curriculum teach?

We never got anywhere. We got stuck at the very beginning. Should we teach students that they should not hit each other?

"How can we teach that?" said one committee member, echoing several more. "Some cultures value the physical expression of difference, and who are we to say otherwise?"

The odd thing about this committee was that nobody thought that students should hit each other, and nobody knew of any culture anywhere that valued students hitting each other. It was just the very possibility that some culture somewhere valued "the physical expression of difference" that caused the committee members to lose confidence in their own beliefs.

The county in which this school board is located is relatively liberal. Not every school board in the country would have ended up stuck at the beginning—good liberals afraid to assert something they all believed in. Cultural relativism made cowards of them all. Whether this is a problem with liberalism itself, or just with ordinary everyday liberals not too thoughtful about their own beliefs, is an important question that cannot be addressed here.[1]

Well, I quit the committee at that point, but they went on and did some work. Several years later, I ran into one of the members in the local supermarket. I asked what they finally came up with, and the statement they finally agreed on was, "Keep your body parts to yourself." It was not about sexual abuse. It was the cowardly, bureaucratic way of saying, "Do not hit each other."

What I Think Happened

People pretty much agree on the precepts of natural law; that is, the principles that should guide our relationships with each other. A simple example is that it is not right for kids to hit each other in school. Trouble is, most people do not believe they have any basis for their beliefs, certainly not in natural law. Or if they do, they feel their beliefs are private, religious, personal, and so they have no basis to criticize or judge others. This is a loss not of the content of natural law, but a sense of its moral force, especially regarding others. Many people hold to the content of natural law, but to relativism as a theory of knowledge.

The tragedy of modern man and woman is that they cannot trust in what they already know, and the more they look for grounds among intellectuals, the more insecure they are going to become. Indeed, academics are often a hindrance, seeing universals as instruments of repression, teaching students to be critical of everything, but putting nothing in its place.

As Joseph Biden once put it against the possibility that Clarence Thomas believed in natural law: ". . . [n]atural law dictates morality to us, instead of leaving matters to individual choice." But do we really want to leave morality to individual choice? About who to have sex with and when? Maybe. About whether to kill? Or rob? Or rape? I think not.

---

1. The most important recent book on this topic is John Rawls' *Political Liberalism*. By "liberalism," political theory means a tradition that makes the individual the center of all value. This differs from the everyday use of the term.

Second Story: What if Someone Rejects the Universal Declaration of Human Rights?

We were talking about the foundations of morality in one of my classes, and several students mentioned the United Nations Universal Declaration of Human Rights. The Declaration was adopted in 1948, shortly after the Second World War, shortly after the Holocaust. It says what one might expect:

> **Article 1.**
> All human beings are born free and equal in dignity and rights. They are endowed with reason and conscience and should act towards one another in a spirit of brotherhood.
>
> **Article 3.**
> Everyone has the right to life, liberty and security of person.
>
> **Article 18.**
> Everyone has the right to freedom of thought, conscience and religion . . .

And it goes on, a total of 30 articles similar in nature.

I found myself in almost complete agreement with the UN Declaration, but then I started wondering, what if someone simply said, "No, some humans are superior to others, some people deserve to be tortured, and freedom of thought and expression are too dangerous to be left to anyone but an elite few"?

What would I, what would anyone, say to this person? The UN Declaration offers absolutely no help here. It asserts these rights, but it offers not a single argument for them, unlike the United States Declaration of Independence, which refers to "the laws of Nature and Nature's God," which maintain that "all men are endowed by their Creator with certain unalienable rights." Still, even about the U.S. Declaration, one wonders what one might say to someone who replies, "No they are not; there is no Creator and no rights, just power."

The Historical Context of the UN Universal Declaration

The UN Declaration was not written in a vacuum. It was written in response to a problem faced by the Allies at the end of World War II. Almost everything the Germans did was totally legal, according to German law. The

Germans were scrupulous about the law, passing laws to strip Jews of their citizenship, laws to deport them to the death camps, and so forth.

When it came time for the Allies to put the architects of the Holocaust on trial in 1945 in the city of Nuremberg, there was a problem. The German defendants said that they were just following German law. How could they be found guilty for following the law?

In response, the allies held a series of trials, the prosecution claiming that the allies had the right to find the architects of the Holocaust guilty because even though they were following German law, they should have known better. Every human being with reason knows that it is wrong to deliberately murder innocents. Hermann Goering, one of the chief organizers of the Holocaust, told the court that the trial had been nothing more than an exercise of power by the victors of a war: justice, he said, had nothing to do with it.

The trial court claimed differently: that about such things as the murder of innocents, there exists a higher law that every normal human being must know. We may disagree about the details, but every normal human being must know that laws that proclaim the murder of innocents violate the conscience of humankind. Though the allies never used the term "natural law," this was the idea behind the trial: it was not just the victors punishing the vanquished. The trial recognized that every human being knows, or should know, that certain terrible acts, whether or not they are in accord with human law, are wrong, and not to be committed.

Natural Law Is about Living Together Well

The natural law is not just a theological or philosophical concept. It was the basis of the conviction of Nazi mass murderers, and it is the foundation of the Declaration of Independence and the UN Universal Declaration of Human Rights. People do not talk about it very much these days, but the natural law goes to the heart of living together: what do we owe other people, or what do they owe us? It exists not to settle arguments, but to remind us what it means to be a human being among others.

Third Story: "Written on the Heart"

"Written on the heart" is a term often used to describe natural law. What it means is, merely by virtue of being a human being, you know it. You cannot help knowing the natural law, even if you do not know you know it, even if you have forgotten it. Life may have become so painful that you have chosen to forget it.

Imagine that during your second year in college you became good friends with Tom. You study together, go drinking together, and gradually learn that you see life pretty much the same way. You make each other laugh.

Sometime early in your senior year he disappears. You wonder about him, but you are busy applying to graduate school and so forth, and so do not think about him too often. One day, his mother calls, sick with worry. She has not seen him in months, but someone told her he is living in a rundown area of the city. She even has a street address. Would you go find him and at least persuade him to call home?

A couple of days later, you set out to find him, and you do. He lives in a crummy apartment in a crummy and dangerous-looking part of the city. When he answers the door, he is so gaunt and ragged that you barely recognize him. When he talks, he slurs his words, like he is coming down from something. He smells like he has not bathed for a week. He is dressed in a torn undershirt and boxer shorts. To get to his apartment, you passed some pretty dangerous-looking characters in the halls, looking like they were doing drug deals. The place stinks of stale urine.

Tom invites you in, and this is what he says:

> Man, dropping out of school, that's the best thing I ever did. No more f-ing teachers telling me what to do. For the first time in my life, I'm happy. Sure, I do drugs. And I deal them too. But I feel free, and when I'm high, nothing can touch me. "Just say no to drugs." Sure, that's what they tell you. What they don't say is how good it feels. They don't want you to know that. I can honestly say that I've never been happier. Say, do you want to shoot up with me? I've got some pretty good stuff here.

With that, you make your goodbyes and almost run to your car. When you get back to your room, you call his mother and say you could not find Tom. That seems like the kindest thing to do.

The Moral

Natural law tells us that Tom is living a lie, that he has made a terrible mistake with his life. He thinks he is happy, but he is not. He is mistaken about his own happiness. In our culture of subjectivity, some may argue that this is impossible. It is not. Natural law is not just about what *not* to do. Natural law tells us in a very general way what the good human life consists of:

- health
- friendship
- family
- education
- a chance to develop one's talents and abilities
- a chance to work and play
- an opportunity to appreciate beauty

The list is incomplete, but it is enough to give you the idea. Tom has missed the boat. He fails to understand the good human life, and is headed in the wrong direction. He has confused happiness with anesthesia, or the pleasure of the moment. Anyone who seriously thinks about this must know this, even if some of Tom's so-called friends hanging out in the halls do not. Happiness is a well-lived human life.

How do I know this? How does anyone know this? Most natural law theorists stress reason, but I am drawn to the explanation of Jacques Maritain, who helped draw up the UN Universal Declaration of Human Rights. Maritain says that we know the natural law by inclination, by which he means intuition, what happens when we look and feel deep inside ourselves. Knowledge by inclination, says Maritain,

> consults the inner leanings of the subject—the experience that he has of himself—and listens to the melody produced by the vibration of deep-rooted tendencies made present in the subject.[2]

The is not the clearest explanation in the world, but about some things, clarity is not the highest value. Often, we feel what we know before we know it. Natural law is like that. Natural law challenges a philosophy and science that puts clear definitions and empirical evidence first. Natural law asks us to trust our cultivated feelings. This depends on a sound upbringing, good teachers, and good examples—role models, as they are now called.

---

2. Maritain, "On Knowledge through Connaturality," 34–35.

36

Do Human Rights Depend on God? Natural Law?

I CANNOT STOP WONDERING whether a belief in human rights depends on God. The answer depends on what you mean by "depends." I am going to be moving around between the terms "God," "natural law," and "religion." They are not synonyms, and I will distinguish them when I think it is important, but do not get too hung up on terms.

I believe in human rights because humans are vulnerable, and in need of protection, including from their own governments. I believe that humans are uniquely valuable and special, and this specialness deserves protection. I believe that, about the fundamentals, people are basically the same: we want to be loved, cared for, challenged, housed, clothed, fed, free of disease, and all the other basics. So, no, my belief in human rights does not depend on God. It depends on what I believe about humans.

But Can I Justify My Belief?

Perhaps the justification of human rights is not the most important thing. Paying attention to what is going on around you—from the people in your neighborhood to people all over the world—is probably more important than justification. For if you look closely, you will be horrified. If you want to persuade people that human rights are important, a movie about suffering people who, for all their difference, are basically like you and me, is often more persuasive than a belief in God.

Nevertheless, it is worth asking whether there any intelligible secular versions of the claim that every human being is sacred, or is the claim inescapably religious? When challenged, can the idea of human rights stand on its own? I think not, and Michael Perry agrees.[1] Terms are obviously

---

1. Perry, *Idea of Human Rights*, 5.

important here, and Perry uses the term "religious" in a wide sense to mean a view opposed to Albert Camus's experience of absurdity, in which I find myself alone in a radically unfamiliar, unresponsive, perhaps even pointless universe. Religion says that the world is finally hospitable to our deepest human yearnings, that the world was in some way made with the human being in mind. From this way of thinking about humanity's place in the universe comes that well-known saying from the *Talmud*:

> He who destroys one person has dealt a blow at the entire universe, and he who sustains or saves one person has sustained the whole world."[2]

Christ's teaching that we should "love one another as I have loved you" invokes a world in which we are all part of one family, and should therefore receive the same gift of each other's loving care. (John 13:34–35) Human rights stem from a vision in which every human life is sacred because the world is hallowed ground, part of a universe in which every life has a purpose and a place, no matter how obscure.

What happens when one tries to justify human rights without the religious story behind it? Some hold that, without religion, not just Christianity, but morality itself becomes explicable only in Nietzsche's terms: as a strategy by which the weak intimidate and suppress the strong. Give up religion, and one must give up any claim to universal brotherhood, the equal value of every life because we are all brothers and sisters in God.

Nevertheless, the question remains. What does someone say to a person who asks, "Why should I think of someone who lives in Outer Mongolia as a member of my human family?" Evolutionary biology tells us that we are not naturally made to identify with distant others in different groups, but with our own group, which is not to say that identification with distant, even anonymous, others cannot be taught. Indeed, it can be taught in such a way that anonymous others no longer exist.

Humans are creatures of imagination and narratives. Judeo-Christianity is the greatest imaginative narrative ever told, capable of bringing an entire universe into its creation story, and so rendering the world and its inhabitants less alien. (I simply do not know enough about Islam to include it here.) The tragedy, of course, is that rather than uniting people, religion is so often used to divide them. Blame this on human nature in groups, not religion.[3] People often write as if religion is the cause of difference and conflict. No, religion is just the tool that people who seek conflict use to divide us.

2. *Jerusalem Talmud*, Sanhedrin 4:8 [37a]).
3. Alford, *Group Psychology*.

Natural Law and Human Rights Are Not the Same

One of my favorite philosophers is Leszek Kolakowski, but about natural law and human rights I think he was mistaken. For him, there is no difference.

> There is no substantial difference between proclaiming "the right to life" and stating that natural law forbids killing. Much as the concept may have been elaborated in the philosophy of the Enlightenment in its conflict with Christianity, the notion of the immutable rights of individuals goes back to the Christian belief in the autonomous status and irreplaceable value of the human personality.[4]

But there *is* a difference. Human rights hold that the individual is the most important thing, that the individual is the locus of all moral value. Individuals are born with rights attached. Natural law comes at human rights from the opposite direction, that of the community. The individual is uniquely valuable because he or she is embedded in a community of others. Not individual human rights, but the principle of brotherhood, is central. I do not have rights because individuals have rights. I have rights because I am a member of a community in which I have an obligation to treat others decently, and they have a similar obligation to me. This community can be as small as the family, or as big as the world.

The point is that the thinking is different. Human rights thinking says the individual is sacred, period. Natural law thinking says the individual is sacred, because he or she is bound by bonds of love, care, obligation, and affection to other members of the community. Human rights are based on individualism; natural law bases rights on relationships of brotherhood and sisterhood, relations that include everyone on the planet, even if they are more easily seen in communities.

Both Are Based on God

Both natural rights and natural law lead back to the same place: we are created by God, and for that reason, have unique value that it is the obligation of others to respect. Nevertheless, there is a difference between an approach that puts the individual first and an approach that puts human brotherhood and sisterhood first.

How much difference this makes in practice is hard to say, but it is worth noting that the United Nations Universal Declaration of Human

---

4. Kolakowski, *Modernity*, 214.

Rights, adopted in the aftermath of World War II, is based on the natural law approach. Referring to every person's membership in the human family as the basis for rights, it was this document, and this reasoning, that eventually 173 countries agreed to, and none opposed.[5] All, it is safe to say, have violated this Declaration, some far more than others. But if hypocrisy is the tribute that vice pays to virtue, then this remains an important first step.

5. Glendon, *World Made New*, 228

Part VI: Topics and Heresies

37

Process Theology and a God of Strong Breasts

THERE ARE A LOT of synonyms for God, particularly in the Old Testament, as Christians call it. One of the more frequent is God Almighty (*El Shaddai*). But strange things happen as ancient words are translated, and the term *El Shaddai* is just as readily translated as "God of the strong breasts." This comes from the term *shadayim*, which means a pair of breasts in Hebrew. *Shad* means breasts and *ai-im* signifies a dual noun. The idea seems to be that God is fertile and giving.[1]

Most images of God, including God Almighty, signify God's strength, power, and magnificence. God is too frequently modeled on the idea of the ancient tyrant. A God of breasts hardly fits with this model, which is why this translation is generally ignored.

Process theology argues that God is strong, but not strong enough to overcome the will of humans, or to overcome the past. God lures us to the best choice, meaning most in keeping with our self-development as persons. But God does not compel, not because he chooses to give us our freedom, but because he lacks the ability to compel. Instead, God is "the great companion—the fellow-sufferer who understands."[2]

Charles Hartshorne, who, along with Alfred North Whitehead, is the founder of process theology, argues that, God, "with infinite subtlety

---

1. http://www.hebrew4christians.com/Names_of_G-d/El/el.html
2. Whitehead, *Process and Reality*, 351.

and appropriate sensitivity, rejoices in all our joys and sorrows in all our sorrows."[3] I will summarize process theology as best I can. Then I will list objections. I agree with these objections, while finding much in process theology that remains attractive.

Heresy or Freedom?

Process theology is more radical than it first appears. Both Judaism and Christianity hold that God is eternal, unchanging, and impassable. That is, God does not feel pleasure or pain from the acts of others, including humans. Process theology rejects these claims. For process theists, God is involved in the world. "God is the supreme Receiver, gathering together in His consciousness all that creatures do and responding appropriately to it." What we do changes God. This claim is made by W. Norris Clarke, a Jesuit philosopher, who argues that "God's consciousness is contingently and qualitatively different because of what we do."[4]

From this perspective, we might say that we are all held in the mind of God because we are in God. The power he exercises over us is persuasive power, the power to order the world so that we are faced with alternatives. Without God, nothing new would ever enter the world, which would be governed by entropy and materialism. Everything would be caused, and nothing new could enter this closed system.

God opens the world and confronts us with choices. Some choices will make us better human beings, which for process theologians means we will have come closer to being the best we possibly can. God tries to make these choices more attractive, but the cost is often dear, as we must abandon ways of life to which we have become accustomed.

A Weak God or a Caring One?

Some reject process theology because God is no longer omnipotent. God remembers us; everyone who ever lived has a place in God's mind. In this respect alone, humans are immortal. God also frees us. But God cannot make humans choose wisely, he cannot overcome natural forces, such as a tornado, and God can only present us with the choices that history has made possible. God cannot change the past, or the limits the past sets on the future.

---

3. Hartshorne, *Divine Relativity*, 54.
4. Clarke, *Philosophical Approach to God*, 92–93.

God did not create the universe *ex nihilo*, but *ex materia*. That is, he created the universe from material already present in chaotic form, matter that resists God's will. This account is entirely compatible with the first sentence of the Bible as rendered in Greek (*Septuagint*), the only ancient language I understand. *En arche epoiesen ho Theos.* "In the beginning God made. . . ." *Epoiesen* just as readily applies to something made from raw materials as it does something out of nothing. Indeed, the former sense is its usual sense in ancient Greek, for it is an ordinary word. *Ex nihilo* is a theological doctrine, not a Biblical one. Compare the creation account in Job 38:1–40, where God must overcome terrible forces to create the world.

The Problem of Evil

God orders chaos, creating the past, present, and future. But even God does not know the future, for while God exists forever, he exists in time, not outside of it. A great advantage of this view is that it overcomes the problem of evil. The problem of evil is this: if God is all powerful, all knowing, and all good, why would he allow the suffering of innocents? Why would he allow Hitler to be born?

The usual answer is that God has chosen to give us our freedom, and with it comes all sorts of terrible things. I ask whether the cost need be so horrifically high. If God is omnipotent, could he not occasionally intervene?

Process theology has a simpler answer. God lacks the power to intervene; he does not because he really cannot. "God is the divine Eros urging the world to new heights of enjoyment."[5] "Enjoyment" is Whitehead's term for self-fulfillment, as measured by God, not man. Some will reject this option. That too is their freedom.

The most common argument against the process theological answer to the problem of evil is that a God without omnipotence is a God too small to worship. David Griffin is a process theologian. About his God, Roth says:

> A God of such weakness, no matter how much he suffers, is rather pathetic. God though he may be, Griffin's God is too small. He inspires little awe, little sense of holiness.[6]

Christians, particularly, should be receptive to process theology, for Christ is an ideal example, his strength made perfect in weakness. (2 Corinthians 12:9) Jesus does not overcome the world; he weeps for it. "Jesus wept" is the shortest, and perhaps the most important sentence in the Bible. (John 11:35)

---

5. Cobb and Griffin, *Process Theology*, 26.
6. Roth, *Critique of Griffin*, 121.

The gospels remain good news. God is with us and for us totally. (Matthew 1:23) He weeps for us, and shares our joy. We are in God (remembered by God) forever.

Criticisms of Process Theology

Among the most powerful criticisms is that process theology eliminates the mystery of God. We now know who God is, what he wants, and what he wills. To my way of thinking, religion is still built on the leap to faith, which includes the inexplicable. Whitehead says that he introduced God to solve a metaphysical problem. If all is process and change, what holds everything together, what prevents the triumph of entropy, and what allows for the introduction of novelty and newness? The answer is God, who creates by setting limits, for example, between past, present, and future.[7]

Trouble is, in practice, process theology often proceeds by asking, in effect, "How do I want God to be?" To be sure, humans participate in creating the God they subsequently discover. Nevertheless, the Bible sets constraints, and process theology ignores those constraints it does not like, such as when God acts like a capricious tyrant, destroying the innocent and guilty alike. (Exodus 23:23) It is good to remember that we are the created, not the creators.

Another problem is the claim that God "lures" us to the best choice. Perhaps he does, but the concept of "lure" is underdeveloped. The claim that "God is the divine Eros urging the world to new heights of enjoyment" is unclear, even if we understand enjoyment as the fullest development of human potential, as we should.[8] Does he lure us by knowing what each of us likes, or does he lure by constraining the choices open to us? I suspect the latter, but process theology is inventing God as it goes along.

Since ancient times, redactors of the Bible have done this, as when God restores Job's fortunes at the end of his trials. (Job 42:7–16) Most scholars believe that the prose conclusion of Job is an addition by later editors, designed to render God less mysterious and more benign. While process theology is not the first to create the God it wants to find, sometimes it seems overly eager to do so.

---

7. Cobb and Griffin, *Process Theology*, 42–43.
8. Cobb and Griffin, *Process Theology*, 26.

Conclusion

Most people encounter process theology as a solution to the problem of evil. More interesting to me is the idea that God need not be all powerful in order to be God. A God who orders the world, remembers the suffering and joy of each one of us, sharing both, while luring (but not compelling) us to make the best choices, is powerful enough for me. It also reminds us to separate goodness and power, something that many people have great difficulty in doing (chapter 3 of this work).

38

God Is the One Who Remembers

GOD IS THE ONE who remembers. Everything. Everyone, every being, is remembered by God, a God who understands human weakness, but also a God who judges each of us. Everything you or I do matters, because it will be remembered by God. Those who made the Holocaust possible will be remembered by God. My grandson, who contributes a large portion of his small salary to charity, will be remembered and judged by God. For all eternity. But that's it. God does not punish the bad or reward the good. In the end, we return to the stardust from which we came. But God knows. Forever. Kind acts and cruel acts are not the same. God knows the difference and remembers, even when humans have forgotten. Everything you do is of eternal significance.

But how could God remember every little thing? The simple and complete answer is he remembers because he is God. From this perspective, God resembles a cosmic memory. But this is not how I prefer to think of God. I think of God as an eternal being, one who has eternity to notice and remember. This is how C. S. Lewis explains it.[1]

Eternity

Our life comes to us in moments, one moment disappearing before the next arrives. This is the way time works. But if God is eternal, then he is not in time. His experience of time is not like ours. If I act this way or that way, God need not be present at that moment to know, remember, and judge. He has all eternity to do so, for an eternal God would experience all things as present to him at once. There are no moments for God. He has eternity to notice and remember one small thing. An eternity to notice and remember everything that each of us does. I do not, however, think this is a particularly

---

1. Lewis, *Mere Christianity*, 167–8.

important problem. Much simpler to say God notices and remembers because that is what God does; that is who he is. But some people seem to like this explanation, or at least feel a need for it.

A God Who Suffers

So far, my account of God has been theistic: God is at a great remove. But I think Christianity has brought to us something quite wonderful, a God who suffers with us. Think of it: God became human (or part of him did) in Jesus Christ to experience human suffering, so that he could know what it was like, as well as how vulnerable, kind, hateful, and cruel humans can be.

Most Christians do not see Christ in this way. They see him as sent to earth to save us from the wages of sin. The singular moment in Christianity is the resurrection of Christ, demonstrating his salvific power. Is my view heresy?

It is often noticed that the Bible says almost nothing about Christ between the years he visited the temple in Jerusalem at twelve years of age (Luke 2:41–51), and his reappearance at about thirty, three years before his death. More than half of Christ's life is unaccounted for. I imagine that Christ spent the time traveling and listening and sharing in humanity, the better to know who we are. I cannot imagine that he came to love humanity during that time, for we are not a lovable species, but evidently he did.

As important as what Christ shared with us is what he taught us. His teachings are called the *kerygma*, as noted earlier. His most important lesson is the simplest, but not easy: "Love one another as I have loved you." (John 13:34) Too much is made of Christ's suffering, and not enough about his message to the living and loving. The love Jesus is speaking of is a self-sacrificing love, in which the best interest of the other person comes first. Jesus takes this love to its ultimate conclusion: "There is no greater love than to lay down one's life for one's friends." (John 15:13)

What about Prayer?

About prayer, the same idea applies. God listens, remembers, and judges. Do you pray for yourself, or others? Is there a connection between your prayers and your deeds? Do you try to bargain with God? The principle of prayer is simple: not my will but Thy will be done. Prayer is not so much supplication as it is acceptance. A thoughtful prayer from a sincere person is worthwhile in itself. God does not answer prayers; he remembers them.

A Christian Heresy

My account of God is a Christian heresy. I focus not only on what Christ taught, but what he learned, in order that a distant God might know what it is to live among humans. I could pick Biblical passages to support this view, but I am not out to offer a labored biblical defense. Better a heretical view of God than to imagine that he does not matter.

God matters, because he judges and remembers everything we do. In a curious way, my view resembles Nietzsche's doctrine of the eternal return.[2] Act as if everything you have done, experienced, and suffered will be repeated for eternity. Are you strong enough to stand it?, asks Nietzsche. In my version, it is not the eternal return but the eternal significance of what you do, because your acts (I do not know about thoughts) will be remembered for all eternity. How will they be judged? By the standards of the *kerygma*, Christ's teachings. That is enough God for me.

---

2. Nietzsche, *Gay Science*, paras. 245, 381.

39

What Is So Great About Faith?

WHAT IS SO GREAT about faith? It depends on what you mean. Most people today seem to regard faith as a so-called leap of faith in which we simply choose to believe something that cannot be demonstrated or proven (chapter 9.1 of this work). Society, or one's own needy self, says that I need to believe, and I do, keeping quiet about my doubts, if I even let myself have any. Real faith is given by the grace of God. We do not choose faith; faith chooses us. Nevertheless, there are things we can do to receive it. Prime among these is humility, and living as Christ would have us live, as though we were men or women who deserve grace.

How Do I Know if I Have Received Grace?

There are two answers. If you have to ask, you have not received it. If you think you have received grace, you have not. Just continue to live as though you were worthy of grace. In the end, perhaps this is the most we can hope for. What is more important: to know that you have grace, or to be worthy of it?

Revelation

Revelation is central to religious faith. We do not simply have faith in things unknown, like ghosts. To have faith is to believe in revelation, as it is expressed in the Holy Scriptures. Christianity is a revelatory religion, originating in the person and sayings of Jesus, whom Christians believe is a man-God who entered into history at a particular time and place.

The historical evidence supports time and space. Paul's letters and the gospels support the rest. But is it reasonable to believe in revelation and faith?

A little basic philosophy of knowledge (epistemology) helps. Objective statements, such as scientific statements, can be shown false. Yet this is not quite right, because even science is never certain. Think of all the scientific statements once thought true that are now held to be false. What is special about science is not that its statements are guaranteed true, but that its statements can be shown false by comparison with objective facts as they are known at the time.[1]

Lots of important statements cannot be shown false. They are neither objective nor scientific. Love cannot be shown false (unless you think it is all about pheromones), but love can be real, deep, fatuous, and many other things. Many of the most important things in life, such as the beauty of a poem, or the pain of loss, are subjective truths: statements that become true because we feel or believe them. Faith in God is more like love or beauty than it is like science. Faith in God may be subjectively true or false (I have it or I do not), but it cannot be proven or disproven. The same goes for the claim that faith in God is reasonable or unreasonable. It is neither more, nor less, reasonable or unreasonable than love, beauty, or poetry.

Faith Should Not Be Blind

Pistis, the word almost always translated as "faith" (more than 240 times in the New Testament) was used regularly by ancient Greeks to refer to the presentation of evidence. It is also used to mean "to be persuaded" by the evidence.

> Christian faith is not belief in the absence of evidence. It is the proper response to the evidence.[2]

Faith is not blind. It is not guaranteed by the scriptures, but it uses the scriptures as evidence. However, since the first accounts of Christ appear more than two generations after his death (Paul's First Thessalonians, circa 50 AD), we must assume that Paul was relying heavily—if not exclusively—on oral tradition.

The first gospel was written by Mark sometime around 70 AD, relying on an oral tradition and written sources now lost. Matthew, Luke, and John were written several decades later. Faith in "scriptural inerrancy" makes no sense, primarily because the gospels were written with an agenda. One part of the agenda was to show that Christ fulfilled the prophecies of the Old

---

1. Popper, *Logic of Scientific Discovery*.
2. https://www.bethinking.org/truth/faith-is-about-just-trusting-god-isnt-it

Testament, the other to demonstrate that he was divine. He may have been, but while the scriptures provide evidence, they are not proof.

Faith should be approached in this light. Those who base their faith on sound scriptural evidence have done what they can, as much as faith can ask. Faith cannot ask for more (or it would not be faith), but neither should it be judged by less.

The Biggest Enemy of Faith Is the Common Culture

Less than two centuries ago, almost all North Americans and Europeans would have had subjective certainty about God: his existence, the existence of heaven and hell, and so forth. Today, most lack this certainty, and many hold their beliefs casually, as though they hardly matter. The result is change, but can one with any certainty say that it is progress?

Not progress, just cultural plausibility, is the reason for the loss of faith, and rise in religious skepticism, as science and technology unravel nature, and smartphones take the place of God. (I am only half joking: your smartphone never sleeps, and always knows where you are, and many owners seem to treat them as sacred objects.) It is not just smartphones, of course, but progress in science, technology, and medicine that have made God seem less plausible. But none of these bear on subjective truth, the realm of faith.

Faith depends on imagination, the ability to imagine a world other than it is: mere matter. Scientists imagine how matter can be rearranged, and so sometimes change how we experience the world. But poets have been changing and rearranging how we experience the world, and how we feel about it, for millennia. Faith comes closer to poetry, and we have been losing our poetic and metaphysical imaginations for some time now.

Faith Communities and "the Individual"

If the common culture is the biggest threat to faith, then faith communities can be the greatest threat to authentic faith. How is it that most Christians seem to have the same experience of God? Because God *is* the same for most Christians, or because faith can too easily fall victim to group suggestion and group pressure?

Subjective truth is the most creative truth, and the truth most vulnerable to group pressure—intended or unintended. This is what one of my favorite religious writers, Søren Kierkegaard, was thinking about when he said that he wanted his tombstone to read simply "the individual" (it does not). Kierkegaard believed that Christianity can be true even if only one person in the world believes. He is wrong; religion is a communal experience, as the Jews and first Christians understood. But faith is an individual experience; it happens one by one. If it does not, then it is not faith, but something else, like conformity.

The Problem Is Insoluble

The problem is insoluble. Faith is an experience of revelation through scripture. But these experiences of revelation are so socially impressionable, and so difficult to separate from socially held beliefs, that they are in constant danger of becoming little more than consensus and tradition. Both have their place, but not at the heart of faith. The best we can do, I think, is to ask people who make faith-based claims what the scriptural authority for that claim is. Doing so would mean taking faith seriously, not just something someone wants to believe, or is afraid not to.

40

Do you Have Soul?

I IMAGINE THAT MOST Jews and Christians believe they have a soul. I imagine most believers of all faiths believe in the soul, though what they mean by "soul" varies considerably. Surprising then is how unclear the concept of the soul is within Christianity itself. The Bible has two different accounts of the fate of the soul, and attempts to reconcile them are clumsy.

Some passages of the Bible suggest that when you die, your soul goes immediately to heaven. Jesus promised this to the thief hanging on the cross beside him when he says, "Truly, I tell you, today you will be with me in Paradise." (Luke 23:43) At other times, Jesus referred to resurrection as *anastasis*, which most likely refers to the raising up of the dead at the end of the present age. (Matthew 22:29–33) Other books of the Bible emphasize the resurrection of the body.

> It is the same way with the resurrection of the dead. Our earthly bodies are planted in the ground when we die, but they will be raised to live forever. (1 Corinthians 15:42–43)

The resurrection of the body at the end of days is so central to Christianity that it is included in the Apostles' Creed and the Nicene Creed.

How these Two Views Are Reconciled

The usual way these two views are reconciled is:

- Our soul goes immediately to heaven, where it resides in the Lord's presence.
- Our body is buried until the day of resurrection.
- When Christ returns, we will be raised bodily from the grave.
- Body and soul reunited, and we will be with the Lord forever.

It works but it is clumsy.

I used to think the resurrection of the body was a weird idea. I still do, but I see its advantages. It is sometimes argued that the Christian concept of the soul came from Plato, for whom the soul (*psyche*) is separate from the body, and always longing to be free of the body.

Plato has Socrates' last words as these:

> Crito, we owe a cock to Asclepius. Pay our debt and no forgetting. (*Phaedo* 118 a-b)

Socrates was not delirious from the poison he had been forced to drink. Asclepius was the god of healing. When a person who had been ill recovered, it was traditional to make an offering to the god. Socrates is saying that embodied life is itself like an illness. Health is the separation of the soul from the body, so that it can consort with the eternal ideas, or forms (*eidos*), above all, goodness and beauty. It is not difficult to see how Plato was Christianized.

Embodiment

The advantage of emphasizing the resurrection of the body is that it asserts the value of the body and its experiences. The soul is not body, but it is distributed throughout the body so that soul experience is body experience (though not just body experience), which was roughly Aristotle's view (De anima, 408b, 414a). It is not difficult to see how Saint Augustine baptized Aristotle, as the saying goes.

Too often, Christianity has been directed against the body, as though bodily needs, pleasures, and desires are bad. The embodied soul reminds us that we are not just our bodies, but we are also our bodies.

What Is the Soul?

From one perspective, the soul is just me: my sense of myself as a continuous entity over time, including my hopes, loves, and dreams. The ancient Greek term for soul, *psyche*, lends itself to this psyche-logical perspective. From this perspective, you do not so much *have* a soul as you *are* a soul. You have a body. Personhood is not based on having a body. A soul is required. Consider the late physicist Stephen Hawking. His body was almost useless; he communicated using a single cheek muscle attached to a speech-generating device. Perhaps his body was a burden, but no one would question his rich personhood.

What Does God Have to Do with It?

The problem with making personhood the defining dimension of the soul is that the soul is left to itself. If I am my soul, what does God have to do with it? Is he just a judge sitting on a white throne waiting to send me to heaven or hell? (Revelation 20:11–15) I think it makes more sense to see our souls as merged with God at the same time as he breathed the breath of life into us. (Genesis 2:7) *Pneuma*, breath, is another word for soul. Our souls do not belong to God, or if they do, then we have the power to make them our own. But exercising this power is risky business, for we will have exiled ourselves from the presence that unites the universe.

Ashes to Stardust

That the soul is sacred, shared in some way with God, does not mean that it is immortal in any personal sense. On Ash Wednesday, we are reminded that we are mere mortals, "ashes to ashes, dust to dust," as it says in the Book of Common Prayer. The committal continues: "in sure and certain hope of resurrection unto eternal life."

I am not exactly what "sure and certain hope" is. If it is certain, then it is not hope. If it is not certain, then it is just hope. I think it should run like this: "ashes to ashes, dust to stardust."

"We are stardust" is not just a line from Joni Mitchell about Woodstock. Astrophysicists agree.

> . . . [e]verything we are, and everything in the universe and Earth originated from stardust, and it continually floats through us even today. It directly connects us to the universe, rebuilding our bodies over and again over our lifetimes.[1]

At death, we return to the basic elements of which we are made, and the cycle starts all over again. Our souls are sacred, an expression of the One who made it all, but the soul is not personal. It is what we share with God and the universe.

Do I know this? Of course not. It is just a likely story, but one that has soul.

---

1. Schrijver and Schrijver, *Living with the Stars*.

41

"The Grand Inquisitor," Then and Now

"The Grand Inquisitor" is a short story by Fyodor Dostoevsky in *The Brothers Karamazov*. It is told by Ivan, an atheist, to his brother Alyosha (Alexei) who is studying at a monastery. Ivan's fable begins with Christ's brief visit to Spain in the middle of the Spanish Inquisition. Rather than arriving on clouds of glory, Christ quietly appears amid a crowd of people, healing some, and raising a dead child. Though he speaks not a word, everyone knows who he is. The Grand Inquisitor has Christ jailed.

The people do not want you, says the Inquisitor, because all you can offer them is freedom and salvation. What people really want is magic, mystery, and authority. Add bread, and they will follow you anywhere. Christ made the mistake of offering them freedom.

> Instead of the strict ancient law, man had in future to decide for himself with a free heart what was good and what was evil, having only your image before him as a guide.[1]

It is not enough. More than that, the quiet reappearance of Christ disrupts the authority of the church and the rules it has laid down. The inquisitor will have Christ burned at the stake the next day.

Christ is silent, and the Grand Inquisitor continues. The Church, he says, is led by the few men who are strong enough to accept the burden of freedom, the knowledge of nothingness. It is the Roman Catholic Church to which the Inquisitor refers, but his arguments apply to almost any organized religion. Under the leadership of the strong few, humanity will live and die in happy ignorance. Though he leads them only to "death and destruction," they will be happy along the way. "Anyone who can appease a man's conscience can take his freedom away from him." Most would give it gladly.

---

1. Dostoevsky, *Brothers Karamazov*, book 5, c 5.

Christ wants what he never can have: for people to choose the way of Christ with perfect freedom to do otherwise. It is the free choice of men and women of His way that is most precious to him. As the Inquisitor puts it to Christ, "the freedom of humanity's faith was the dearest of all things to you." Christ wants people to believe for the right reasons, not just eternal life, but an eternal life that participates in perfect communion with God.

Trouble is, people are not like that. Take away their earthly bread, and they will do anything and believe anything to get it back. The Inquisitor is part of a small regime that has taken on the burden of freedom, so that men and women can be happy in the few short years they spend on this planet between the nothingness before birth and the extinction of death. Having not spoken a word the entire time, the silent Christ walks over to the Grand Inquisitor and kisses him full on the lips. Continuing on his way, Christ walks quietly into the darkness; he has not yet reappeared.

What if the Grand Inquisitor Is on to Something?

Every Christian believes that Christ arose from death after three days, and that this is a promise to all believers. But, does not this promise resemble a bribe? What if it is simply good to believe in the values embodied by Christ because these are good values? Christianity is good for its own sake, not just for the sake of eternal life.

We become the best we can be when we love God and love each other. This is more than the Golden Rule, because it puts Christ, not just my own needs and desires, at the center. Christ was pointing in this direction when he said:

> Thou shalt love the Lord thy God with all thy heart, and with all thy soul, and with all thy mind. This is the first and great commandment. And the second is like unto it, Thou shalt love thy neighbor as thyself. On these two commandments hang all the law and the prophets. (Matthew 22: 35–40)

Christ was pointing in this direction because it is not just "do unto others . . .," but love them. Love their lives as you love the lives of your children. Is this the hidden moral of The Grand Inquisitor? Choose God not for the sake of eternal life, but because God is worthy of our love, which includes following Christ's example inasmuch as humans can.

How many would remain Christians after this? I am not sure. Many people, I hope, could be convinced of the value of a Pauline community (chapter 28.1 of this work). Exactly what such a community would look like, I know not. I do know that Paul had the right idea.

> For Paul, [love] had (for want of a better word) a *social* meaning as well. The social form of love for Paul was distributive justice and nonviolence, bread and peace.[2]

Bread and Nationalism

Bread was important to the Grand Inquisitor as well. Give them bread and they will follow you anywhere, he says. What if we think of this bread as the bread of communion, making us part of one body? For, the problem that religion addresses and the Grand Inquisitor exploits is the isolation and loneliness of mass society. No amount of magic and mystery can take the place of community, but community can help fill the need addressed by magic, mystery, and tyrannical authority. Nationalism is fake community, in which people are bound together by common hatreds instead of love.

2. Borg and Crossan, *The First Paul*, 204.

42

What Is So Great About Eternity?

For all its importance in Christian thought, the concept of eternity in the Bible is remarkably unclear. The two most important Christian thinkers, Saints Augustine and Aquinas, place God outside of time, in what is called the *nunc stans*. *Nunc stans* is the opposite of the way we ordinarily think of eternity: as time going on forever. In the *nunc stans*, you experience all of time in a single moment. Or you would if you were God.

As Augustine put it, we pass through God's today.[1] The experience would be something like seeing time as though it were space, a plane spread out before you. You might focus on one part of the plane or another, but all time is there to be experienced in a moment. The term is Latin (no surprise). *Nunc* means "now," and *stans* refers to "stand." In the *nunc stans*, all of time stands before you now.

Not in the Bible

Trouble is, this way of thinking about time is nowhere in the Bible. (I will confine myself to the New Testament, but the problem is found in the Old Testament as well.) The Greek term *aionios*, for which so many translations mistakenly use the word "eternal," is derived from the noun "aeon." "Aeon" means "age," or "ages." Thus, the word translated as "eternal" really refers to an aeon or age, not forever. When Jesus says, "I am with you always, to the end of the age," he does not mean forever, but until the end of the present age; that is, until the eschaton. *Aidios* is the ancient Greek term for "eternal," and it is used only once in the Bible in reference to God. (Romans 1:20)

While Augustine and Aquinas interpret eternal as meaning the *nunc stans*, their interpretation is not so much Biblical as it is philosophical, a way perhaps to preserve God's dignity. For the Bible, "eternal" means a very long

---

1. Augustine, *Confessions*, bk 11, section 17.

time. For God, it is perhaps a time so long as to be the same as forever, but it is a forever *in* time, not *outside* of it.

In translations and discussions of the Bible, "eternity" is often used as a synonym for "eternal life." But once again, the concept is remarkably unclear. Nowhere are the Greek terms *aidios* and its equivalents employed. But rather than go further into this issue, I want to mention a few problems that arise with the concept of eternity today.

Rage, Rage against the Dying of the Light

In commenting on a verse from the well-known poem by Dylan Thomas, the author of a book on eternity asked,

> Who, for instance, would not resonate with one of the most famous poems of our time? "Do not go gentle into that good night, Old age should burn and rave at close of day; Rage rage against the dying of the light."[2]

Well, I do not resonate with it, if "resonate" means something like "agree." Eire continues,

> ... [w]e as a species tend to find the very concept of *nothing* and the thought of *not existing* unimaginable and abhorrent.[3]

Acceptance has its place, particularly in old age (and I am getting there). Happiness wants eternity, but hell *is* eternity. I cannot imagine just going on forever. It is death that makes life meaningful; it is death that gives not just poignancy but intensity to life. Everything we do matters more, because about the most important things there are no second chances.

Not only does death give intensity and meaning to life, but it is simply the case that, for many, the thought of nonbeing is a relief. Murder, the death of a child: we rage at that. But for many, and not always the old, death is a relief. I am not saying this is how it should be. This is how it is. For many, the thought of an ending brings as much comfort as it does fear.

Death Equivalents: What We Really Fear

Sigmund Freud argued that we cannot fear death, for we cannot imagine nonbeing. Robert Jay Lifton, a psychiatrist, writes that we fear not death, but "death equivalents," such as separation, loneliness, darkness, and

---

2. Eire, *Brief History*, 12.
3. Eire, *Brief History*, 15.

abandonment (chapter 32 of this work). This makes sense to me. We are creatures of attachment; people die of loneliness. What is so often confused with death are images, feelings, and experiences of abandonment. But death is not abandonment. Death is nonbeing.

Dying alone and uncared for is a terrible experience of abandonment most of us fear. Nonbeing is terrifying to the degree that we confuse it with death equivalents, an easy thing to do, especially in an individualistic world, where the possibility of abandonment in illness and old age is real. The fact that we can be abandoned by our own minds, as in dementia, is equally scary. I am not saying there is nothing to fear about death. There are many things to fear, including what is sometimes called a "bad death," but it is really a bad end of life, such as pointless medical intervention and poor pain control.

Transience Does Not Devalue Anything

I think the transience of life makes life sacred. Because there are only so many tomorrows, each day is more important. Evidently, this is not how many people reason. Eire argues that, without eternity, every evil is ephemeral.

For, how can anything transient be condemned, even the worst atrocities?[4] This makes no sense. Transience mitigates nothing. Would we say that because a torturer tortured his victim for "only" an hour, that it is transient, of no great importance? Of course not. The most important things in life are not measured by eternity, but by the quality of our lives, including how deeply we care for others. Transience allows us to feel deeply, for we could not sustain certain feelings for a lifetime, nor would we want to. An endless kiss is a good line for a song (Bruce Springsteen), but in reality, it would be hell.

A Glimpse of Eternity

Pope John Paul II wrote that, in the absence of eternity, the present requires too much importance.[5] No matter how much we have, we will never be satisfied, for only eternal things truly satisfy. In one respect, John Paul was correct. As long as humans remain as we are—vulnerable creatures of attachment—certain values will always be right, and other values wrong. It is always good to care for life, always wrong to destroy life, even if there are exceptions. In pursuing these values, we participate, inasmuch as humans possibly can, in the eternity of universal values. We do not become eternal, but we share in things eternal. Is that not enough?

4. Eire, *Brief History*, 198.
5. John Paul II, *Sollicitudo Rei Socialis*.

43

Christianity and Technology

BEGINNING IN 1943, A small group of Christian intellectuals began to think seriously about the postwar world. The United States and Britain had talked about victory since the beginning of the war, but no one was certain, and many had grave doubts. But by 1943, victory was in sight, even if its details were not.

These Christian intellectuals included Jacques Maritain, W. H. Auden, C. S. Lewis, Simone Weil, and T. S. Eliot. Auden and Eliot were poets, and Lewis, an Oxford don, is probably best known for his children's work of fiction, *Chronicles of Narnia*. The relationship among these men and woman was rich, complex, and varied. Some worked together, some alone. This work devotes several chapters to Weil and Lewis.

The Problem

The problem they worried about is what sort of people the winner of this war of civilizations would become. What values could substitute for that of winning the war? Would the technological thinking that won the war destroy the values we fought for? It might, they argued, and the only thing that could stop it was an education that fosters humanity, sensibility, and pity.

> ...Weil echoes Maritain and Lewis in calling for an education that trains the sensibility and affections at least as seriously as it attends to the mind: "To show what is beneficial, what is obligatory, what is good—that is the task of education."[1]

> ... [i]t is inevitable that evil should dominate wherever the technical side of things is either completely or almost completely sovereign.[2]

1. Jacobs, *Year of Our Lord*, 164.
2. Weil, *Need for Roots*, 200–201.

It seems an old-fashioned and odd idea that a humane education in the liberal arts should be thought to be the answer to the crisis of civilization that came out of World War II. The crisis is not that we do not have the answers, but that the questions no longer seem important: who am I, what should I do, how should I live, and what may I hope?

I recently retired after forty years of teaching ancient Greek and medieval philosophy to undergraduates at a large state university in the United States. Most students were worried about how much their education was costing, and whether they would they get a good job. More than a few openly questioned the value of what I was teaching. Yet in my own small way, I often thought I was doing my part to preserve a tradition concerned with the issues Maritain and his companions were concerned with.

Sometimes I still think so. At other times, I think the day it might have mattered is long gone, and unlikely to return. In 1943, it still seemed possible that the end of the war would bring a more humane world, and Christianity could make a difference. Interestingly, none of the people discussed here thought it would be a good idea to teach Christianity. It would be a good idea to teach the arts and literature, which help humanize us. Religion is not so much taught as learned.

The Social Beast?

Maritain, like Lewis and Weil, is concerned that the social beast—that is, mass society—will subordinate the individual in a soft and comfortable totalitarianism, one that even feels like freedom.

> . . . [w]hat Americans need to learn from Europe's catastrophe is the danger of failing to cultivate intellectual and spiritual aspirations beyond what one's everyday culture encourages.[3]

I am a professor, but I think they are wrong. An acquaintance with the worlds of art and literature is valuable, but more important is how we live every day. The bonds of family and community are more important than the bonds of nations. A healthy community, one that respects its members and gives every man and woman a chance to make a decent living, is more important than philosophy. Everyday life *is* mundane, but that is what mundane means, and it is OK.

The crisis in America today has only a little to do with the decline of art and literature, and a great deal to do with economic and cultural insecurity. Economic insecurity is obvious. Cultural insecurity is best seen as the

---

3. Jacobs, *Year of Our Lord*, 129.

loss of anything to believe in. Here religion is important, but it should not be seen as "spiritual Benzedrine for the earthly city," as one of them put it. The job of religion is not to strengthen state and society, and foster loyalty among its citizens. Here C. S. Lewis is right. Everyday life may be mundane, but people are not.

> There are no *ordinary* people. You have never talked to a mere mortal. Nations, cultures, arts, civilization—these are mortal, and their life is to ours as the life of a gnat. But it is immortals whom we joke with, work with, marry, snub, and exploit—immortal horrors or everlasting splendours.[4]
>
> To embrace this account of the human person, which is of course a traditional Christian one, is to decenter the world of politics—not to ignore it, but to shift it toward the periphery, to see it as among the second rather than the first things.[5]

Respect for our friends and neighbors, recognizing that everyone has a valued place, is the goal. I believe that Lewis's perspective helps, but it is possible to know these things simply by living among others who act this way. It helps if they can explain why this way is good to others in terms even a child could understand. Healthy communities are their own reward, generally self-perpetuating unless outside forces intervene. Economics and politics as they are currently practiced are outside forces.

And Today . . .

World War II was not a war between technocratic Nazis and something else, but between two highly developed technocratic-industrial societies. Technocracy threatens community, which is not all bad. Community itself always threatens to become closed and closed minded. But nationalism does not open communities; it destroys communities. The result is citizens who feel displaced, disoriented, and devalued. It is happening in the United States today. If fascism ever comes to America, it will be called "Americanism" (my riff on a great quote).

We are a long, long way from fascism, and there are powerful countervailing forces. But the concerns of this small group of intellectuals were not about the renewed rise of fascism. They were worried about what happens when there is nothing left to fight for. They worried about a way of life that isolated the individual, making him or her vulnerable to extreme

---

4. Lewis, *Weight of Glory*, 46.
5. Jacobs, *Year of Our Lord*, 56.

ideologies that promised belonging. Nativism is about belonging by making sure others do not.

Finally, they were worried about a world in which religion no longer provided a counterbalance to materialism and the crowd. They were worried about a world in which men might once again mistake themselves for gods, for no vigorous tradition remained to tell them otherwise. They were right to be worried then, and we are right to be worried now.

Part VII

44

Conclusion

A PASSAGE I HAVE quoted frequently, "His strength made perfect in weakness" (2 Corinthians 12:9), captures so much of what I have tried to say in this book. It means that God chose to suffer as humans do so that he, Jesus Christ, could come to know every human experience. The view that Jesus suffered crucifixion so that humans might have eternal life, so central to Christian doctrine, has never seemed as important to me as a God who would humble himself so that he might know human suffering, as well as human joy. From this perspective, the eschaton has already happened. It happened the moment Christ entered human history. Rather than waiting for Advent, we should live as though we are already saved. This is sometimes called a proleptic interpretation of the New Testament.

Does "saved" mean eternal life? I do not know, but I think it is not the most important question. Not "am I saved?" but, "do I lead a life that follows the teachings and example of Jesus, insofar as humans can?", is the important question.

Since his crucifixion, God has stepped back from human history. In his place, he left the Holy Spirit, the paraclete, who may subtly guide us, if we are open to his presence. Natural law is, I believe, partly an expression of that guidance. It is not up to God to save us. It is up to us to save ourselves, which means helping make this world a decent place for every human to live. We have a long way to go.

The great contribution of Christianity is the creation of a God who knows human experience from the inside out, a God who promises not eternal life, but his perpetual presence in our lives. That is the *kerygma*.

The World of the Bible Is Long Gone . . . What Is Next?

Since the spirit and wonder world of The Bible, as Bultmann puts it, is long gone, what else can support belief? The only answer is faith, and it is on this answer that so many contemporary Christian thinkers agree, including Barth and Bultmann. It is on this same insight that Kierkegaard founded existentialism in the nineteenth century. But while I am always impressed by people with deep faith, thinking that they make ours a better world to live in, I am not so impressed with faith itself as an answer. Faith means, "I believe it because I choose to believe it," and no more. Kierkegaard showed us the power of that insight, but also its dangers. How is it that millions (perhaps billions) of people just happen to believe the same thing? Is it faith, or is it socialization and the fear of being left out? Not left out of salvation, but left out of the fellowship of humans. If so, faith is not a very firm foundation, and certainly not a spiritually ennobling one. There is an alternative. I have called it the mythical imagination.

In an increasingly scientific and materialistic era, in which even love is explained in terms of pheromones and hormones, and our psychology in terms of neuroscience, it seems that the capacity to imagine an alternative world, a mythical world, has been mortally wounded. The great virtue of not just Christianity, but religion, is that it provides a place to stand that is an alternative to worldliness. This too is the promise of the *kerygma*, that the world of our mythical imaginations is as real as the material world. Winnicott calls this alternative reality "transitional space," and his idea seems right: transitional space occupies that place between the everyday material world and the imaginary worlds of fantasists and mad men.

Myths occupy this space. The question about myths is not whether they are true or false; the question is whether they are rich or impoverished, whether they help us live better, fuller lives.

In calling religion a myth, I am saying no more about its truth or falsity than I would be if I called science a myth. I am talking about narratives, and whether they open us to a wider world, a wonder world of its own. Much science does this, whether it's cosmology, and its world of dark holes and red dwarfs, or the study of the tiniest invisible entities, such as quarks, whose existence remains hypothetical.[1] God too remains a hypothesis, but a good one, for God encourages us to think of each other as sacred, made in his image, and more precious than rubies.

Yet even as I write this, I cannot help but think of all the men, women, and children who have been killed in the name of God. I have argued, against Jon Mills and others, that God is just the excuse. Humans like nothing so much as justified objects of their hatred. Religion provides this, and so I must close on a somber note. While religion provides us with narratives by which we can live more meaningful lives, it is too often used for darker purposes. In our heart of hearts, I believe we all know the difference between love and hate. Love is what Christ teaches. Love is what the natural law is about. But just as natural law can be corrupted by our darker impulses, so can belief in God. Reinhold Niebuhr says that original sin is the only empirically verifiable doctrine of the Christian faith. I believe that he was thinking along these lines. It has not to do with angels and devils, but the conflict in the human heart. Let us be sure that religion is on the right side.

---

1. http://thescienceexplorer.com/universe/how-do-we-know-quarks-exist-if-they-have-never-been-directly-detected

Bibliography

Adorno, Theodor. *Minima Moralia: Reflections from Damaged Life*. Translated by E.F.N. Jephcott. London: NLB, 1974.
Alexander, Eben. *Proof of Heaven: A Neurosurgeon's Journey into the Afterlife*. New York: Simon & Schuster, 2012.
Alford, C. Fred. *After the Holocaust*. New York: Cambridge University Press, 2009.
———. *Group Psychology and Political Theory*. New Haven: Yale University Press, 1994.
———. "Holocaust." In *The Encyclopedia of Political Thought*, edited by Michael T. Gibbons. New York: John Wiley & Sons, 2015.
———. *The Psychoanalytic Theory of Greek Tragedy*. New Haven: Yale University Press, 1992.
Aquinas, Thomas. *Summa Theologica*. Claremont, CA: Coyote Canyon, 2010. [original circa 1270]
Auden, W. H. *A Certain World*. New York: Viking, 1970.
Augustine, Saint. *Confessions*. Translated by Sarah Ruden. New York: Random House. [original 400 CE]
Bacevich, Andrew J. "Introduction" to Reinhold Niebuhr, *The Irony of American History*, 45–218. Chicago: University of Chicago Press, 2008.
Bainton, Roland. *Here I Stand*. Nashville, TN: Abingdon, 1983.
Banks, Russell. *The Sweet Hereafter*. New York: Harper, 2011.
Barker, Kenneth, ed. *NIV Study Bible*. Grand Rapids, MI: Zondervan, 1995
Barth, Karl. *The Word of God and Theology*. Edinburgh: T&T Clark, 2011.
Bash, Anthony. *Forgiveness and Christian Ethics*. New York: Cambridge University Press, 2007.
Bauckham, Richard. *The Theology of Jürgen Moltmann*. Edinburgh: T&T Clark, 1995.
Beale G. K., and David Campbell. *Revelation: A Shorter Commentary*. Grand Rapids, MI: Eerdmans, 2015
Berger, Benjamin Lyle. "Qohelet and the Exigencies of the Absurd." *Biblical Interpretation* 9.2 (2001) 141–179.
Berger, Peter. *A Rumor of Angels: Modern Society and the Rediscovery of the Supernatural*. New York: Open Road Media, 1970.
Blanshard, Brand. The Gifford Lectures: Reason and Faith in Kierkegaard. https://www.giffordlectures.org/books/reason-and-belief/chapter-vi-reason-and-faith-kierkegaard
Bonhoeffer, Dietrich. *The Cost of Discipleship*. Translated by R. H. Fuller. New York: Macmillan, 1963. [German original 1937]

———. *Ethics*. Translated by Neville Horton Smith. New York: Simon and Schuster, 1995. [original 1949]

———. *Letters and Papers from Prison*, enlarged ed. Translated by Reginald Fuller and Frank Clark. New York: Simon and Schuster, 1971.

———. *Life Together*. New York: Harper & Row, 1954.

———. *Sanctorum Communio: A Theological Study of the Sociology of the Church*. Philadelphia: Fortress, 2009.

Borg, Marcus J. and John Dominic Crossan. *The First Paul: Reclaiming the Radical Visionary Behind the Church's Conservative Icon*. New York: HarperCollins, 2009.

Brooks, David. "Obama, Gospel and Verse." *The New York Times*, April 26, 2007.

Brown, Raymond. *The Gospel According to John*, vol 2. New Haven: Anchor Bible, 1970.

Brzezinski, Zbigniew. *Out of Control: Global Turmoil on the Eve of the 21st Century*. New York: Touchstone, 1993.

Buber, Martin. *Between Man and Man*. Translated by Ronald Gregor Smith. New York: Routledge, 2002. [reprint of the 1947 ed.]

———. *I and Thou*. Translated by Walter Kaufmann. New York: Scribner, 1970.

———. *The Legend of the Baal-Shem*. Translated by Maurice Friedman. New York: Harper and Row, 1955.

Bultmann, Rudolf. *The New Testament and Mythology*. Edited and translated by Schubert Ogden. Minneapolis, MN: Fortress, 1984.

———. *This World and the Beyond: Marburg Sermons*. New York: Scribner, 1960.

Byrne, Brendan. *A Costly Freedom: A Theological Reading of Mark's Gospel*. Collegeville, MN: Liturgical, 2008.

Camus, Albert. *The Fall*. Translated by Justin O'Brien. New York: Vintage, 1991.

———. *The Myth of Sisyphus and Other Essays*. Translated by Justin O'Brien. New York: Vintage, 1955.

———. *Notebooks*, vol. 1, 1935–1942. Translated by Philip Thody. Chicago: Ivan R. Dee, 2010.

———. *The Plague*. Translated by Stuart Gilbert. New York: Vintage, 1972.

Carson, D. A. *The Gospel According to John*. Grand Rapids, MI: Eerdmans, 1991.

Chesterton, G. K. *Introduction to the Book of Job*. London: Cecil Palmer and Hayward, 1916. http://www.chesterton.org/introduction-to-job.

Clarke, W. Norris. *The Philosophical Approach to God: A Neo-Thomist Perspective*. Winston-Salem, NC: Wake Forest University Press, 1979.

Cobb, John B. Jr. and David Ray Griffin. *Process Theology*. Louisville, KY: Westminster John Knox, 1976.

Congdon, David. *Rudolf Bultmann: A Companion to His Theology*. Eugene, OR: Cascade/Wipf and Stock, 2015.

Cooney, John. "Thomas Merton: the hermit who never was, his young lover and mysterious death." *The Irish Times*, November 9, 2015. https://www.irishtimes.com/culture/books/thomas-merton-the-hermit-who-never-was-his-young-lover-and-mysterious-death-1.2422818

Crouter, Richard. *Reinhold Niebuhr: On Politics, Religion, and Christian Faith*. Oxford, UK: Oxford University Press, 2010.

Des Pres, Terrence. Review of *The Broken Connection: On Death and the Continuity of Life*, by Robert Jay Lifton. *The New York Times Review of Books* (November 4, 1979), 3.

Didion, Joan. *The Year of Magical Thinking*. New York: Vintage, 2006.

Dor-Shav, Ethan. "Ecclesiastes: Fleeting and Timeless." *Azure*, 2004 (no. 18). http://azure.org.il/include/print.php?id=214

Dostoevsky, Fyodor. *The Brothers Karamazov*. New York: Farrar, Straus and Giroux, 2002.

Edwards, James. *The Gospel According to Mark*. Grand Rapids, MI: Eerdmans, 2002.

Ehrman, Bart. *How Jesus Became God: The Exaltation of a Jewish Preacher from Galilee*. New York: Harper, 2014.

Eire, Carlos. *A Very Brief History of Eternity*. Princeton, NJ: Princeton University Press, 2010.

Eissler, Kurt R., *The Psychiatrist and the Dying Patient*. Madison, CT: International Universities Press, 1955.

Epictetus, *Discourses*. Translated by W. A. Oldfather. Cambridge, MA: Harvard University Press, 1925.

Erikson, Erik. *Young Man Luther: A Study in Psychoanalysis and History*. New York: W. W. Norton, 1958.

Evans, C. Stephen. *Kierkegaard: An Introduction*. Cambridge, UK: Cambridge University Press, 2009.

Fiorenza, Elisabeth Schüssler. *In Memory of Her: A Feminist Theological Reconstruction of Christian Origins*. Chestnut Ridge, NY: Crossroad, 1994.

Freud, Sigmund. *Civilization and its Discontents*. Translated by James Strachey. New York: W. W. Norton, 1961. [original 1929]

———. *The Future of an Illusion*. Translated by James Strachey. New York: W. W. Norton, 1975.

———. "Thoughts for the Times on War and Death." In *The Standard Edition* of the *Complete Psychological Works of Sigmund Freud*, vol. 14, 275–305. London: Hogarth, 1971.

Friedman, Maurice. *Encounter on the Narrow Ridge: A Life of Martin Buber*. Saint Paul, MN: Paragon, 1993.

Funk, Robert et al. *The Five Gospels: What Did Jesus Really Say? The Search for the Authentic Words of Jesus*. Farmington, MN: Polebridge, 1993.

Gilkey, Langdon. *On Niebuhr: A Theological Study*. Chicago: University of Chicago Press, 2001.

Glendon, Mary Ann. *A World Made New: Eleanor Roosevelt and the Universal Declaration of Human Rights*. New York: Random House, 2001.

Grotius, Hugo. *On the Law of War and Peace*. Hoboken, NJ: Wiley, 1964. [original 1625]

Gutiérrez, Gustavo. *On Job: God-Talk and The Suffering of the Innocent*. New York: Orbis, 1987.

Hartshorne, Charles. *The Divine Relativity: A Social Conception of God*. New Haven: Yale University Press, 1948.

———. *Omnipotence and Other Theological Mistakes*. Albany, NY: State University of New York Press, 1984.

John Paul II, Pope. *Encyclical Letter Sollicitudo Rei Socialis*. Washington, D.C.: Office of Publishing and Promotion Services, United States Catholic Conference, 1988.

Jung, Carl. "Symbols of the Mother and of Rebirth." In *Collected Works*, vol. 5. Princeton, NJ: Princeton University Press, 2014. [digital ed.]

Hauerwas, Stanley. *The Hauerwas Reader*, edited by John Berkman and Michael Cartwright. Durham, NC: Duke University Press, 2001.

———. *The Peaceable Kingdom: A Primer in Christian Ethics*. Notre Dame, IN: University of Notre Dame Press, 1983.
Hauerwas, Stanley and William H. Willimon. *Resident Aliens: Life in the Christian Colony*. Nashville, TN: Abingdon, 2014.
Havel, Václav. "Forgetting That We Are Not God. *First Things* 51, 49–50, 1995.
Jacobs, Alan. *The Year of Our Lord 1943: Christian Humanism in an Age of Crisis*. New York: Oxford University Press, 2018.
Jones, Gregory L. *Embodying Forgiveness: A Theological Analysis*. Grand Rapids, MI: Eerdmans, 1995.
Kainz, Howard. *Natural Law: An Introduction and Re-examination*. Chicago, IL: Open Court, 2004.
Kierkegaard, Søren. *Concluding Unscientific Postscript to Philosophical Fragments*. Edited and translated by Howard V. Hong and Edna H. Hong. Princeton, NJ: Princeton University Press, 1992.
———. *Fear and Trembling*. Translated by Alastair Hannay. Princeton, NJ: Princeton University Press, 1983.
———. *Journals of Søren Kierkegaard*. http://www.naturalthinker.net/trl/texts/Kierkegaard.Soren/JournPapers/
———. *Philosophical Fragments*. Edited and translated by Howard V. Hong and Edna H. Hong. Princeton University Press, 1985.
———. "Strengthening in the Inner Being." In *Eighteen Upbuilding Discourses*, 80–101. Princeton, NJ: Princeton University Press, 1990.
———. *Works of Love*. Translated by George Pattison. New York: Harper Perennial, 2009.
Klay, Phil. *Redeployment*. New York: Penguin, 2015.
Kolakowski, Leszek. *Modernity on Endless Trial*. Chicago, IL: University of Chicago Press, 1990.
Kolb, Martin. *Martin Luther, Confessor of the Faith*. New York: Oxford University Press, 2009.
Kolitz, Zvi. *Yosl Rakover Talks to God*. Translated by Carol Brown Janeway. New York: Vintage, 2000.
Kraybill, Donald, Steven Nolt, and David L. Weaver-Zercher. *Amish Grace: How Forgiveness Transcended Tragedy*. San Francisco, CA: Jossey-Bass, 2007.
Kruse, Colin G.. *John*. Downers Grove, IL: InterVarsity, 2003
Lemert, Charles. *Why Niebuhr Matters*. New Haven: Yale University Press, 2011.
Lerner, Melvin J. *The Belief in a Just World: A Fundamental Delusion*. New York: Plenum, 1980.
Levinas, Emmanuel. *Ethics and Infinity*: Conversations with Philippe Nemo. Translated by Alphonso Lingis. Pittsburgh, PA: Duquesne University Press, 1985.
———. *Nine Talmudic Readings*. Translated by Annette Aronowicz. Bloomington, IN: University of Indiana Press, 1990.
———. "A Religion for Adults." In *Difficult Freedom: Essays on Judaism*. Translated by Séan Hand, 11–23. Baltimore, MD: Johns Hopkins University Press, 1990.
———. *Totality and Infinity: An Essay on Exteriority*. Translated by Alphonso Lingis. Pittsburgh, PA: Duquesne University Press, 1969.
Lewis, C. S. *Mere Christianity*. San Francisco: HarperOne, 2012.
———. *A Grief Observed*. New York: HarperCollins, 2009.
———. *The Problem of Pain*. New York: HarperCollins, 2008.

———. *The Weight of Glory*. New York: Harper Collins, 2001.
Lifton, Robert Jay. *The Broken Connection: On Death and the Continuity of Life*. New York: Simon and Schuster, 1979.
Luther, Martin. *On the Bondage of the Will*. New Orleans, LA: Scriptura, 2015. [original 1525]
Maimonides, Moses. *The Book of Knowledge: From the Mishneh Torah of Maimonides*. http://www.torahlab.org/download1983/rambam_sourcesheet.pdf [original twelfth century CE]
Marcuse, Herbert. *The Aesthetic Dimension*. Boston: Beacon, 1978.
———. *Eros and Civilization: A Philosophical Inquiry into Freud*. Boston: Beacon, 1966.
Maritain, Jacques. "On Knowledge through Connaturality." *The Review of Metaphysics* vol. 4, 473–81, 1951.
McCullough, Lissa. *The Religious Philosophy of Simone Weil*. London: I. B. Tauris, 2014.
McLellan, David. *Simone Weil: Utopian Pessimist*. New York: Palgrave, 1989.
Merton, Thomas. *Conjectures of a Guilty Bystander*. London: Sheldon, 1977.
———. *Faith and Violence: Christian Teaching and Christian Practice*. Notre Dame, IN: Notre Dame Press, 1994.
———. *The Journals of Thomas Merton*, 7 vols. New York: Harper, 2009–2010.
———. *Redeeming the Time*. London: Burns & Oates, 1966.
———. *Thomas Merton on Zen*. London: Sheldon, 1976.
Metaxas, Eric. *Bonhoeffer: Pastor, Martyr, Prophet, Spy*. Nashville, TN: Thomas Nelson, 2010.
Meyer, Marvin W., ed. *The Nag Hammadi Scriptures*. New York: HarperCollins, 2009.
Mills, Jon. *Inventing God: Psychology of Belief and the Rise of Secular Spirituality*. London: Routledge, 2017.
Milton, John. *Paradise Lost*. New York: Penguin Classics, 2003. [original 1674]
Mitzman, Arthur. *The Iron Cage: An Historical Interpretation of Max Weber*. Piscataway, NJ: Transaction, 1984.
Moltmann, Jürgen. "The Crucified God." In *Jürgen Moltmann: Collected Readings*, edited by Margaret Kohl, 35–64. Philadelphia, PA: Fortress, 2014.
———. "God in Creation." In *Jürgen Moltmann: Collected Readings*, edited by Margaret Kohl, 103–130. Philadelphia, PA: Fortress, 2014.
———. *Jesus Christ for Today's World*. Philadelphia, PA: Fortress, 1994.
———. "Theology of Hope." In *Jürgen Moltmann: Collected Readings*, edited by Margaret Kohl. Minneapolis, MN: Fortress, 2014.
———. "The Trinity and the Kingdom," in *Jürgen Moltmann: Collected Readings*, edited by Margaret Kohl, 7–34. Minneapolis, MN: Fortress, 2014.
Moo, Douglas. *James: Introduction and Commentary*. Carol Stream, IL: Tyndale, 2015.
Morrison, Stephen D. *Jürgen Moltmann in Plain English*. Pickerington, OH: Beloved, 2018.
Moses, John. *Divine Discontent: The Prophetic Voice of Thomas Merton*. London: Bloomsbury, 2014.
Mumma, Howard. *Albert Camus and the Minister*. Orleans, MA: Paraclete Press, 2000.
Murdoch, Iris. *The Sovereignty of Good*. London: Routledge, 1970.
———. "The Sublime and the Good." In *Existentialists and Mystics: Writings on Philosophy and Literature*, edited by Peter Conradi, 205–220. London: Penguin, 1999.

Niebuhr, Reinhold. *Beyond Tragedy: Essays on the Christian Interpretation of History.* New York: Scribner, 1937.

———. *The Children of Light and the Children of Darkness: A Vindication of Democracy and a Critique of its Traditional Defense.* Chicago: University of Chicago Press, 1944.

———. *Faith and History: A Comparison of Christian and Modern Views of History.* New York: Scribner, 1949.

———. *The Irony of American History.* Chicago: University of Chicago Press, 2008.

———. *Major Works on Religion and Politics*, edited by Elisabeth Sifton. Boone, IA: Library of America, 2015.

———. *Man's Nature and His Communities.* New York: Scribner, 1965.

———. *The Nature and Destiny of Man: A Christian Interpretation*, 2 vols. New York: Scribner, 1941–1943.

———. "The Power and Weakness of God." In *The Essential Reinhold Niebuhr*, edited by Robert McAfee Brown, 21–32. New Haven, CT: Yale University Press, 1986.

———. "The Things That Are and the Things That Are Not." In *Reinhold Niebuhr, Major Works on Religion and Politics*, edited by Elisabeth Sifton, 104–108. Boone, IA: Library of America, 2008.

Nietzsche, Friedrich. *The Gay Science.* Translated by Walter Kaufmann. New York: Vintage, 1974. [original 1882]

———. *On the Genealogy of Morals.* Translated by Michael Scarpitti. New York: Penguin, 2014.

Nussbaum, Martha C. *The Fragility of Goodness: Luck and Ethics in Greek Tragedy and Philosophy*, 2nd ed. New York: Cambridge University Press, 2001.

Oates, Joyce Carol. *A Widow's Story: A Memoir.* New York: HarperCollins, 2011.

Onimus, Jean. *Albert Camus and Christianity.* Translated by Emmett Parker. Tuscaloosa, AL: University of Alabama Press, 1970.

Pagels, Elaine. *Beyond Belief: The Secret Gospel of Thomas.* New York: Random House, 2003.

———. *The Gnostic Gospels.* New York: Random House, 1979.

———. *Revelations: Vision, Prophecy, & Politics in the Book of Revelation.* New York: Viking, 2012.

———. *Why Religion?: A Personal Story.* New York: HarperCollins, 2018.

Perry, Michael J. *The Idea of Human Rights: Four Inquiries.* New York: Oxford University Press, 1998.

Popper, Karl. *Logic of Scientific Discovery.* New York: Routledge Classics, 2002.

Pugh, Jeffrey, *Religionless Christianity: Dietrich Bonhoeffer in Troubled Times.* Edinburgh: T&T Clark, 2008.

Rorty, Richard. *Contingency, Irony, and Solidarity.* New York: Cambridge University Press, 1989.

Roth, John K. "Critique of Griffin." In *Encountering Evil: Live Options in Theodicy*, edited by Stephen T. Davis, 119–123. Louisville, KY: John Knox, 1981.

Samuelson, Scott. *The Deepest Human Life: An Introduction to Philosophy for Everyone.* Chicago: University of Chicago Press, 2014.

Scheindlin, Raymond. "Introduction to The Book of Job." In *The Book of Job*. Translated by Raymond Scheindlin. New York: W. W. Norton, 1988.

Schimmel, Solomon. *Wounds Not Healed by Time: The Power of Repentance and Forgiveness.* Oxford, UK: Oxford University Press, 2002.

Schrijver, Karel and Iris Schrijver. *Living with the Stars: How the Human Body is Connected to the Life Cycles of the Earth, The Planets, and The Stars*. Oxford, UK: Oxford University Press, 2015.

Shaw, Mark. *Beneath the Mask of Holiness*. New York: Palgrave Macmillan, 2009.

Singer, Peter. *Practical Ethics*, 3rd ed. New York: Cambridge University Press, 2011.

Smith, Huston. *Why Religion Matters: The Fate of the Human Spirit in an Age of Disbelief*. New York: HarperCollins, 2007.

Strong, James. *Strong's Exhaustive Concordance of the Bible*. Nashville, TN: Abingdon, 1986. [original 1890]

Tillich, Paul. *Dynamics of Faith*. New York: Harper Collins, 2001.

———. *The Courage to Be*, 2nd ed. New Haven: Yale University Press, 2000.

———. *The Essential Paul Tillich: An Anthology of the Writings of Paul Tillich*, edited by F. Forrester Church. Chicago: University of Chicago Press, 1987.

———. *Systematic Theology*, vol. 1. Chicago: University of Chicago Press, 1973.

Todd, Olivier. *Albert Camus: A Life*. New York: Carroll and Graff, 1997.

Ulanov, Ann Belford. *Finding Space: Winnicott, God, and Psychic Reality*. Louisville, KY: Westminster John Knox, 2001.

Urbano, Ryan. "Approaching the Divine: Levinas on God, Religion, Idolatry, and Atheism." *Logos* 15, 50–80, 2012.

Waugh, Evelyn. *Brideshead Revisited*. Boston: Little, Brown, 1945

Weber, Max. *The Protestant Ethic and the Spirit of Capitalism*. New York: BN, 2009. [original 1930].

Weil, Simone. *Gravity and Grace*. London: Routledge, 1952.

———. "The Iliad, Poem of Force." In *The Simone Weil Reader*, edited by George Panichas, 153–83. Wakefield, RI: Moyer Bell, 1977.

———. *Letter to a Priest*. New York: Penguin, 2003.

———. "The Love of God and Affliction." In *The Simone Weil Reader*, edited by George Panichas, 439–68. Wakefield, RI: Moyer Bell, 1977.

———. *The Need for Roots*. Translated by Arthur Will. London: Routledge, 1952.

———. *The Notebooks of Simone Weil*. Translated by Arthur Willis, 2 vols. New York: Routledge, 2013.

———. "Reflections on the Right Use of School Studies with a View to the Love of God," In *The Simone Weil Reader*, edited by George Panichas, 44–52. Wakefield, RI: Moyer Bell, 1977.

———. *Waiting for God*. Translated by Emma Craufurd. New York: HarperCollins, 2001.

Whitehead, Alfred North. *Process and Reality: An Essay in Cosmology*, edited by David Ray Griffin and Donald W. Sherburne. New York: The Free Press, 1978. [original 1929]

Wiesenthal, Simon. *The Sunflower: On the Possibilities and Limits of Forgiveness*. New York: Schocken, 1997.

Wills, Gary. *What Paul Meant*. New York: Penguin, 2006.

Winnicott, D. W. "The Child in the Family Group." In *Home is Where We Start From*, 128–141. New York: W. W. Norton, 1986.

———. "Creativity and its Origins." In *Playing and Reality*, 65–85. New York: Routledge, 1971.

———. "Morals and Education." In *The Maturational Processes and the Facilitating Environment*, 93–107. Madison, CT: International Universities Press, 1965.

———. "Playing and Culture." In *Psycho-Analytic Explorations,* 203–6. London: Karnac, 1989.

———. "Transitional Objects and Transitional Phenomena." In *Playing and Reality,* 1–25. New York: Routledge, 1971.

———. "The Use of an Object and Relating Through Identifications." In *Playing and Reality,* 101–121. New York: Routledge, 1971.

Wright, N. T. *Paul: A Biography.* New York: Harper, 2018.

Wyschogrod, Edith. *Emmanuel Levinas: The Problem of Ethical Metaphysics,* 2nd ed. New York: Fordham University Press, 2000.

Yourgrau, Palle. *Simone Weil.* London: Reaktion, 2011.

www.ingramcontent.com/pod-product-compliance
Lightning Source LLC
Chambersburg PA
CBHW062011220426
43662CB00010B/1286